Theatrical Worlds

Beta Version

Orange Grove Texts *Plus*

UF | **College of Fine Arts**
School of Theatre and Dance
UNIVERSITY *of* FLORIDA

UNIVERSITY PRESS OF FLORIDA

Florida A&M University, Tallahassee
Florida Atlantic University, Boca Raton
Florida Gulf Coast University, Ft. Myers
Florida International University, Miami
Florida State University, Tallahassee
New College of Florida, Sarasota

University of Central Florida, Orlando
University of Florida, Gainesville
University of North Florida, Jacksonville
University of South Florida, Tampa
University of West Florida, Pensacola

Theatrical Worlds

Beta Version

Edited by Charlie Mitchell

University Press of Florida
Gainesville • Tallahassee • Tampa • Boca Raton
Pensacola • Orlando • Miami • Jacksonville • Ft. Myers • Sarasota

Library of Congress Control Number: 2014903773
ISBN 978-1-61610-166-4

Orange Grove Texts *Plus*

Orange Grove Texts *Plus* is an imprint of the University Press of Florida, which is
the scholarly publishing agency for the State University System of Florida, comprising Florida A&M University, Florida Atlantic University, Florida Gulf Coast
University, Florida International University, Florida State University, New College
of Florida, University of Central Florida, University of Florida, University of North
Florida, University of South Florida, and University of West Florida.

University Press of Florida
15 Northwest 15th Street
Gainesville, FL 32611-2079
orangegrovetexts.org

Frontispiece: West 45th Street theatres in Manhattan.

Contents

Part One

Creating a World

1 Mapping Reality

An Introduction to Theatre

Charlie Mitchell and Michelle Hayford

Nothing has as much potential as a stage. In all of its incarnations, it is a world of imagination, limitless possibilities, and the site of passionate labor. Consider the following moments repeated countless times from antiquity to today. An audience has assembled, full of anticipation, to witness a performance. The appointed time draws near. Perhaps these patrons are seeing this work for the first time. Maybe they have heard or read the opinions of others. It is possible that they have seen another version of the show created by other hands. Nevertheless, it is a certainty that this experience will be unique; every performance has a singular, organic nature—no two can be the same. Among the crowd, perhaps a playwright nervously sits, anxiously waiting to see what will become of his words. The director who shaped this production, once a powerful creative force, is now helplessness. Backstage, hidden from the curious eyes of the audience, actors fight with nerves. As they run their lines and movements in their heads, they adjust their costumes, or check on items they might use in the show. Some may have preshow rituals such as physical and vocal warm-ups. Others may simply enter a psychological state of preparation. All the hours of preparation will now be put to the test. Will the audience celebrate or reject what has been created?

It is time to begin. The actors take their places. Suddenly a signal is given to the audience—the theatre darkens, music is heard, a curtain rises, or actors simply enter the performance space. This is the moment of creation. In the next moment, a new world will appear where none existed, crafted to say something about the nature of our existence. This world, in turn, is the product of many others, one of practitioners who have shared their creativity in the service of this experience. If they have done their best, an everlasting impression will be made and lives may be changed forever.

This book seeks to give insight into the people and processes that create theatre. Like any other world—be it horse racing, fashion, or politics—understanding its complexities helps you appreciate it on a deeper plane. The intent of this book is not to strip away the feeling of magic that can happen in the presence of theatre but to add an element of wonder for the artistry that makes it work. At the same time, you can better understand how theatre seeks to reveal truths about the human condition; explores issues of ethics, gender, ethnicity, class, sexuality, and spirituality; and exists as a representation of the culture at large.

The benefits of studying theatre can be immense. Think of it as a structure that houses other domains of knowledge. It touches and has influenced disciplines such as languages and literature, psychology, music, science, law, journalism, and business. It enables you to cross cultural boundaries and bridge the distance that separates understanding. In the future, anthropologists will examine our contemporary theatre as a cultural artifact in order to help them understand who we were, how we saw ourselves, and what we aspired to be.

Studying theatre also adds a great deal to your overall cultural literacy. Because it has had such a profound social presence in everyday life, understanding references to plays, playwrights, theatrical movements, and production practice helps you communicate with the past and present. For example, look at how the theatre has permeated our language. Against a "backdrop" of anticipation, some could be viewed as "acting out," taking "center stage" or "standing in the limelight" while people "work behind the scenes." You can be accused of being "melodramatic," "upstaging" the work of others, or forcing them to "wait in the wings." And with a nod to the high-stakes struggle found on stage, you can even engage in a "theatre of war."

Of course, the best way to learn about and learn from theatre is to create it yourself; you do not have to pursue a professional career in the arts to gain its benefits. Employers have found that theatrical practice answers the need for enhanced cognitive ability in the workplace. Analysis of texts, the interpersonal and collaborative skills gained in production, and the development of the creative mind gives students an advantage in whatever field they pursue. Theatre is a training ground for successful thinkers and doers.

Basic Elements

For all of the intricate ways that theatre produces meaning, its core elements are simple. Legendary British director Peter Brook puts it best in his book *The Empty Space* when he writes: "I can take any space and call it a bare stage. A man walks across this empty space whilst someone else is watching him, and this is all that is needed for an act of theatre to be engaged." This space could be anything from a vintage Broadway theatre to a high school auditorium to a claimed space in a public park. All that is needed are boundaries, agreed upon by performer and audience.

A variety of artists and other members of the theatrical community dedicate their time and efforts to supporting the creation of fully realized productions. However, nothing more is required than an actor, an audience, a space, and the intent to create a fictional world. The popularity of improvisational theatre reminds us that a script is not even mandatory. This type of performance also disproves the absolute need for a director, the person usually responsible for providing a single artistic vision for a production. That position, in its current incarnation, has been around for only a hundred years, a small span of time when you think about the lengthy history of the theatre. Prior to its creation, staging had been shared by actors, producers, and playwrights, usually with very little rehearsal by today's standards.

There are not even a requisite number of audience members for something to be called theatre. Take Ludwig II (1845–1886), the eccentric king of Bavaria, who took this idea to its logical extreme. Convinced he could not enjoy himself surrounded by others, he arranged more than two hundred private viewings of operas by composer Richard Wagner and others. Unfortunately, this chronic shyness was later used by his enemies as a symptom of mental illness, and he was ousted from his throne.

Today, you can still live like a king. Since 2009, the area known as Times Square, the epicenter of commercial theatre in the United States, has been the site of Theatre for One. A four-foot-by-eight-foot portable theatre booth is erected and for six days, only one person can enter at a time. Once a partition lifts, a five-to-ten-minute show is given by a single performer, a strange oasis from one of the most chaotic places on the planet.

Fine Art and the Qualities of Theatre

Theatre, along with music and dance, has been labeled a fine art as well as a performing art; it can be found in performing arts centers and taught in colleges and departments of fine art. But these terms lead to larger issues. By the twentieth century, educational programs had been broken down into classifications, all of which were historically tied to economic class. In many cultures of the ancient world, work was done by slaves. Consequently, physical labor was imagined to be degrading and associated with a lack of nobility. The Romans, for example, called any activity where money changed hands the vulgar arts (*vulgares artes*) or sordid arts (*sordidæ artes*), also translated as "dirty arts." By the Middle Ages, the designation changed. The term *mechanical arts* was adopted to mean skilled activities accomplished by manual labor. In the seventeenth century, **useful arts** appeared, and with the arrival of the machine age in the nineteenth century, it was replaced with *industrial arts*, a term still in use today.

In the ancient world and beyond, proof of high status was having leisure time to pursue self-improvement of the mind or to serve the public good. Therefore, philosophy, history, languages, math, and science were given the term **liberal arts** ("arts befitting a freeman"). Now the term simply means subjects separate from science and technology and implies an education that is not particularly specialized. Therefore "liberal," in this sense, is not a political term and is not meant to contrast any "conservative" mode of thought.

> "I think art describes the vacuum. Art describes what isn't there -- the thing that needs to be said -- the missing element of the current dialogue that is going on in the world."

John Patrick Shanley, playwright

The third branch, separate from *useful* and *liberal*, was given the term *fine arts*. Coined in the eighteenth century, it was meant to include sculpture, painting, music, and poetry. Later, the performing arts were added along with disciplines such as printmaking, photography, and collage. "Fine" was not intended to suggest art that was "acceptable" or "delicate"—it was supposed to classify artistic endeavors that were beautiful for their own sake and not compromised by serving any practical function. In other words, a craftsman could make a stunningly beautiful cabinet, but once it stored clothes, it ceased to be art. An architect could design a building that was a pleasure to behold, but since it provided shelter, his work was considered only useful.

Clearly, the exchange of money and the association with leisure time has been abandoned as a dividing line between fine and useful art. However, the remaining concept of beauty for its own sake leaves us with a variety of con-

"Life beats down and crushes the soul and art reminds you that you have one."

Stella Adler, actor

flicts, questions, and ambiguities. Many works communicate images or use material that we may not regard as beautiful. Still, we would not hesitate to label them as art. Theatre deals in conflict, sometimes using subject matter that can make some feel uncomfortable. Does it cease to be art when no pleasurable feeling is derived from it? Many would argue that even though the arts do not serve any domestic function, they can be extremely useful as a means of interpreting our world and spiritually nourishing our lives. Is that not useful? When does an object or performance stop being artistic and start being art? Are there rules that must be satisfied or is it simply in the eye of the beholder? Does the quality of something determine if it qualifies as art? To ask and engage with these sorts of questions is to practice **aesthetics**, a branch of philosophy that deals with beauty and taste.

A working definition of art that is elastic enough to bridge different mediums of expression has occupied us for centuries. The Greek philosopher Plato called it an imitation of nature but for that same reason, condemned it as artificial, a copy of a copy, and believed actors should be banned from what he saw as an ideal republic. Many have tried to adopt the poet William Wordsworth's definition of poetry for art in general—"the

This is a word cloud, a type of data visualization where more frequently used words become larger than others. It was created by comparing two dozen definitions of art from classical to modern sources.

spontaneous overflow of powerful feelings" from "emotion recollected in tranquility." Novelist Leo Tolstoy wrote that experiencing art was "receiving an expression of feeling" from the artist.

Contemporary critics have also chimed in. Susanne Langer called art "the creation of forms symbolic of human feeling," and Ellen Dissanayake claimed that art is "a specialness" that "is tacitly or overtly acknowledged." The frustration in creating a unifying theory of art has led some to claim that even the attempt is self-defeating. Playwright Oscar Wilde once lectured, "We want to create it, not to define it."

So what separates theatre from the other arts? What are the qualities particular to theatre that, collectively, make it unique? Theatre certainly deals in the **imitation** of human action. We can trace the origins of theatrical practice in the Western world to the citizens of the Greek city-state of Athens in the fifth century BCE. Theatre began with *dithyrambs*, a chorus of fifty men with a leader who told stories about a fertility god named Dionysus through song and dance. Eventually, innovations were made such as performers imitating individual characters. In addition, the chorus was greatly re-

"Artists are created, not made. To be an artist you just have to find your path, and there's no short-cuts to it, and nobody can really help you, and you've got to find it."

Peter Sellers, theatrical director

duced and changed to represent the men or women of a city where a play took place. Presented at festivals, this form became what we know today as Greek tragedy.

Sitting in the audience was Aristotle. The student of the philosopher Plato, he could be called our first drama critic. His collected notes form the basis for a treatise called *Poetics* (dated between 335 and 322 BCE), which described what he thought were the components of a good tragedy. He began by defining his subject, calling it "the imitation of an action that is good and also complete in itself and of some magnitude." This could be interpreted as requiring that drama artfully depict the actions of someone; have a beginning, middle, and end; and be of an appropriate length. Independently, an Indian critic named Bharata came to a similar conclusion in a text called the *Natyashastra*. Written sometime between 300 BCE and 300 CE in a now-dead language called Sanskrit, he defined drama as "an imitation of people's demeanor, attitudes, conditions, and joys and sorrows."

Here, both authors speak to a fundamental aspect of humanity. It is our nature to imitate the actions of others—psychological studies confirm that imitation is a major part of our social development. Mimicry strengthens the bond between parent and child. Newborns copy the facial movements of their parents. Toddlers learn to speak by imitating and sifting through the sounds they hear. When we observe an action, it has been shown that the neurons in our brain respond as if we were performing the same action. Our capacity for empathy is based on this hardwired ability. In acting classes, one of the most common exercises to get scene partners to connect emotionally is called mirroring. Actors are paired, facing each other, and one performs all of the physical movements of the other until they are told to switch leaders. Duplicating actions is the fastest way to get two people to reach synchronicity.

Our skill in patterning behavior is also one of the reasons that actors—and the theatre in general—have often been greeted with suspicion throughout history. Even though psychologists have established that children as young as twelve months can recognize the concept of pretense, there has always been a belief that viewing or participating in fictional worlds can warp our moral core, regardless of age. In 1999, two teenagers entered Columbine High School in Colorado and killed twelve students and a teacher before ending their own lives. Soon after, many tried to tie their violent behavior to the playing of video games.

This type of role playing was seen as tantamount to being trained to point and shoot weapons. A lawsuit was brought against gaming companies, but in the end, a judge decided that "there is social utility in expressive and imaginative forms of entertainment, even if they contain violence." When California tried to ban selling violent video games to children in 2011, the Supreme Court overturned the law, finding it a violation of free speech.

This leads us to how an imitation-based definition of theatre is lacking. Simply to watch the actions of others would brand too much of everyday life as theatre. However, imitation in the sense of representing a fictional or real person creates a better dividing line between performance and an action that is performative. In the brief but effective words of critic Eric Bentley, "A impersonates B while C looks on." A sporting event or a fashion show has performers and an audience, but these "actors" are not pretending to be someone else. Theatre needs **a pretense of self**—a presentation of character. This is a useful definition to limit the scope of your study, but as you will see, many avant-garde and postmodern performers have sought to challenge this idea by blurring the line between real life and fiction, audience and performer.

Potentially, a great many people can participate in the creation of this pretense. Unlike other solitary forms of art, theatre is often **highly collaborative**. Although the actor is its only requirement, theatre has developed numerous artistic and support personnel such as directors, designers, and stage managers who may contribute to the final product. This is one of the reasons that theatre studies are so valuable—they teach teamwork in the service of excellence.

Theatre has other qualities that, collectively, make it distinct from other art forms. The economics of producing plays is one reason theatre is no longer a mass medium. Film and television can reach greater audiences because their product can be broadcast and played simultaneously on millions of screens. Additionally, computers can now stream the same content on demand. Theatre can never be as profitable or match the scale of these mediums. However, its resistance to duplication is what makes it special. Live performance is **immediate**. When you read a novel or watch a recorded television program, you have total control over the experience by varying your tempo of reading or stopping and starting altogether. The theatrical experience, however, is relentless. It pushes your focus from place to place, forcing you to reflect on the events on the fly, during intermissions, or after the show. That is the reason it is **ephemeral**. Performances can have no true reproduction. Anyone who has participated in the creation of theatre can attest to the strange, emotional moment when the run of a show has ended, sets are removed, and nothing remains but an empty stage. In dressing rooms and backstage walls of many theatres, you will find lines from shows scribbled by actors, a poignant attempt to live beyond the temporary world of a production run. While it is true that performances can be captured on film or video, the true experience of live theatre cannot be truly duplicated. Once it is finished, it lives only in memory.

This transitory quality of theatre is due to the **dynamic between the actor and the audience**. There is a feedback loop—energy is exchanged. Each produces signals that are perceived by the other, which, in turn, can profoundly affect how the performance evolves. This is more difficult to perceive in serious drama but is especially evident in comedy, where laughter influences the delivery and timing of lines or the intensity of an individual performance. Actors complain of tough or dead audiences and celebrate the ones that seem to take an emotional journey with them, inspiring them to make bolder choices.

The idea of pretending that the audience is not present is a relatively new one. In many theatrical traditions, actors commonly spoke directly to their audiences. Readers of Shakespeare often ignore that his famous soliloquys, monologues in which a single character shares his or her innermost thoughts, are direct appeals to the audience. The audience members become characters in the play, confidants who can seemingly solve the problems they are being asked to hear.

This relationship between actors and audiences has changed over the centuries. In many theatrical traditions, the audience has been a much more influential "actor" in the performance. In eighteenth-century France and England, wealthy patrons could sit right on the stage in full view. As much as we complain about the annoyances of cell phone use and texting during performances today, to a nineteenth-century audience, our behavior would seem downright passive. It was common practice for people to vocalize their criticism by booing and hissing at villains during their entrances or heckling actors when it was thought a performance was subpar. Vocal reactions to onstage action built to such a crescendo that newspapers often complained of theatrical rowdyism.

How to See a Play

The following observations were written by a German traveler to a theatre in the United States in 1833:

> ... freedom here degenerates into the rudest license and it is not uncommon, in the midst of the most affecting parts of a tragedy, or the most charming 'cadenza' of a singer, to hear some coarse expressions shouted from the gallery in a stentor voice. This is followed, according to the taste of the by-standers, either by loud laughter and approbation, or by the castigation and expulsion of the offender. .... It is also no rarity for some one to throw the fragments of his 'gouté' [snack], which do not always consist of orange-peels alone, without the smallest ceremony, on the heads of the people in the pit or, or to shail them with singular dexterity into the boxes; while others hang their coats and waistcoats over the railing of the gallery and sit in shirt-sleeves.

We certainly have come a long way! Although politeness is a relative idea, it can be said that theatre-going today has some common rules of etiquette to follow so everyone can have an enjoyable experience. We list them here to save you any future embarrassment:

> Arrive on time. Finding your seat in a dark theatre is disruptive
>   to those in your wake.
> Do not talk during the show.
> Do not use your phone or smartphone. It is best to turn it off
>   completely. Vibrating phones can be just as attention-getting
>   as a ring tone.
> Do not eat or drink during the show.
> Do not open candies with loud wrappers.

Violating these rules breaks the reality the actors are trying so hard to create as well as greatly annoying patrons around you (although they may not say it). You do not want to be the person everyone complains about after the show.

If there is an intermission between the acts, some theatres will blink the lights or broadcast a tone to let you know it is time to take your seat. At the end of the show, applaud the actors for their efforts instead of darting for the door. It is the only way they know you enjoyed their work, and they appreciate it immensely. Standing ovations should be reserved for outstanding performances.

And now for backstage superstitions. Do not say "Good luck" to an actor before a show; it is considered bad luck to do so. "Break a leg" is the proper way to give your good wishes. It is also believed by some that it is bad luck to whistle in a theatre. This probably originated back when ex-sailors used to work in theatres to operate the ropes and pulleys that raised and lowered scenery. They communicated by whistling, so an errant one could cause pandemonium on stage. Today, however, all communications are done through intercoms. But these infractions are trivial compared to saying "*Macbeth*" in a theatre. Supposedly, disaster will befall any show if this word is spoken aloud. We have seen many a seemingly mature and levelheaded actor go into a histrionic tizzy at the mention of Shakespeare's play. Calling it "the Scottish play" is imagined to be a harmless alternative. The fanciful legend connected to this irrational belief is that Shakespeare observed the rituals of a real witches' coven and included their spells in his play. Outraged, the witches placed a curse on the play. If its title is said by accident, actors have developed elaborate rituals to combat this "curse," involving spinning, spitting, and/or circling the theatre a number of times.

Finally, many theatres claim to have a kindly ghost in residence. It is likely that an apparatus referred to as a "ghost light" contributes to this one. This bare lamp mounted on a pole is put on stage whenever the theatre is not in use and all the lights are shut off. It is a safety measure but also saves on electrical costs. Its eerie light has convinced many a green actor that a ghostly presence is nearby.

Other cultures have a more casual relationship between actor and audience. For example, in some puppet theatre traditions like the *wayang kulit* in Indonesia, shows are played from evening until dawn, and it is common practice for spectators to move about, talk, and feast during the show. Nevertheless, actors and audiences are ultimately partners. Theatre's primary strength comes from the fact that it is a medium of imagination that depends on the *suggestion* of reality rather than slavish photorealism.

How Theatre "Means"

How theatre generates meaning is both simplistic and highly complex. Think of the theatrical space as a machine that constantly generates meaning. A bare stage can become any location by using language or gesture — our minds fill in the blanks. Actions on stage forge what we call a **convention**, an unspoken agreement between actor and audience concerning a fictional reality. As long as this covenant is unbroken, other fictions can be built upon it. A fun example of this concept comes from a play called *Black Comedy* by Peter Shaffer. The show opens in darkness but when the characters in the play experience a blackout caused by a short circuit, the stage suddenly becomes illuminated. As the actors grope around in the "dark," we realize the convention. When the lights are on, the reality is that the characters are experiencing darkness. When the lights are out, the lights in the house have returned. Following this logic, if a match is struck or a flashlight is switched on, the stage lights dim.

Entire styles of performance can be created through conventions. In musical theatre, a performer interrupts a scene to break into song. In doing so, he has constructed a world where singing as a means of expression is an accepted reality. In poetic drama, characters speak in patterned language and as long as the other characters do the same, it establishes a norm.

Of course, the audience must be willing to participate in this enterprise. Back in 1817, Samuel Taylor Coleridge coined the expression *"the willing suspension of disbelief"* to describe a reader's encounter with supernatural poetry. The theatrical community has since adopted that phrase to describe the decision by an audience member to put aside any doubts about the narrative being presented. In other words, the audience chooses to believe as long as the actors hold up their end of the bargain and support the established reality.

At the outset, nothing on the stage has any inherent meaning. The symbolism that is generated is entirely based on context. Visualize a chair in a performance space. At its most basic, it represents a simple piece of furniture. However, if used as a throne, it becomes a sign of power. If physically toppled, for example, it can change into a symbol of the overthrow of monarchy. In many ways, a stage is no different from a painting—everything inside the frame is open for interpretation—but theatre can constantly morph to create other meanings. In August Wilson's play *Fences*, a character named Troy builds a fence around his house at the insistence of his wife, Rose. On the surface, it seems to symbolize a barrier to protect the family from the threat of the outside world. However, as the play progresses and facts about his behavior outside the home come to light, the fence comes to symbolize a kind of emotional prison shared by both husband and wife or the emotional barriers that keep people apart.

Because theatre cannot help but generate meaning, it has a strong tendency to be allegorical. If a play depicts a single romantic relationship triumphing over adversity, a strong message that "love conquers all" might be communicated. If multiple couples are shown with different outcomes to their relationships, the result becomes more complex. This is why it is problematic to have a person of a particular background or ethnicity represented in a negative light when there is no positive counterpoint. Nevertheless, playwrights of color have struggled with this idea. Some believe the theatre is an opportunity for positive portrayals, while others bristle at the thought of being "ghettoized" and want to represent the human condition without being a spokesperson for their race or gender.

Of course, the reception of art does not begin and end at the theatre. The conclusions we reach about the onstage world we experience are greatly influenced by the personal and cultural baggage we bring with us. Our background—socioeconomic status, history of personal relationships, familiarity with the subject matter, and so on—all influence how we interpret the fictional lives and outcomes we see. One of the major strengths of the theatre is that it helps us transcend our own preconceptions by intimately exposing us to new ideas, cultures, and subcultures.

It should also be noted that stories that are deeply rooted in our own cultural traditions often have little or very different meaning to people from another one. An American anthropologist named Laura Bohannan discovered the fallacy of "universal understanding" in 1961 when she was living with a tribe called the Tiv in southeastern Nigeria. Pressed to tell a story by the elders of the village, she attempted to recount the story of *Hamlet*. When she told them that the ghost of a dead king appeared to demand revenge, they rejected the idea. They insisted it must be an omen sent by a witch or a zombie and that Hamlet's father should have taken more wives. As she continued the story, it was determined, among other reinterpretations, that the only explanation for the behavior of Hamlet and Ophelia was bewitchment. "Tell us more stories in the future," said one of the elders, "and we will instruct you in their true meaning." Theatre practitioners forget their audience at their own peril.

The Uses of Theatre

We certainly look to theatre for entertainment, but many believe that using it as a source of pleasure or escape is not its only purpose. A series of practices called **drama therapy** is described by its national association as when "participants are invited to rehearse desired behaviors, practice being in relationships, expand and find flexibility between life roles, and perform the change they wish to be and see in the world." It is a mix of theatre and clinical and psychological practice, and master's degrees in drama therapy are now offered nationally and internationally to train specialists to work with special populations such as troubled children and adolescents, the elderly, substance abusers, people with developmental disabilities, and those who have experienced traumatic events such as wars or natural disasters. Drama therapists might also work with dysfunctional families or individuals seeking help with life problems. One example is called playback theatre, in which an audience member tells a story about his life and then a troupe of actors recreates it through artistic improvisation. This allows the storyteller to actively and immediately reflect upon an event—choices and dynamics can be reexamined and insights can be gained. At the same time, audiences can find parallels in their own lives.

Role play can even be valuable for the clinicians themselves. Today, prominent hospitals and medical schools commonly hire actors to portray the sick to help aspiring doctors learn to relate to patients. Encounters are recorded and reviewed by supervisors in order to improve students' bedside manner.

Although it can be argued that all plays teach by presenting an outlook that can be accepted or rejected by the spectator, numerous groups have sought to use theatre to educate throughout history. In the Christian world, for example, theatre was widely used to provide a moral education. During the Middle Ages in Europe, most people were illiterate and could not speak Latin, the language of the Bible and the Christian service. To share biblical stories and teach Catholic doctrine, priests oversaw the creation of plays that were performed by amateurs belonging to the local community. At first, plays were presented inside the church, but they were later moved outside to temporary stages. Each of these stages, called *mansions*, represented a specific location such as heaven or hell with an open space called a *platea* used for the playing space. The audience would then follow the action from set to set. It was not uncommon for these shows to have elaborate special effects such as flying machines to raise and lower actors (Jesus' ascension and flying demons), smoke and fire, and mirrored lighting to simulate a halo.

Today, churches continue to use theatre for instruction. Many use skits, with varying degrees of sophistication, to illustrate points made in sermons, and Easter plays continue to dramatize the crucifixion and resurrection of Christ. Other religious uses of theatre can be quite controversial. Since the 1990s, many evangelical Christian churches have presented Hell House, a yearly alternative to the traditional Halloween haunted house. Performed by teenagers and targeted to their age group, it follows the same structure and spirit as a medieval theatrical presentation. An actor playing the devil or the devil's helper shepherds the audience from one graphic and disturbing scene to the next in an effort to frighten the audience away from behaviors it considers sinful. After depictions of gay lifestyles, drugs, suicide, occultism, drunk driving, or domestic violence, characters involved are dragged away by demons to eternal damnation. At the end of the tour, the crowd moves to some representation of heaven, then is invited to pray and possibly join the congregation.

Secular forces have also made full use of the theatre's persuasive possibilities. Public opinion has been swayed by plays designed to inform the public about important social issues. In the 1840s and 1850s, alcohol consumption was considered an enormous threat to the American family, so much so that a temperance movement was established in order to preach abstinence and pressure the government to restrict and/or abolish its use. One of their strongest weapons was a play called *The Drunkard* written by a former alcoholic actor with help from a Unitarian minister.

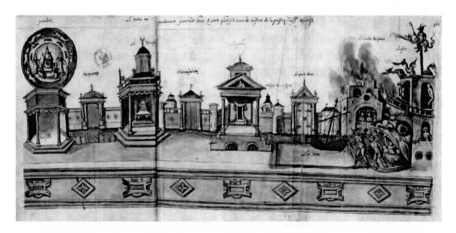

During the medieval period, the Bible was available only in Latin and could not be understood by an illiterate public. To address this problem, the Catholic church used theatre to illustrate stories such as the Creation, Cain and Abel, and the Last Supper. Performed by amateur actors from the community, these plays were funded outside the church and often had elaborate sets and special effects. This print recreates one type of performance called a **passion play**, which depicted the suffering, death, and resurrection of Christ. It was presented in Valenciennes, France, in 1547; took twenty-five days to perform; and had one hundred roles for seventy-two actors. On the left, you can see a depiction of paradise with God on his throne surrounded by angels and saints. On the right, Satan and his devils control the entrance to hell or "hell-mouth." Fire and smoke effects were designed to strike fear into the hearts of any audience members that dared to sin. Courtesy of Bibliothèque Nationale de France.

A 2013 passion play presented on Good Friday in Trafalgar Square, London. Photo by Elena Dante.

Images from a 2008 Hell House created by an evangelical church in Cedar Hill, Texas. A "demon guide" ushers the audience to disturbing scenes such as this simulated school shooting. The Hell House phenomenon began in 1995 with a church in Arvada, Colorado, that went on to sell kits to other churches. Approximately three thousand Hell Houses are presented each year. Some churches have drawn sharp criticism for their controversial interpretations of immoral behavior. Soon after the 9/11 terrorist attack, a Waco, Texas, Hell House contained a scene in which a woman's abortion was followed by her announcement that she was to accept a new job at the Twin Towers. Photos by Marcus Junius Laws.

It portrays a good-natured landowner who is destroyed by liquor and abandons his wife and child only to be saved from a life of shame by a wealthy philanthropist. It became one of the most successful plays in American history and was one of more than one hundred plays dedicated to showing the evils of drink.

Equally influential were the many dramatizations of *Uncle Tom's Cabin*, an anti-slavery book by Harriet Beecher Stowe, already one of the most popular books of the nineteenth century. Audiences throughout the country could watch the story of runaway slaves Eliza and George and their escape from cruel masters and slave traders along with the travails of Uncle Tom, a faithful slave rewarded only with misery. Because of a lack of copyright laws, some adaptations had a pro-slavery bent, but most questioned the immorality of the institution and humanized its sufferers.

Today, plays like *The Drunkard* might be called **engaged theatre**, drama that aspires to promote dialogue and social justice through performance. It can take many forms: community-based theatre, theatre in education, health education, theatre for development, prison theatre, museum and memory theatre, and theatre for social change. Engaged theatre also answers to many names: applied theatre, civically/socially/politically engaged theatre, ethnodrama, and documentary theatre, to name several. As currently practiced, it can trace its emergence to the

The Metropolitan Playhouse's 2010 revivals of *Uncle Tom's Cabin* (featuring Marcie Henderson, directed by Alex Roe) and *The Drunkard* (featuring Michael Hardart, directed by Frank Kuhn). Photos by Debbie Goldman.

early 1990s intersection of anthropological research into theatre and community-based performance. However, if we consider its ethos of democratic participation, we find that its origins are the same as Western theatre itself. Athenian theatre of the fifth century BCE relied on an engaged citizenry for its development. In addition to tragedies, playwrights Aeschylus, Sophocles, and Euripides wrote comedies for a demanding democratic public who judged the relevance and relative merits of their work by how it engaged the current political debate. The archetypal characters created on stage stood in for competing philosophies, and major political figures could be criticized for their excesses.

Documentary or Verbatim Theatre

Some performers have sought to represent not only characters, but pivotal events as well. They do it by constructing plays using material directly from firsthand interviews as well as historical or contemporary documents. Unlike so-called reality television, which often asks us to negatively judge its subjects, these "verbatim plays" ask us to empathize and see multiple sides of a single issue. The following are some contemporary examples.

Actor Anna Deavere Smith's work began in the 1970s when she traveled the country, interviewing interesting people with a tape recorder and then transforming this material into a series of monologues in which she would play all of the parts. Her most famous plays are about race relations that have erupted into riots. *Fires in the Mirror* takes you to Crown Heights, Brooklyn, in 1991. Tensions turned into violence in this African American and orthodox Jewish neighborhood after two shocking events: a black child was killed by a car transporting a rabbi, and a Hasidic man was stabbed by a group of black men. By portraying real people from both communities who experienced the riot, she brought both perspectives into sharp focus. Later, she performed *Twilight: Los Angeles, 1992,* a piece she created after the violence following the acquittal of several white police officers who had been videotaped repeatedly beating Rodney King, a black man pulled over for drunk driving.

The Laramie Project (2000) was devised by members of the Tectonic Theater Project. They sought to understand the rural community of Laramie, Wyoming, where Matthew Shepard, a gay twenty-one-year-old university student, was savagely assaulted and left to die by two local men. They spent fifteen months in the city conduct-

Anna Deveare Smith. Photo by Kevin Fitzsimons.

CREATING A WORLD

ing interviews with its inhabitants. Some were connected to Matthew Shepard and the events surrounding the murder, and others were simply dealing with its aftermath and what it meant to be a resident of Laramie. The result was a play with seventy-two characters played by eight actors. *The Laramie Project* has been produced worldwide and generated so much interest that a companion epilogue, created from follow-up interviews, was added ten years after Shepard's death.

The following two shows have dealt with the inequities of our criminal justice system. *The Exonerated* (2002), by Jessica Blank and Erik Jensen, was constructed from interviews with six death row inmates who were freed when new evidence proved their innocence. *Doin' Time: Through the Visiting Glass* (2004) was developed by actor Ashley Lucas by interviewing prisoners in California, Texas, and New York; their families; and people connected to the prison system. She also added material from her own childhood dealing with an

A high school production of *The Laramie Project*. In this scene, members of Westboro Baptist Church protest the funeral of Matthew Shepard. Mary Institute and Saint Louis Country Day School, 2008. Photo by Anthony Chivetta.

incarcerated father to help audiences gain perspective into prison life and its effect on families.

A perennial favorite in the theatre community is *The Vagina Monologues* (1996). Eve Ensler conducted interviews with two hundred women about a body part that she thought deserved celebration rather than shame or embarrassment and created an entire evening dedicated to it. Now performed on countless college campuses, this series of monologues is usually presented by a group of women instead of a single performer and has been used as a fund-raiser for charities that deal with violence against women.

Do these plays have a point of view, or does the fact that they are made out of the words of real people prove their objectivity? Keep in mind that although they are made from primary sources, they are still forms of artistic expression. Out of the sum total of material collected, points of view are chosen, others go unused, and the texts are arranged for some kind of overall effect. Regardless, they have the potential to create powerful theatre and are an indelible link to historical moments from which we can learn and initiate change. In the words of Anna Deavere Smith, "I think when things fall apart—you can see more and you can even—be a part of indicating new ways that things can be put together."

While we can see the embrace of democratic ideals of participation since the inception of Western theatre, more recent developments in engaged theatre have sought to extend these ideals to their logical conclusions—why not involve the community as creators of theatre instead of solely as observers? To subvert the notion of theatregoers as consumers, this kind of theatre empowers community members to produce their own art—a passive audience is not the goal. Even in work that does not have explicit audience/community participation in the creation or performance, the content will be relevant to the audience as it speaks to community social realities. So what does engaged theatre look like?

Case Studies

Hallie Flanagan was an American experimental theatre director who used theatre to address the struggles of everyday people. She accepted a Guggenheim Fellowship in 1926 to study theatre abroad, and while in Russia, she attended "living newspapers," performances that delivered the news and politics of the day through theatre. When Flanagan was called on to serve as the director of the U.S. Federal Theatre Project (FTP; 1935–1939), one of many stopgap programs to put people to work during the Great Depression, she accepted her post and instituted the same type of performances in the United States. She had already earned a reputation directing a script she had adapted in 1931 with Margaret Clifford titled *Can You Hear Their Voices?* It was based on a newspaper's true account of Arkansas farmers raiding a Red Cross station to get food during the Dust Bowl, a time when droughts and violent dust storms destroyed once-fertile land and left farmers destitute.

Flanagan's commitment to telling real stories that were vital to local and national communities was evident in the way she organized

The 1938 production of *One-Third of a Nation*, a living newspaper that opened with this scene depicting a burning tenement. Concerned with the poor state of urban housing for the poor, the show included a history of the New York real estate market, newspaper headlines, government statistics, and speeches by political figures as well as some fictional characters. During the run of the show, the content was updated to reflect new developments, and when presented in other cities, local facts were included. The play took its name from a speech by then-president Franklin Delano Roosevelt, who said "I see one-third of a nation, ill-housed, ill-clad, ill-nourished." Courtesy Library of Congress, Music Division, ftp0068.

the Federal Theatre Project. The FTP produced many theatrical works and employed thousands of theatre artists to create children's theatre, community-specific ethnic theatre companies that embraced the nation's diversity, and productions that dealt with political issues of local and national concern. Plagued by accusations of socialist and communist designs, the FTP was halted shortly after Flanagan was called before the House Un-American Activities Committee in 1938. In 2010, Flanagan's *Can You Hear Their Voices?* was revived by the Peculiar Works Project theatre in New York City.

Augusto Boal (1931–2009) was a Brazilian theatre director and founder of Theatre of the Oppressed. His early career was spent directing at Arena Theatre of São Paulo, where he laid the groundwork for the theatre's nationalist productions and directed classical work with an eye to making it relevant to Brazilians. In 1971, Boal was kidnapped, arrested, tortured, and exiled because of his cultural activism, which was perceived as a threat to the Brazilian military regime. During his exile, he wrote *Theatre of the Oppressed* (1973). In this book, Boal argues for the direct participation of the audience in theatre, rather than their traditional role as passive spectators, recasting the audience as "spect-actors." Upon his

Augusto Boal in 2007. Photo by Teia/Flickr.com 2007.

CREATING A WORLD

return to Brazil, his commitment to working for human rights and issues of citizenship resulted in his serving one term (1993–1997) as a city councilman for Rio de Janeiro and developing a new form named *legislative theatre*. Boal sought to transform voters into legislators by conducting performative town hall meetings that considered proposed laws.

El Teatro Campesino, located in San Juan Bautista, California, was founded by Luis Valdez in 1965 at the Delano Grape Strike picket lines of Cesar Chavez's United Farm Workers Union. In order to raise awareness of poor working conditions, farmworkers performed *actos* (short improvised skits) on flatbed trucks and in union halls. These shows toured and were later honored in 1969 with an Obie Award for "demonstrating the politics of survival" and with a Los Angeles Drama Critics Award in 1969 and 1972. More recently, El Teatro Campesino and Monterey Bay Aquarium partnered to create *actos* for children that deal with global warming and conservation issues, titled *Basta Basura* and *Watt a Waste*.

Reverend Billy and the Church of Earthalujah are a New York City–based performance group that is not affiliated with any religious organization. Through the guise of the Reverend Billy character, Bill Talen and his

A performance by El Teatro Campesino, 1966. Courtesy of Walter P. Reuther Library, Wayne State University. Photo by John A. Kouns.

Reverend Billy at the 2011 Theater Festival Impulse in Wuppertal, Germany. Photo by Robin Junicke.

gospel choir bring their activist performance art to many fronts where he feels the need to take a stand against consumerism, corporate greed, and the degradation of the planet. Reverend Billy began performing in Times Square, where he preached to any who would listen to cease their thoughtless spending. His act has since grown to include a forty-person choir and a five-piece band. In 2011, Reverend Billy and the Church of Earthalujah completed an Occupy Tour, voicing their support of the 99 percent of Americans who are not the wealthiest 1 percent of the population.

Juliano Mer-Khamis was an actor, director, and activist who was murdered in 2011 because he created theatre that engaged his conflicted community. He said of his identity: "I am 100 percent Palestinian and 100 percent Jewish." His allegiance to intercultural peace and liberal views, including teaching theatre to Palestinian youth by integrating boys and girls together, was controversial to some in the community. His Freedom Theatre at the West Bank's Jenin Refugee Camp persisted in its difficult work of fostering Arab-Israeli peace since its founding in 2006. The theatre continues today in Mer-Khamis's name. At its heart, engaged theatre practice shares Mer-Khamis's commitment and passion for both art and

Palestinians demonstrating in Ramallah on April 4, 2012, the one-year anniversary of the murder of Juliano Mer-Khamis. Despite their urgings, the Palestinian police have not found his killer. Photo by Oren Ziv/Activestills.org.

community. Most simply put, it is a creative representation that is produced out of intimate engagement with a community.

Living newspapers and groups such as El Teatro Campesino have been referred to as **agitprop theatre**, a blending of the words *agitation* and *propaganda*. Designed to provide new information and galvanize the public to act upon it, this type of political action is often practiced as street theatre. Humor has been an effective tool to spread the message of its creators. The following two groups have employed the same strategy — mocking conservative ideology and practices by acting ridiculously conservative themselves:

Ladies Against Women (LAW) began in the 1980s as a feminist reaction to Reagan-era politics and periodically surfaces to attack what it considers repressive attitudes toward women. Both sexes dress up as 1950s housewives and hold public "consciousness-lowering" events. With protest signs such as "Make America a Man Again" and "Abolish the Environment," they have marched in parades and held bake sales for national defense, pretending to sell Twinkies with a million-dollar price tag. Here is an example of one of their songs:

(sung to the tune of "My Bonnie Lies over the Ocean")
My body belongs to my husband
Decisions do not concern me
My thoughts must not stray from my housework
So please make my choices for me

Please make, please make
Oh please make my choices for me

My body belongs to our nation
The judges know what's best for me
My ovum have more rights than I do
So please make my choices for me.

Billionaires for Bush (or Gore) was another group that used irony as a form of protest. However, they used it to target corporate welfare and the influence of money on the political system. Creator Andrew Boyd writes:

The Billionaires campaign was devised to educate the public about the twin evils of campaign finance corruption and economic inequality. With the pay gap between CEOs and workers at 475 to 1, both Democrats and Republicans renting themselves out to big money donors, and 97% of incumbents running for re-election being returned to Congress, these problems had reached crisis proportions by the 2000 presidential election. Our idea was to create a humorous, ironic media campaign that would spread like a virus via grassroots activists and the mainstream media.

Their performances were often designed to coexist with serious events. The campaign kicked off with a "Million Billionaire March" where activists wearing tuxedos, top hats, and cocktail dresses arrived at the Democratic and Republican conventions waving fake money, holding signs such as "Corporations are people too!" and chanting slogans such as:

One, two, three, four, we just want to earn much more!
Five, six, seven eight, don't you dare tax our estates!

A 2007 Billionaires for Bush performance in New York City. Photo by Fred Askew.

Whose president? Our president!
Whose money? Our money!
Whose media? Our media!

Materials about starting your own chapter were made available on a Web site, and soon independent groups sprang up in different cities, tailoring performances to their own message. After Barack Obama was elected, the organization morphed into Billionaires for Wealthcare and has shown up at Republican fund-raising events pretending to oppose healthcare reform and to lobby for corporate loopholes so the wealthy can avoid providing healthcare to their employees.

A Serbian youth movement called **Otpor!** ("resistance") used this same kind of humorous, nonviolent consciousness-raising to overthrow Slobodan Milošević, the president of Yugoslavia accused of war crimes and corruption. It began in 1998 when fifteen students at Belgrade University decided to protest repressive laws that attacked freedom of speech. By 2000, the organization had expanded to 20,000 members, but unlike traditional political parties, Otpor! expressed dissent in unusual ways. For example, barrels with Milošević's face were made available on the street and people walking by could hit one with a stick for one dinar. Theatre-like events became an important part of these protests. When arrests of activists became common, Otpor! arranged a parade of mock support for Milošević populated by a small herd of sheep carrying signs that said "We support the Socialist Party." Other movements have since adopted their methods and their symbol of a clenched fist.

Theatre and Propaganda

Sometimes theatre has been used for abhorrent propaganda. Before World War II, the Nazi regime held elaborate outdoor pageants called *thingspiele* ("meeting or judgment plays") in specially built theatres called *thingplätze* such as this one near Heidelberg. With thousands of performers collected into huge choruses, these plays tried to conjure up a mythological German past in order to celebrate German fascism and Nordic supremacy. After a short period of success, the public lost interest in these spectacles and the program was scrapped. Of the two hundred theatres planned for construction, approximately forty-five were built. Today, the few theatres that survive are used for rock concerts and other events.

A *thingplatz* near Heidelberg, Germany. Photo by matthiashn/Flickr.com.

Show Business: An Interview with Broadway
Producer Ken Davenport

Ken Davenport has produced such shows as the Tony Award-winning musical *Kinky Boots, Godspell, Chinglish, Oleanna, Speed-the-Plow, Blithe Spirit,* and Will Ferrell's *You're Welcome America.*

How would you define the role of the producer?

It's a difficult question to answer, but the analogy I often use is that the producer is very much like the CEO of any business or chairman of the board. We are responsible for all aspects of the business of putting a show together. We have to hire the management team. We have to find a product that we are going to sell—that would be the show. We have to find a location to sell that product. So it's similar to owning a hardware store or restaurant or anything else. In fact, especially nowadays, as I hear every politician on both sides of the dial screaming about how the future of this country is in small business, that's what we are: we are small businessmen and small businesswomen.

How much influence does the producer have over the finished product?

We have a lot of control over the finished product. At the same time, theatre is one of the most collaborative art forms there is. You're counting on a producer, of course, and for a musical, you're counting on a book writer, a composer, a lyricist, a director, a choreographer. Obviously, we are bringing money to the table and the distribution of that product. To the inventor of that product, which is the authors, we certainly have a big say in it. But at the same time, I don't hire artists that I don't trust and believe in. So often, we are just facilitating their voice, to make sure that it's heard. I often say that my goal as a producer is to make sure that my shows run as long as possible because the longer a show runs, the better chance my investors have of getting their money back. And the longer a show runs, the more people have a chance of hearing my author's voice and spreading whatever messages they want to spread. So I have a lot of control or influence over the finished product, but it's a collaborative effort.

How do you find material worthy of producing?

A number of ways. Many of the shows that I have produced I've developed myself, ideas that were born out of my head or something I was inspired by, something that I saw as a kid, or something I have always just been very passionate about. Or sometimes it's from writers, scripts . . . I have people that look for shows. Inspiration for a production can come anywhere. I just kind of live life with my eyes open, looking for something I believe can have an effect on an audience.

Can you give me an example of something that leapt from your mind and found its way onto the stage?

The very first show that I ever produced is a show called *The Awesome 80s Prom*, and it's an interactive show set at a high school prom in 1989. It's basically the dream, fantasy prom that I always wanted to have when I was in high school. And I'm also a big fan of the John Hughes movies, and that's what it is, a kind of a John Hughes movie live on stage, happening all around you. That's something I was very passionate about, thought I could make a lot of fun, and it's still running eight years later.

How did you get started?

I started as an actor. When I was about five years old, my parents dragged me to an audition for *The Steadfast Tin Soldier* and I was obsessed with it until I was about twelve or thirteen when I became too cool for it. I thought I was going to play for the Boston Celtics. I stopped growing, so that didn't work out so well. And then I was going to be a lawyer. I went to a small, private college prep school in central Massachusetts that churned out a lot of doctors and lawyers, and I said, "I'll be one of those lawyers." But I got re-bit by the bug my senior year of high school when I did the musical *Les Misérables* and saw the kind of effect it could have. I went to Johns Hopkins University for a year and ended up doing more theatre there than anything else so I transferred to Tisch School of the Arts at NYU, where I continued to act. And then I got a very fortunate position as a production assistant on a Broadway show, and that opened my eyes to all the other different roles that were available on a Broadway production including the producer and company manager, which is what I did for about ten years. And I learned the ins and outs of how to make a musical from the administrative side and the marketing side. Then I left and leapt out into producing about nine years ago now.

What is the most difficult part of being a producer?

There are two parts. Finding product that you love is a very difficult thing to do, which is one of the reasons I started coming up with it on my own. Raising money is certainly a difficult part, but that being said, when you find great product, money is very easy to raise. I do believe in the philosophy, "If you build it, they will come." I think the hardest thing to do these days is marketing and advertising a show. We live in a very cluttered advertising world now and, especially in New York City, live entertainment is a cluttered sphere. So to make your show stand out in that group is very, very challenging.

So what is a good quality for a producer to have?

It's passion. Theatre producers have to be unbelievably passionate about what they do, about the theatre and about their shows. With that kind of passion you can accomplish anything. Without it, they'll never produce a show.

How has technology/the Internet/social media changed what you do?

We found another way to reach audiences, find audiences, and see who is talking about us. We're still catching up with the rest of the world in terms of how we deal with it. The theatre industry is about twelve years behind, or ten years behind in terms of its use of technology, partly because our audience is about ten years behind. Remember, we cater to an older group. We are not the pop music world where they need to be on the cutting edge of technology because the kids that are downloading the top forty are already there. The average theatregoer is about forty-four years old and female, and the average age of a Facebook user is thirty-eight. They haven't picked up as fast as some other demographics. But it's a way for us to find new audiences, cultivate new audiences. It's very important and certainly will be for the audience of tomorrow.

How do you see the future of Broadway? How would you like to see it change?

If you follow Broadway statistics, you'll see our gross has been going up every year. Like a telethon, we are very proud to say, "Hey, look! We did better than last year!" Which is fantastic. But if you look at the other statistic about how many people are coming to Broadway shows, you'll see that attendance is typically very flat. So we're grossing more money, but we're not putting any more butts in seats. That is not a sustainable business model. It means that we are raising ticket prices—same numbers, just paying higher prices. And at some point, that will cap out. I would like to see those graphs rise at the same proportion. I would like to see us adding dollars and putting more people in the seats, because that means we'll have a big audience for tomorrow.

Origins of Theatre

So how did theatre come into being and why does it persist? It is commonly believed that Western theatre began with the ancient Greeks. But if we are to include the performance traditions of the rest of the world, images from unrecorded history remind us that this impulse to perform has always existed. In various parts of the world, records of artistic human expression have been found in the form of drawings on cave walls that are more than forty thousand years old. Even before written language, our need to record life experience was so great that we represented ideas in symbols that could be understood by others. Looking at images such as people, bison, and horses on cave walls, it is hard to imagine that all of these images were merely decorative. Instead of mere imitation, it is far more likely that many represented a story, one important enough to live longer than its narrator. For all the technological trappings that come with today's theatre, we often forget that storytelling is still its primary concern. For all of our imagined sophistication, we still yearn to be emotionally involved in the lives of others and live vicariously through their struggles. The primary question we still ask of one who has witnessed a show is not of theme but of story. What is it about? It is no accident that all world religions teach through parables. Stories allow us to put ourselves into someone else's universe, feel their anticipation of the unknown, and learn from their actions. Theatre artists are not trained to be solely self-expressive—they are taught to tell stories better.

Our propensity to engage in ritual can also be considered a factor in the origin of theatre. Long before we singled out art as a distinctive experience from the rest of everyday existence, human beings have looked to influence uncertainties around us, organize our lives, and satisfy our psychological needs through formalized action. Although every culture has developed performative rituals to positively influence fortune, good weather, plentiful crops, fertility, and victory in war, when we learn about the formal rituals of non-Western cultures, we often make the mistake of viewing them in a paternal way. In other words, we see them as currently existing in a primitive state that eventually evolves into something similar to our own. However, if you look beyond religious observances that we readily acknowledge such as church services, weddings, and funerals, you will notice that we engage in a host of civic rituals that also establish landmarks and transition people from one state to the next (graduations, award ceremonies, and sorority/fraternity initiations, to name a few). Although we now tend to identify ourselves as members of nations and not tribes, we still create and seek out ritual experiences that provide a fundamental need. Theatre can be seen as part of that impulse for collective experience and our need to be transformed by it.

Many historians look to Africa for the first example of impersonation performed as part of a ritual. Sometime between 1870 and 1831 BCE, there was a yearly festival in Abydos, Egypt, commemorating the death and rebirth of Osiris, a king who came to be worshipped as an important god. During this festival, there is evidence that a priest played Osiris' son, Horus, and told exciting parts of the story along with other priests and priestesses who played other major roles. Next, thousands of participants bloodlessly reenacted the combat between the forces of Osiris and Set, his brother. We can find the same type of commemorative performances today in the re-creations of famous battles from history such as the American Civil War or the English War of the Roses.

However, you cannot have impersonation without a natural impulse to play, a willingness to pretend. Today, this impulse is under siege. Since the 1970s, children have lost an average of nine hours of free playtime per week. Television, smartphone, and video game use are not the only culprits. Parents have increasingly structured the lives of their children

Like the ancient Abydos participants, we continue to duplicate important cultural events. This photo shows a 2008 Civil War reenactment in Moorpark, California. Photo by Kent Kanouse.

On hundreds of college campuses, a large-scale game of tag is played called Humans vs. Zombies. The backstory is that a zombie infection has taken root and humans must fight for their survival. Human players must kill zombie players with toy guns, but if a zombie touches ("infects") them, humans must change sides. Zombies "die" if they do not feed in forty-eight hours. This photo is from a 2010 game at the University of Florida. Photo by J. Hunter Sizemore.

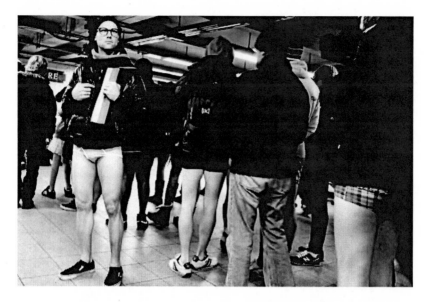

Improv Everywhere, a self-proclaimed "prank collective," arranges what they call "scenes of chaos and joy." Their audiences are simply passersby who, going about their daily lives, suddenly find themselves witnesses to quirky events. One of them, the "No Pants Subway Ride," has become an annual event. In the dead of winter, "agents" enter a train without pants pretending not to notice each other, much to the embarrassment and delight of the people around them. The event has become so popular that it has been duplicated in other subway cities. Photo by Karen Blumberg, www.flickr.com/specialkrb.

or converted free time to adult-supervised activities. This is unfortunate because instead of being frivolous or unproductive, playing is an important part of our development. It increases imagination, allows us to explore ideas, improves problem solving and decision making, and helps us cope with stress. Theatre helps us tap into this important element of our psyche, as both participants and observers.

How to Read a Play

Reading a play may be a new experience for those used to other forms of fiction. Keep in mind that theatre is not a literary form. Plays are meant to be performed, so scripts should be looked at as blueprints for action (ones that are meant to be only read are called **closet dramas**). In this way, plays are inert and incomplete until brought to life by theatre artists. This is why play-going is the best complement to play reading. We can marvel at the transformation and discover meanings we did not know existed.

Theatre and Games

Games can be seen as a formalized version of play. Like theatre, they have structure, rules, and an absolute outcome. Theorist James Carse defines two kinds of games—finite and infinite. In a finite game, you effect a kind of metaphorical death of the opposition by defeating him within the parameters of the agreed-upon rules. In an infinite game, the object is to prolong the game. The emphasis is on play itself and not the outcome. According to Carse, performance is more akin to infinite games. Everybody wins when a performance is aesthetically satisfying and artfully executed.

Although we associate games with children, we forget that adults expend an enormous amount of energy and resources on sports, which are merely games with a physical component. Worldwide, we spend between $480 and $620 billion a year on sports events. It would be difficult to even calculate how much money is spent adorning ourselves in the trappings of our favorite sports teams.

Anthropologist Claude Lévi-Straus would describe sports as having a "disjunctive effect." In other words, unlike ritual, which brings groups together, sports divides individuals or groups into winners and losers where there was originally some kind of equality.

A scene from Dallas Theatre Center's 2012 production of *The Elaborate Entrance of Chad Diety*. Photo by Karen Almond.

Although theatre is a kind of ritual, it still provides us with the same basic element we seek out in sports—conflict. Because theatre is about people in extraordinary circumstances, it inevitably leads to clashes between powers. Actors are taught to discover what their character wants in a scene and find ways to fight other characters that stand in their way.

Although many specific elements of a play can be interpreted, the object of a production is usually to pursue the vision of the playwright and find the best means to showcase his or her ideas. This is one area where theatre and film diverge dramatically. A film script is a commodity and when it is sold, the screenwriter ceases to have any influence over the end product. Another writer or a team of writers can completely rewrite it. In addition, directors and star actors may decide that lines or scenes should be altered as well. In television, a room full of writers may get their hands on a script even though only one may end up being credited. In both cases, the result can be a polished gem, a hodgepodge of different points of view, or anything in between. In theatre, even though production teams may have radically different ideas about how to interpret a script, the playwright still holds an honored position. His favor is sought by directors and actors who seek to create a definitive live realization of his words. Playwrights or their estates have even pulled the rights to perform a play because they felt a production diverged too radically from the original intent.

Play reading is an exercise in imagination. Some plays contain extensive notes as to how the work should be staged and how each line should be delivered. Others keep it spare to leave room for artistic interpretation. Look at the beginning of the play *Waiting for Godot*, by Samuel Beckett:

(*A country road. A tree. Evening. Estragon, sitting on a low mound, is trying to take off his boot. He pulls at it with both hands, panting. He gives up, exhausted, rests, tries again.*)

Which country? What kind of tree? Early evening? Late evening or early evening? What does Estragon look like? How old is he? Is the business with his boots a sad or a comic moment? As you read any play and imagine the details of the environment—how the actors should look, how the lines are delivered, and their physical actions—what you create in your head may be very different from the imaginings of your peers. But that is how it should be. That is the nature of art. And that is why there can be endlessly different productions of the same play.

Every play has what is called a **protagonist**. Identifying that character helps you understand the play overall. It is not necessarily the one with the most lines, nor does this character need to be noble or heroic. The protagonist carries the main theme of the play and usually goes through the greatest change. The concept of theme is tricky for some. Every play wants to tell you something about the way we live our lives, but theme is not the same as "the moral of the story." Sometimes the best ones leave us with nothing but questions that we must answer for ourselves. Theme is the subject of thought, and there can be a variety in a single play. Since a protagonist struggles for something, there is often an **antagonist** who hinders the protagonist in his or her journey.

The "wright" in *playwright* means "maker." It is useful to remember that plays are constructed; they have a shape that is chosen for a reason. Think of a play as a fictional universe consisting of characters' lives, from birth to death, that intersect and conflict with each other. We call the place in this universe where the playwright picks up the story the **point of attack**. Presumably, he has chosen this point as the most effective way to tell this particular story. A late point of attack is one where the story begins in the midst of conflict and we find out important details about the past on the way to a much greater conflict. An early point of attack, or epic structure, takes us from the beginning of a story and allows us to experience each point of the timeline leading up to the main conflict. Plots with early points of attack tend to emphasize the past. Those with late points of attack seek to make us understand the dynamics that lead up to a conflict. One is not better than the other. It is simply two ways a playwright can attack a story.

The classic example of a late point of attack comes from the Greek tragedy *Oedipus the King*, by Sophocles, considered by many to be a masterpiece of plot construction. The story begins in the city-state of Thebes in front of the royal palace. A group of elders (or chorus) has gathered to beg King Oedipus to deliver them from a mysterious plague that has struck the city. He appears before them and listens to how disease has killed their loved ones, crops, and cattle. Oedipus tells them that he has already sent his brother-in-law, Creon, to the shrine of Apollo, god of truth, to find out how to save the city. This is the **exposition** or background of the play, which lays the groundwork for all of the play's action. Suddenly, Creon enters and gives his report from the oracle. We find out that the previous king, Laius, was killed by someone who remains in Thebes. It is this unsolved murder that has cursed the city with disease. Oedipus is eager to help and vows to find the killer. So begins the first murder mystery in theatrical history.

As the play progresses, we are reminded that Oedipus became king after the death of Laius, at a time when Thebes was being terrorized by a merciless creature called the Sphinx, a terrible monster with the head of a woman, the body of a lion, an eagle's wings, and a serpent's tail. At the entrance to the city, all who came upon it were asked a riddle and then killed when they could not answer it. Bravely, Oedipus approached it and wisely solved the riddle, which caused the Sphinx to kill itself in frustration. In gratitude for freeing the city, he was made king and married Laius' window, Jocasta, who bore him four children.

Tension builds in the play during the next phase, called **rising action**. The leader of the elders suggests that Tiresias, a blind fortune-teller, come forth and give details about the crime. Again, Oedipus has anticipated this request and Tiresias enters, led by a small boy. When first asked for information, he refuses. When pressured, Tiresias states that Oedipus is the murderer. Outraged, Oedipus accuses Creon of paying Tiresias to lie so Creon can become king. Creon denies the charge, but Oedipus threatens him with banishment and death. After much arguing, Oedipus' wife, Jocasta enters. She tries to put their minds at ease by stating that human beings cannot be prophets of the future. To prove it, she recounts an old prophecy made by a priest of Apollo that did not come true. It stated that the son of Laius and Jocasta would kill the king. In order to prevent it, Laius ordered their three-day-old son to be left on a mountain to die. Since Laius was killed by a traveler at a place where three roads met and not by their son, says Jocasta, prophecies are not to be believed.

Oedipus is shaken by the news. He questions Jocasta and finds out that the king's shepherd survived when he was killed on the road. She says this man begged to be sent out to the mountains when Oedipus was crowned. Oedipus orders the shepherd's return and then reveals a crucial moment from his past. When he lived in the city of Corinth, a drunken man claimed Oedipus was adopted and not the son of King Laius.

Reassured by his parents that it was not the case, he traveled to Delphi and consulted the oracle. There, he was told he would murder his father and share a bed with his mother. To avoid this monstrous outcome, he left Corinth. On the road, he was pushed aside by the driver of an old man's carriage. Oedipus retaliated, but the old man was angered by this action and struck Oedipus as he passed by. Oedipus hit him back with his staff and killed him along with the rest of his men in the ensuing struggle.

Oedipus is now desperate for these pieces not to fit together. Jocasta tries to soothe his fears by reminding him of the rumor that it was a band of thieves who killed Laius, not one. Then, a messenger arrives with fortunate but sad news. His father is dead from old age and the people of Corinth wish Oedipus to return and become their king. But with this news comes a terrible revelation. The messenger confirms that Oedipus was adopted, given to the family by a shepherd. Grief-stricken, Jocasta runs into the palace. Now, the testimony of a lowly shepherd controls everybody's destiny. He enters and when he is questioned by Oedipus, he describes how he was ordered to murder the child but, unable to do so, gave it to a man who brought it to the king's palace in Corinth. In this horrifying moment, the truth is now undeniable. All predictions were true— he has unknowingly committed an unspeakable taboo. This moment of painful self-knowledge is the **climax**, the highest emotional point in the play. The next section is called the period of **falling action**, followed by the **denouement**. The denouement (meaning "untying" or "unraveling") is when the all of the final loose ends of the plot are resolved.

Oedipus moves into the palace, but soon a servant emerges and describes the terrible scene he just witnessed. Oedipus had searched for Jocasta in a rage but found that she had hanged herself. After taking her down, he took her golden brooches from her dead body and plunged them into his eyes, blinding himself. Destroyed by the light of truth, Oedipus wishes only darkness. Creon enters and sees the pathetic Oedipus emerge bloody from the palace. Oedipus begs to be banished to the mountains. Creon agrees but insists the children stay behind. The elders tell the audience:

Men of Thebes: look upon Oedipus
This is the king who solved the famous riddle
And towered up, most powerful of men.
No mortal eyes but looked on him with envy,
Yet in the end ruin swept over him.

Let every man in mankind's frailty
Consider his last day; and let none
Presume on his good fortune until he find
Life, at his death, a memory without pain.
(trans. Dudley Fitts and Robert Fitzgerald)

According to the play, fate is something we cannot escape no matter what our station. We seek knowledge but have to live with the answers. Oedipus has shown us the limits and frailty of human happiness. But if Oedipus is the protagonist, who is the antagonist? You might imagine Oedipus to be his own antagonist or name those who sought to stand in the way of revealing the truth about his life. Even fate could be called the culprit since it was believed in Sophocles' time that the destiny of men was supernaturally determined.

Finding the protagonist and antagonist and charting the dramatic action is not just an exercise in dramatic analysis. It helps theatre creators shape their production. Directors must be able to answer the question, "Whose play is it?" in order to emphasize the right character through action onstage. They must also guide performances so the climax is properly highlighted. Actors must also know the highest emotional point so they can adjust their performance accordingly. Plot is the engine that drives a production.

Theatre and Advertising

Theatre companies are always looking for creative ways to attract new audiences using social media. However, Quebec's Théâtre du Nouveau Monde took a more creative step than a mere Facebook page. For their production of Molière's *The Bourgeois Gentleman*, a French comedy from the seventeenth century, they created Twitter accounts for the play's fictional characters, allowing the public to follow and converse with them. As a result, the show sold out and they had to offer additional performances. Some theatres have even created so-called "tweet seats," a reserved seating section of the auditorium where patrons are allowed to use their phones or tablets to tweet about the performance as it is happening.

Courtesy of Théâtre du Nouveau Monde.

As theatres find ways to reach out to the marketplace, it is important to note that the marketplace has often used the theatre for its own purposes. Long before product placement was commonplace in films, leading stage actors would be paid by designers to wear their clothes, songwriters paid to have their tunes included in musical revues, and for a price, some producers would make sure everything from watches to Scotch whiskey would get verbal and visual plugs in their shows. Recently, self-described "guerrilla marketers" have even paid actors to go to public places and converse about products in the hopes that word of mouth will be more effective than traditional ads. However, the strangest union of theatre and advertising has to come from Papua New Guinea in the 1990s. An advertising company needed a way to sell products to a large portion of the population that could not be reached by television, radio, or print ads. Their solution, called Wokabout Marketing, used a theatre company to travel to isolated villages and present plays that praised consumer goods such as laundry soup, Coca-Cola, and toothpaste.

Part Two

Theatrical Production

2   Acting

Charlie Mitchell

One of the first images that spring forth when people think of actors is glamorous red carpet award shows filled with pampered stars whose pictures fill supermarket checkout magazines. Many assume a glamorous life of public attention, steady work, and colossal paychecks. But the reality of the average actor's life is starkly different, especially in the world of live theatre. There are extremely few overnight successes. Most actors toil for years before getting any high-profile acting jobs. Auditioning more than they work, they can face constant rejection from casting agents, directors, and producers. Most have studied for a long time to hone their skills, and even after establishing themselves, many continue to take classes or meet with coaches to keep their instincts sharp. Since lucrative acting jobs are hard to find and usually offer no permanent financial security, most actors have to support themselves through other work. This is where the cliché of the "actor/waiter" originates; it is one of the few jobs where you can alter your hours to attend auditions.

So why become an actor when most other occupations offer more stable living conditions? Most will tell you no other medium offers the same rush of emotion and immediate connection with the audience. Simply put, they would not be happy doing anything else. Even those who have enjoyed success in film and television often return to the stage to practice their first love. Braving audiences and critics in professional theatre still remains the ultimate test of an actor's ability and courage.

The 2003 production of *The Pillowman* (featuring Adam Godley and David Tennant). Intensely emotional scenes like this one must be duplicated by actors night after night. Photo © Robbie Jack/Corbis.

A Brief History of Acting Theory

Before we delve into the particulars of how an actor approaches a role, reflect on this question: is the actor a craftsman or an artist? You could consider them craftsmen in the sense that they use a set of skills to build a character onstage; they do it by interpreting the lines set forth by the playwright in a manner that will ring truthfully to an audience. Although many of us might have little to say in matters of art, we are all critics of human behavior—we all know emotional truth when presented to us.

"The technique is the craft. It's the individual qualities that make the art."

Stanley Tucci, actor

At the same time, you could call the actor an artist because he applies creativity and imagination to this interpretation, transcending the words on the page to create something highly individual. Ultimately, no two actors can play

THEATRICAL PRODUCTION

a character exactly the same way.

"I think it's a craft...I come at it from the point of view that I need a writer."

Morgan Freeman, actor

No matter how you label it, acting is a paradoxical activity. Actors must explore the emotional world of the character, but at the same time they must meet a set of technical demands such as articulating and projecting their words so they can be understood by an audience, applying a voice and physicality appropriate for their character, following proscribed movements dictated by the director, adjusting to the response of the audience, and dealing with any mishaps that might occur (missing props, actors forgetting lines, etc.). This balancing act, what one critic called a "special gift for double-consciousness," is one of the skills that separate merely competent actors from great ones.

Schools throughout the world offer classes in acting, but there is no singular way to teach it. All acting teachers are, in some way, disciples of other teachers who have struggled with the same questions—when creating a character, what should get the most emphasis, technique or emotion? Should the actor truly feel the emotions of his character, or can they be somehow simulated by physical means? When playing the same character night after night, how personally invested must you be in your performance to give the appearance of truth?

We turn to the originators of Western theatre, the ancient Greeks, to find the first opinion on the emotion vs. technique debate. In Aristotle's *Poetics*, he suggests that when writing plays, playwrights should become actors because "they are most persuasive and affecting who are under the influence of actual passion" because the audience shares "the agitation of those who appear to be truly agitated—the anger of those who appear to be truly angry." This idea that actors must actually feel and not just feign the emotions of their character was adopted by the Romans, whose powerful empire conquered the Greeks and imported their theatre. Although the Romans enjoyed plays among their pastimes and some actors were celebrated, the social status of the actor was at an all-time low.

Acting was left to slaves and noncitizens, which is probably why we do not find debates on the subject during this period.

Performance *was* discussed, however, by the practitioners of public speaking. This was the last phase of education for men of ancient Rome; they needed the ability to argue and persuade to enter public life in politics, administration, or law. To speak well was the hallmark of a powerful Roman citizen. The most notable teacher of what we call **the rhetorical tradition** of performance was a teacher named Marcus Fabius Quintilianus (35–100 CE) known as Quintilian. He ran a school of oratory and produced an influential twelve-volume textbook on the subject. In it, he begins by echoing Aristotle's opinion that the effective player must first feel the emotions present in a speech. He then introduces the idea that after feeling these emotions, they can be "impersonated" later. But how? Quintilian's highly detailed writings offered advice such as the following:

> Wonder is best expressed as follows: the hand turns slightly upwards and the fingers are brought in to the palm, one after the other, beginning with the little finger; the hand is then opened and turned round by a reversal of this motion.

This notion that physical movements such as gestures can simulate true emotion would linger for centuries as Quintilian's work was periodically forgotten and rediscovered. Still, to put his writing in context, there was no understanding of the complexities of the circulatory system or psychology. The belief was that our bodies were giant containers of four fluids or *humors*—blood, yellow and black bile, and phlegm. It was thought that our behaviors were affected by any imbalance in the composition of these components. It was also assumed that if you simulated emotions (called "passions") through proscribed movements but went too far in their execution, the result would be a poisoned body.

This is where **decorum** came into play. Modulating your performance to avoid any excess was considered a great skill, especially when you switched quickly from one emotion to another. The most famous example of this dictum comes from *Hamlet*. In William Shakespeare's play, the title character gives thorough instructions to an actor he has hired to perform a play he has written:

A statue of Quintilian in Calahorra, La Rioja, Spain.

Speak the speech, I pray you, as I pronounced it to you, trippingly on the tongue; but if you mouth it, as many of your players do, I had as lief [I would prefer] the town-crier spoke my lines. Nor do not saw the air too much with your hand, thus; but use all gently: for in the very torrent, tempest, and—as I may say—whirlwind of passion, you must acquire and beget a temperance that may give it smoothness.

Not only could Hamlet's advice be considered a demand for a natural delivery of the lines, it could also be a thought of as a plea for personal safety.

By the eighteenth century, new ideas in physiology shifted to the notion that the body was a kind of natural machine. Under stress, it was thought this machine would generate emotions that could be catalogued by observation, much like a zoologist dividing animals into genus and species. Many actors would write about observing "nature" to create their characters, suggesting that a universal code of emotions existed. If you could discover the correct set of movements, supposedly any emotion could be represented.

One theorist who took this idea to an extreme was François Delsarte (1811–1871). Until the late nineteenth century, no *systematic* means of training stage actors existed in the Western theatre tradition. An actor's early career was a process of trial and error or an apprenticeship with a veteran actor where he was often encouraged to imitate the master's style. Delsarte, a French singer and actor studying at the Paris Conservatory, experienced this bias toward imitation. After four different teachers corrected his delivery of a single line in four different ways, a frustrated

Encyclopedia Britannica

6th ed, vol 7, 1823

The actor, in studying his part before a large mirror, where he can see his whole figure, in order to determine the most proper expressions for every thought, should consult nature, and endeavor to imitate her. But in this imitation, he should take care not to make too servile a copy....The theatre is intended to exhibit an imitation of nature, and not nature itself.

Acting is generally agreed to be a matter less of mimicry, exhibitionism, or imitation than of the ability to react to imaginary stimuli.

Encyclopedia Britannica

online
2013

Delsarte decided to do his own scientific study of how people moved and reacted. After observations in parks, cafés, hospital wards, churches, and even mortuaries, the result of Delsarte's research was what he called his "Science of Applied Aesthetics." The positioning and movement of every part of the body and head was broken down into an extensive list, with a description of the corresponding emotion accompanying each item. For example, various combinations of eye and eyebrow movement could indicate disdain, moroseness, firmness, or indifference. Different movements of the head could suggest abandon, pride, or sensuality, and certain arm and hand positions could indicate acceptance, horror, or desire. Delsarte wanted an emotional connection to the words to accompany his physical system. However, the bastardized popular version taught by enthusiasts made his system a victim of its own success. In Europe and the United States, "Delsarte clubs" sprang up where simply posing and freezing was presented as artistic entertainment.

Photo of François Delsarte taken by Étienne Carjat in 1864. Courtesy of Bibliothèque Nationale de France.

In video games such as *The Sims*, the Delsartian idea is still alive—all characters have the same animation to represent emotions such as sadness and anger. However, the idea that physical poses can represent a finite number of emotional states is now out of favor in theatrical circles. Some anthropologists even disagree as to whether emotions are biologically universal. They hold that many emotional definitions such as happiness, sadness, and fear are shaped by the culture in which people live. A notable exception is clinical psychologist Dr. Paul Ekman, who claims that everybody's facial muscles are involuntarily activated in exactly the same way when feeling certain emotions. According to Ekman, these "microexpressions" last for a fraction of a second and can be useful in detecting deception, an idea that formed the basis for the 2009 television crime drama *Lie to Me*.

The Stanislavsky Revolution

One person who was determined to overturn mechanical and unrealistic performance styles was the Russian actor and director **Konstantine Stanislavsky**. His ongoing "system" of techniques would go on to revolutionize twentieth-century acting. Today, most Western training is based, wholly or in part, on his innovations.

Born in 1863, Konstantine Sergeyevich Alekseyev was the second of nine children. His father was a wealthy textile manufacturer who liked theatre, opera, circus, and ballet. In order to entertain guests with his children's performances, he converted a room in their country house into a theatre and eventually, a family theatre troupe was born. However, instead of embracing the amateur nature of their efforts, a fourteen-year-old Konstantine kept notebooks filled with serious questions about the acting process. He would spend hours in front of a mirror practicing his role and agonizing over his costumes. In his twenties, he became determined to pursue a theatrical career but was concerned about his family's reputation. Therefore, he adopted the stage name Stanislavsky and appeared in risqué amateur shows in Moscow until his parents showed up at one of his performances. His father demanded that if he was to be an actor, he should work with professionals and apply himself to reputable material.

In 1888, Stanislavsky formed and financed a group called the Society of Art and Literature. Rejecting the "star system," where prominent actors received much attention when preparing a production while actors with small parts received almost no direction, the society strove for a sense of ensemble. Stanislavsky was a strong believer in the adage "There are no small parts, only small actors," and every actor on stage was expected to have an inner life. For Stanislavsky the director, his highly detailed productions received positive attention, but as an actor, he continued to struggle to find truth in his own performances. In 1897, he came under the notice of Vladimir Nemirovich-Danchenko, a critic and playwright, who requested a meeting. After an eighteen-hour conversation, the two men decided to create a new professional troupe that would overturn the artificiality of Russian theatre. It came to be known as the **Moscow Art Theatre** (MAT).

Postcard of Stanislavsky performing the role of Gayev in *The Cherry Orchard,* 1922. He also directed the production.

The entrance to the Moscow Art Theatre, where visitors are greeted by a photo of playwright Anton Chekhov. Photo by Pablo Sanchez.

The first great success of this new theatre was *The Seagull* by Anton Chekhov. A doctor and short story writer, Chekhov pioneered a new kind of play that had none of the heroes and villains found in the melodramas of the time. Instead, his characters are flawed human beings struggling for personal happiness. Despite his complaints that Stanislavsky's direction of *The Seagull* was too serious and theatrical, Chekhov allowed him to produce his subsequent plays, *Uncle Vanya*, *Three Sisters*, and *The Cherry Orchard*. Engaging with this new style of writing led Stanislavsky to consider a new approach—creating a role from the inside out rather than the false external physical means he had always relied upon.

Eventually, Stanislavsky's concerns about his own acting reached a crisis point. At the time, it was common for theatres to present plays in repertory, that is, showing the same plays in rotation for a number of years. Over time, it was easy for a part to feel lifeless. Stanislavsky believed his work was still full of bad theatrical habits and tricks and was desperate to save his roles from what he called "spiritual petrification." What made his situation worse was that the other actors felt his situation too common to be a concern. Reflecting on the performances of his past, Stanislavsky realized that when he played the same role for a period of time, his most inspired performances came when he entered something he called "the creative mood" or "creative state of mind." He wondered if there were systematic, technical means by which to make it appear and began to develop a series of exercises.

Years later, while directing nonrealistic drama, he began to put new ideas about this creative mood into practice during rehearsals and studio acting classes held at the MAT. Although the actors resisted at first, his approach soon became adopted as the theatre's primary training method. From 1909 until his death in 1938, he continued to develop his system, often with the help of other members of the MAT. Hundreds of exercises were tried, rejected, or refined. Stanislavsky never stopped experimenting and scolded his pupils who published details about his early methods. Nevertheless, successful international MAT tours elevated Stanislavsky's notoriety, and many actors became intensely curious about these new techniques. Soon, Russian actors who emigrated began teaching early versions of the system, creating a false impression of a fixed set of rules instead of the provisional nature he wished to convey.

The culmination of his views on actor-training, *An Actor's Work on Himself*, did not appear in print until 1938. In the American edition, the material was divided into three books, translated as *An Actor Prepares* (1936), *Building a Character* (1948), and *Creating a Role* (1961), which was created from his notes. All took the form of the fictitious diary of an actor reporting his experiences of being taught by a teacher much like Stanislavsky.

The features of his early system centered on ways to inspire relaxation, concentration, naïveté, and imagination. Relaxation was meant to address muscular tension, which Stanislavsky believed blocked emotional truth and physical expression. Exercises in concentration developed an actor's ability to focus on objects and sensations, allowing the actor to direct the focus away from the audience. Naïveté and imagination improvisations were meant to produce a childlike state that would allow actors to believe in the imaginary circumstances of the play.

What would later become the most controversial technique was called **affective memory**. It was designed to produce emotional states appropriate to a scene; actors were asked to recall details about a strong emotional moment in their lives such as fear, sadness, anger, love, or joy. Emotions were not meant to be accessed directly. Instead, actors would recall sensory details about the people and places involved. Although this method was at the heart of Stanislavsky's program for some time, he later would consider it only as a last resort.

What eventually displaced affective memory in his system was an approach he called the **method of physical actions**. Stanislavsky believed that the link between the mind and body is inseparable. Therefore, if an actor pursued an action, the emotional life connected to that action would follow. Based on the given circumstances of the play, the actor would decide what his character wanted in the play overall (the superobjective) and then what he wanted in each scene (objective). All actions onstage would be in the service of these objectives. Acting would now be action-based rather than driven by emotion. Instead of trying to stir emotional states or copying the observed emotions of others, Stanislavsky would ask actors to practice what he called "the magic if." Actors would ask themselves: "What would I do if I were this character? What actions would I take to reach my objectives?" Unfortunately, these later developments were not as widely disseminated. As used today, the label "method acting" applies to American teachers such as Lee Strasberg who emphasized affective memory techniques.

Generations of teachers continue to build upon or refine Stanislavsky's work with their own exercises and imagery to produce desired results. Some even define themselves in opposition to his approach, proof of its continued importance. Today, you can find a host of training techniques for body and voice that have been created for actors or adapted from other disciplines to help performers broaden their skills as well as prepare and sustain a role. Examples include two Stanislavsky protégés, Michael Chekhov and Vsevelod Meyerhold, who developed their own unique actor training techniques. In the field of movement and body awareness, Rudolf Laban, Frederick Matthias Alexander, and Moshé Feldenkrais have had a great influence. For vocal training, important

"Acting is not about being someone different. It's finding the similarity in what is apparently different, then finding myself in there."

Meryl Streep, actor

innovators include Kristin Linklater, Arthur Lessac, Catherine Fitzmaurice, and Cicely Berry. Today, actors are usually exposed to a variety of different methods, eager to find the best tools to realize human truth on the stage and elsewhere.

Reading Plays Like an Actor

Although most of us will not become professional actors, there is still a great value in reading a play like one. Seeing a play through an actor's eyes helps to build a greater, more nuanced understanding of a dramatic text. Actors treat each character they play like a riddle to be solved based on clues provided by the playwright. Here are some places to start:

Name: Begin with the character's name by looking up its etymology. Is it accurate or ironic? Take the character of Blanche DuBois from Tennessee Williams's play, *A Streetcar Named Desire*. Derived from the French word *blanc*, meaning white, the name eventually came to mean fair or pure. In the play, Blanche, a former schoolteacher, has come to New Orleans to visit her sister Stella (derived from the Latin meaning "star") because she is trying to leave behind her troubled past. Later, it is revealed that she was fired for having an affair with a student and was ejected from a hotel for numerous encounters with men. But her name is not entirely ironic. The related word "blanch" also means to lose color, and as the play progresses, she is revealed as someone who has lost her former wealth, beauty, and energy.

Past: Before the move toward realism, characters in melodramas were either good or bad, heroes or villains. However, with the influence of thinkers such as Charles Darwin and Sigmund Freud, the idea that we are shaped by our environment as well as our past took hold. Now it is not unusual for actors to construct a backstory for their characters based on the text. In doing so, they can gain insight into why specific choices are made throughout the play.

Language: Language is a quick way to divine a character's nature. Is profanity used in every sentence, only in extreme circumstances, or not at all? Do they use short blunt sentences or poetic language with an extensive vocabulary? Word choice and use or misuse of grammar can tell us volumes about their background and how they relate to the world.

Stage directions: Pay special attention to the stage directions associated with a character, separate from his or her words. Car dealers have a saying, "Buyers are liars," meaning customers often misrepresent their true feelings when trying to get a good deal. The same could be said for most characters in a play. As in real life, we want what we want, but we often do not openly say what we want. For example, a man could state his unconditional love to a woman, but if he slowly inches toward the exit during a scene, we could have reason to doubt his sincerity. Frequently, we find out what a character truly wants toward the end of a scene. This is because they must become more direct since they have used up all of their other tactics.

References: What does the character say about herself? At the same time, what do other characters say about her? Sometimes there is a great disparity between our conception of ourselves and true reality.

Objective: Ultimately, all of the factors above may influence the answer to the most important puzzle—what does the character want in each scene? Choosing a character's objective profoundly changes a performance and colors the reading of every line.

3   Directing

Kevin Browne

Of all of the collaborators who create live theatre, the stage director's contribution may be the least visible and least understood. The playwright's words can be heard or read. The producer raises and spends money. Designers create costumes, scenery, lights, and sound. Actors create a direct and immediate relationship with the spectators. All of these are easily visible and apprehended as separate components. The title of director *sounds* important. But what exactly does he or she do?

Simply put, the director is the "captain" of the collaborative team, responsible for all artistic aspects of the production. He is the person who makes sure that all of the pieces are put together to make a coherent, effective, and entertaining artistic whole. Above all, the director provides the overall artistic vision for the production, organizing and leading the entire collaborative process to ensure that the production is artistically unified according to this vision. In this capacity, the director stands in for the audience throughout the preparation and rehearsal of the production; he is the spectator's eye.

If the playwright is the author of the words on the page, we can consider the director as *the author of the production*. He does not "author" its *pieces*, but rather uses them to "write" the staged production. While some directors are more authoritarian than others, the best encourage the full creative powers of all of the artists involved. The collaborative director leads, coaches, encourages, cajoles, and mentors, but trusts and respects the artistic processes of each of the teammates. The collaborative director does not force results, but guides the process according to his or her vision for the production.

In practical terms, the director's main functions can be broken down as follows:

1. Interpreting the script and developing a vision or concept for the production.
2. Working with the design team to develop the visual, oral, and spatial world of the production.
3. Casting the actors.
4. Rehearsing the actors.
5. Integrating all of the elements into a unified whole.

The Development of the Modern Director

Directing as a completely separate function is a relatively recent development in the history of the theatre. In all theatrical traditions, someone has usually been on hand to supervise the process of preparing a play for performance, running rehearsals, and coordinating the various elements that make up the theatrical event. Often the playwright or a leading actor carried out these tasks. Rehearsals were often short and cursory. Even when a person was specifically designated as being in charge, his or her duties were much more executive than artistic.

Most historians locate the emergence of the modern theatre director with the rise of realism in the late nineteenth century. This took place in the context of rapidly changing social and artistic norms. However, some of the changes (both social and theatrical) associated with the birth of modern directing had been evolving for some time. Beginning in the eighteenth century, powerful actor-managers such as Britain's David Garrick (1717–1779) effected great changes in production and acting styles, calling for longer and more thorough rehearsals and greater attention to detail in all aspects of production. But for most actor-managers, the primary concern was to use plays as vehicles for their talents, not to faithfully execute the playwright's intentions. They were actors first and objective interpreters second.

When pressed, most historians will name Georg II, the Duke of the German state of Saxe-Meiningen (1826–1914), and his collaborator Ludwig Chronek as the originators of modern directing. Unlike the actor-managers, Saxe-Meiningen and Chronek neither wrote nor acted in the productions they created, but supervised the proceedings from the viewpoint of the audience. They were meticulous in their preparations, and each production was the result of a strong artistic vision. Beginning with their tours of Europe in the 1870s, the Meiningen players became famous for their historical accuracy and attention to detail. They were particularly lauded for the intricacy and realism of their crowd scenes.

In the late nineteenth century, great social changes blasted conventions and inspired great changes in art, including theatre. While the Meiningen players performed mostly classics and heroic melodramas, a new form of drama arrived in Europe. Developing from a concern with social issues, this new drama sought to portray the truth of human behavior and interaction. It came to be known as realism and its first great dramatists were the Norwegian Henrik Ibsen and the Russian Anton Chekhov. Inspired by the work of Saxe-Meiningen and motivated to create new theatrical methods to bring the plays of Chekhov to life, Russian actor/director Konstantine Stanislavsky put the actor's truthfulness at the center of his theatrical practices. He and other directors of realistic drama understood the importance of detail, specificity, and the absence of false notes on the stage.

The Duke of Saxe-Meiningen in 1914.

The Director and the Script: A Continuum

It is the primary function of the modern director to interpret the script and to develop an artistic vision or **production concept**. This fundamental approach based on their reaction to the script varies along a continuum. Using the faithful approach, the playwright is treated as the production's

In Shakespeare's *Measure for Measure*, first presented in 1604, the Duke of Vienna is disgusted with the moral decay he sees with his people and pretends to take a leave of absence. While in disguise, he observes how his second-in-command, Lord Angelo, is corrupted by power. Director Ralf Remshardt moved the action to the 1960s *Mad Men* era in order to make the forces of control and freedom more accessible to a contemporary audience. Executing his concept, set designer Jamie Frank provided a set with a corporate space above and a background of advertising slogans below. The costume design by Erica Bascom provided a sharp divide between the bohemian citizens of Vienna and the suited figures that rule them. Photos by Jamie Frank.

primary creator. The director serves the dramatist and attempts to realize the play as literally as possible. Using this approach, the director retains the time and place exactly as described and follows all stage directions indicated by the playwright as closely as possible.

The translator approach is probably the most common in today's theatre. The director honors the spirit of the play as received but may depart from many of the specifics. Usually the original dialogue is left intact, but stage directions, the time and place of the action, and many other details may be altered. Productions using this approach are often based on a director's strong vision of the play. In this way, the production finds its own unique style.

Auteur is a French word meaning "author." In this approach, the script serves as raw material that the director feels free to shape and reshape according to his or her artistic intentions. At its most extreme, this approach uses the play as a jumping-off point, adding, subtracting, and rearranging text at will. Bear in mind that what we have illustrated is a continuum, and that the work of any particular director may be located at any point.

A Process for Directing

Although the directing process may widely vary depending on the material and the director's approach, most directors cover the same bases. The steps in the process, as described next, usually overlap to some degree. For example, the wise director is continuously analyzing the play in response to discoveries made throughout the process.

Analyzing and Interpreting the Play

While the director is ultimately responsible for the interpretation taken by the production, *all* of the collaborators we are discussing must engage in a close analysis of the script. In order to engage and utilize the creative powers of the design team, many directors involve them in the early stages of interpretation. Therefore, the earliest **design meetings** comprise a dialogue about the play. The discussion of the text led by the director must include practical questions. What are the given circumstances in this play? What is the play's central action? What is the main conflict? Which character is the play's protagonist and what is he or she fighting for? The director must lead a detailed analysis of the play's structure, the characters in the play, the play's language, and the play's themes. What do we want the audience to go away *feeling*? What do we want them to go away *thinking* about? What does the play mean?

The discussion must also cover the play's genre, mood, and style. What is the world of this play? Is it primarily comic, tragic, dark, or light? Is it primarily realistic, or not? How do the characters fit in this world? This in-depth critical inquiry into the play leads the process into the next steps. Without a firm grasp on the play and a clearly defined creative vision, it will be difficult for the director and his or her team to maintain a steady course.

The Production Concept

The exploration of these questions leads the director to an interpretation, vision, or concept. The concept is often articulated in terms of an overriding metaphor. It can be articulated in the form of a verbal phrase ("a chess game" for *Les Liaisons Dangereuses* by Christopher Hampton), a painting or picture (Munch's "The Scream" for *Marisol* by Jose Rivera), or even a physical object (an early typewriter for *Machinal* by Sophie Treadwell). Concept metaphors can be augmented by verbal descriptions of the world of the play, by a picture or series of pictures, by sounds and music, or by a combination of these elements. However the concept is expressed, it needs to be vivid, motivating, and clear enough to put the whole team on the same page. The concept statement should also communicate the director's approach along the faithful-translator-auteur continuum, and determine such questions as the time and place of the action.

Working with Designers

Next, armed with the production concept, the designers explore the fundamental questions that will help the team develop the visual, aural, and spatial world of the play. These questions are based on the fundamental elements of design—color, texture, line, shape, mass, and rhythm. The members of the team also discuss practical and technical considerations—how many doors are needed, whether the radio needs to work, or how much movement the costumes allow. At each subsequent meeting, these artists present their written or visualized ideas to the director and to the other designers. The designs for the production thus develop as a give and take among the whole creative group.

Casting

Good casting is vital to the production's success and will make the director's job in rehearsal smooth and productive. Conversely, mistakes in casting can irretrievably harm a show. Therefore, it is imperative that the director have a firm grasp of the characters' personalities, their physical characteristics, and how they interrelate. The director should have a strong image of the characters but also remain open to what the actors who audition have to offer.

These are examples of headshots, representative photos that actors give to casting agents and directors. A résumé listing is attached to the back showing acting experience and special skills.

Breakdowns

Who do you see in your mind's eye when you see words like *CEO,
police captain, thug, nurse, judge, mother,* or *leader of a criminal
empire?* Casting can force us to confront the cultural baggage we
carry, which may include stereotypes about race, gender, age, or
body type. For a long time, there was an assumption in the industry
that, unless otherwise indicated, all parts were given to white male
actors. Today, many theatre directors practice what is called **nontraditional casting.** The Actors' Equity Association, the labor union
for theatrical performers, defines it as "the casting of ethnic minor-
ity and female actors in roles where race, ethnicity, or sex is not
germane." Every day, character descriptions called breakdowns are
distributed to the casting industry so they can put forth actors for
auditions. Many will include the instruction "Please Submit Actors
of All Ethnicities." However, some actors still complain that there
is an understanding that words such as *urban, all-American,* and
sassy best friend are euphemisms for specific ethnicities.

The following are real breakdowns from various professional
productions:

[LENNIE SMALL] Late 20s to late 30s, Latino, Filipino or Caucasian. A
large, kind, childlike man. He has a mental disability, perhaps from
an early childhood injury, which has left him emotionally immature,
unable to control his enthusiasm and unable to control his anger.
He is often forgetful, but has great joy for life, and is tremendously
loyal to George. Physically large and extremely strong, he depends
upon George for guidance and protection.

[LUCIA] (age 25–35) Leading role. Ideally Chinese-American, but
would consider women of other ethnicities with same qualities: an
emergency room physician at start. Strong and sensitive, principled.
Very attractive. Loses her fiancé in the 9/11 attacks. Becomes a doctor at Bagram Air Force Base, Afghanistan. Witnesses torture. Becomes a whistle-blower.

[ANTIGONE] (20) An outsider. Scrawny, pensive, passionate, and full of pride. Regal despite her age and stature. Disinterested in her appearance and the expected functions of a princess, but innately mesmerizing and powerful.

[OGUN SIZE] Male actor, African American, late 20s. An auto mechanic; he is the more solid older brother of Oshoosi. His name comes from "war" and "iron" and he has the toughness and resilience of an everyday warrior.

[ROSAMUND] Late 20s, the quintessence of Midwestern charm, beauty, and privilege. She is enchanting and possesses an irresistible laugh. Yet well concealed under the surface is a woman of psychological instability.

[ELOYT CHASE] Caucasian, 5'7" and taller. Male, 35–45, 1930s period piece. Actor must be sophisticated, highly intelligent. Exceedingly charming, he has an acidic wit that he brandishes regardless of the situation. Think George Clooney, Cary Grant, Daniel Craig, Ralph Fiennes, Rex Harrison, Laurence Olivier.

[IAGO] Late 20s–40s. Any ethnicity. Role requires significant experience with classical text. Othello's ensign, a military veteran from Venice. Obsessive, relentless, bold, and ingenious in his efforts to manipulate and deceive the other characters, particularly Othello.

[SARA] Mid–late 30s. An Upper West Side mom who can't quite leave her rock-'n'-roll wild-child past behind. Vital, sexy, and a little tough. A warm and funny mother and wife; unfussy. But she has a reckless streak, and a yearning for the excitement of her youth. A complicated woman.

[TRACY TURNBLAD] A big fat ball of energy and light who was born to dance. She is compassionate, effervescent, optimistic, and enthusiastic but still spends a good deal of time in detention. She believes wholeheartedly that she will be a star despite being from a lower-middle-class, blue-collar family. Her beliefs are revolutionary from fashion to civil rights. Must read as fat and teenaged, preferably under 5'4". Must have excellent 60s pop vocal style (belt low A to Db). Must have great dance skills and a ton of style.

[LENIN] RUSSIAN. 40s to early 50s. The famous Russian revolutionary. Aged 47 at the time of the play. On the eve of the Russian revolution, planning his return to Russia, he is passionate, paranoid, autocratic. And a bit mad.

The audition process unfolds in a number of ways, depending on the production and the type of theatre. In many instances such as theatre festivals and academic theatre, actors are sought by a number of directors for a number of different plays. This process might start with an **open call**, often referred to as a "cattle call." This is a session in which actors present a prepared monologue or possibly a portion of a song in the case of auditions for musicals. From this pool, directors will choose whom to consider further and will invite them to read for particular roles. Auditions of this nature are referred to as *callbacks*, where actors perform *cold readings* from the script, named so because it is unlikely the actor has seen the text prior to auditioning. This is an opportunity to hear and see the actors read together. Because the actors must complement each other, this is also an occasion to experiment with different combinations of actors. Often in professional theatre, there are **closed calls**, where specific actors are invited to read because they are already known to the director, or because they have been sent by a **casting director**. Casting directors, working with directly with actors or through actors' agents, can be useful in trimming the pool of potential performers down to those who will work best for the parts.

The Casting Director: A Few Questions for Alan Filderman

Alan Filderman Casting provides casts for Broadway and off-Broadway shows, national tours, and regional theatres across the country.

What is a casting director?

The casting director is hired by the producer of the project. I read the play. I have discussions with the director and the playwright (if living). I then send out a breakdown of the characters that I am casting and get submissions from agents of actors that they would like me to see. I then make lists using these submissions plus my own ideas. Then auditions are set up . . . we probably have callbacks and then make offers.

How important is physical type?

It differs from role to role. Some roles require very specific physical features . . . others don't. We are always looking for basically one thing in an actor . . . talent.

What does it mean to act "professionally" in an audition?

Be on time, be friendly, and be prepared. I always give out material in advance. Being prepared means that the actor learned the song or worked on the scene.

What mistakes do actors make in audition situations?

Being late, being unprepared, chatting too much, not chatting enough.

How did you become a casting director?

I learned the business by working for a talent manager. I thought that casting looked interesting and told all the casting directors that I was on the phone with all the time that I was looking. One of them bit.

What qualities should a good casting director possess?

I think what sets casting directors apart is their taste. Their ability to see talent, ability, charisma, training . . . again, hard to define.

How do you define talent?

I'm not sure how to answer that. This is where what we do gets very ephemeral. Many people walk through the door. Some are good.

Some aren't. Some are special and charismatic, others aren't. It's almost impossible to define.

What excites you about being a casting director?

It's very fulfilling when you become part of the creative process . . . when playwrights and directors actually listen to you and take your advice. And it's fun getting people work.

How is casting theatre different from casting television or film?

Film and TV is much more corporate. . . . Network execs and studio execs who know nothing about acting have a huge say in the process. Theatre is MUCH more about the art.

What qualities do you think successful actors have in common?

This is a business of flukes and timing and opportunities in addition to being a business of talent and training. I don't think that all successful actors have *anything* in common. Some are gorgeous, others aren't. Some are trained, others aren't. Some have drive and determination, others fell into success.

Is there one casting situation that has stuck with you over time?

My favorite story is when I was casting a replacement for the original cast of *Once on This Island*. Ten women were on time, sang what we had asked to prepare, and then danced. As we were wrapping up, one woman who hadn't showed walked in very late. We said that we would hear her sing. She didn't even have sheet music with her so she had to sing a cappella. Since she was obviously the best of the bunch, she got the job, which goes to prove that talent always wins out in the end and that this is an unfair business.

Rehearsals

The specifics of the rehearsal process and schedule may differ from director to director. They may also differ from production to production depending on the particular demands of the material and the length of the rehearsal period. The essential elements, however, are common to most productions. Although the order and duration of each element may differ, smart directors understand that, like design, rehearsal is a collaborative process.

Usually a first cast meeting is designed to introduce the actors to each other, to the production staff, and to the script. Presentations by the designers are often a preview of the scenery, costumes, lights, and sound. This is an excellent opportunity to share the production concept with the actors and have a first reading aloud of the script. Additional early rehearsals may be devoted to closely exploring the text, a part of the process known as **table work**. During this process, actors read their parts aloud, stopping frequently to discuss elements including the meaning of words and lines, poetic and literary devices the playwright has employed, the characters' objectives, and the play's dominant themes. This allows the entire cast to arrive at the meaning of the play together in order to better communicate it to the audience.

Before the actors can start rehearsing the play on its feet, it is necessary to have developed a **ground plan**. This is a two-dimensional bird's-eye view of the set with the entrances and exits, furniture, and all of the acting areas mapped out. The acting space can then be taped out well in advance of the completion of the set so that the team has the geography of the space in which to rehearse.

Armed with a fundamental understanding of the play, the production concept, and the ground plan, the actors get on their feet and begin the most time-consuming and intensive phase of the rehearsal process, **scene work**, exploring the play in smaller units. Using their own processes, the performers collaborate to find the acting values that will most effectively communicate the play's action. The director's role in this process is both crucial and sensitive: to confidently lead the actors toward his or her interpretation of the action but at the same time allow the actors to pursue their own creativity. This can be a difficult balance. The collaborative director serves as facilitator and coach, questioning the actors to make choices about given circumstances, relationships, and the wants and needs of the characters. The actors are led to the emotional qualities and line readings that will best communicate character, thought, and action to the audience. Forcing results too early can stifle the actors' creative powers but in the end, the director is the editor who decides which choices are right for the production and which must be discarded.

While guiding the acting values, the director also manipulates space by creating **stage pictures**, bodies artfully arranged on the playing space

Director James Lapine speaks with the cast of his play *Amour* during rehearsal at the Music Box Theatre on Broadway, 2003. Photo © Mark Peterson/Corbis.

to communicate ideas. These pictures are created through **blocking** (or staging), a term for the movement and placement of the actors on the stage. This is a powerful tool and is the only element entirely under the director's control. Blocking may come from the play's stage directions or may be deduced from the dialogue. It can be completely planned by the director, but more often it is developed in collaboration between the actors and the director. Depending on the material, blocking can be realistic or nonrealistic. It must, however, be motivated and believable.

The third element the director shapes is time. He or she does so by exerting influence over the pace and rhythm of the scenes. In the theatre, pacing refers not merely to tempo—how fast or slow the action is moving—but to variations in tempo. A performance that plays at the same speed throughout, even if that speed is fast, will ultimately become tedious and will muddy the story. The director needs to decide which moments need to move quickly, and which need to move more slowly. For example, an early expository scene in which the audience is provided with backstory may need to play slowly enough to be absorbed and understood. On the other hand, a climactic action scene may well move at roaring speed.

Quadrants of the Stage

from the actor's point of view

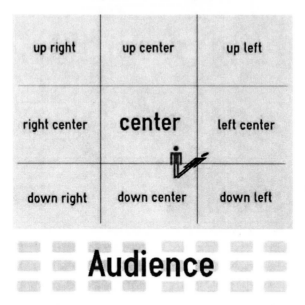

up right	up center	up left
right center	**center**	left center
down right	down center	down left

Audience

In order for directors to tell actors where to move on stage in rehearsals, they must have a shared map to work from. A director might tell an actor originally standing "up left" to cross to "right center," pause, and then end up "down center." In order to make the process easier, blocking is given from the actor's perspective.

Working small units of the play is essential, but it is also essential to get a sense of the whole. Therefore, a director will periodically schedule a **run-through**. Typically the first of these rehearsals will take place as soon as the blocking is roughed in and the actors are **off-book** (free from holding the script, though they may call for lines from the stage manager). This first run-through is commonly known as a **stumble-through** because it is almost always very rough. We may then return to scene work with run-throughs planned regularly until **technical rehearsals**, the period in which all of the technical elements—lights, sound, scene changes—are introduced and integrated. Before the show opens for an audience, **dress rehearsals** run the show in full costume with all of the technical elements as though the audience is present.

The major professional theatres may then offer **previews**. These are performances before audiences with discounted tickets, before the

Color-blind casting is different from nontraditional casting in that it overlooks race entirely as a consideration in casting. Intended to open new opportunities for nonwhite actors, it relies on the suggestive nature of theatre, sometimes at the expense of the playwright's intentions, historical accuracy, or biological reality. Supporters say it rewards talent and makes audiences focus on the story. Detractors find it jarring and say it harms the suspension of disbelief. This photo of the Trinity Repertory Company's 2010 production of *A Christmas Carol* depicts a multiracial Cratchit family observed by an elevated Ebenezer Scrooge. Photo by Mark Turek, www.markturekphotography.com.

official opening of the show. By custom, critics refrain from reviewing during this period, which may last several weeks. Previews give the director, playwright, and, in the case of musicals, the lyricist and composer, the opportunity to fine-tune the show with the benefit of audience response.

During the entire process, from the first design meetings through to opening night, the director's closest partner is the **stage manager**. This person is responsible for running all activities backstage, for maintaining the **prompt book** (a copy of the script marked up with all of the blocking, acting notes, and light and sound cues), and for facilitating communication among the entire production team. Once the show opens, the director's job is done and the stage manager takes control, running the show each evening and ensuring that throughout the run, the production continues the way it was directed.

The stage director employs a unique and complex set of skills. The most important is leadership. The director must be coach and cheerleader, but also must be prepared to make tough decisions. He must be an excellent communicator, know enough about each of the designers' processes to communicate in their language, and know the acting process inside and out. He must also be an expert in theatre history and dramatic analysis. The director shoulders a huge responsibility for the success of his teammates and the experience of the audience.

4   Set Design

Mark E. Mallett

Our word *theatre* is derived from an ancient Greek word, *theat-ron*, a "seeing place" or "place for watching," which suggests that in its most elemental form, theatre involves *both* performers and spectators, joined together in a particular place. In other words, theatre occurs in an environment that enables the actors to bring the script to life and simultaneously becomes a part of the theatrical experience. If we hope to understand theatre and how it works, we must take the places of performance into account.

A simple way to explore the question of the theatrical environment might be to reduce it to two basic categories: the buildings or locations in which theatre takes place and the dramatic worlds of the plays that are performed within them. The former are usually built for the express purpose of housing theatrical events and address a range of functions. As a result, this category also provides a wealth of information for theatre scholars. Buildings are fixed in place, and while they might be altered for particular events, they retain a sense of permanence that transcends the duration of a given performance. The dramatic world, on the other hand, is created afresh for each production and lasts only as long as the needs of the production requires. Yet there is a complex interaction between the two, and the relationship has a profound bearing on the choices made in producing a play for performance.

The success of every theatre building depends on how well it meets three basic demands: facilities for the audience (including entrances into and exits out of the building, a lobby, the box office, restrooms, coat check and refreshment concessions, corridors and hallways for circulation, and finally seating for watching the performance); the stage and its equipment and control rooms or booths; and work and support spaces, such as dressing rooms, construction shops and storage areas for scenery, costumes and properties, and lighting and sound equipment. Typically, the parts of the building that serve the needs of the audience are given the highest priority from an architectural standpoint, the seating area or **house** being the most important. Economic considerations frequently drive the architect to maximize capacity by incorporating as many seats as possible into the design. At the same time, there is an expectation that the stage will be visible and the performers will be audible from every seat. There is also an expectation that the seating will be comfortable and that the auditorium will be reasonably well insulated from unwanted or extraneous light or sound.

Theatres have developed in a variety of ways since their earliest days in Athens, Greece, in the fifth century BCE. They have moved from the outside, where lighting was provided by the sun and performances were always subject to the weather, to specially built rooms indoors where the environment of the performance is controlled artificially. Over the course of this development, it is important to note how the structure and nature of the theatre as a building has not only shaped the qualities of

The National Theatre of Great Britain's touring company production of *War Horse*, Sydney, Australia, 2013. Photo by Eva Rinaldi.

the performances but influenced the plays themselves. It is hard to imagine, for instance, the emergence of the illusionistic realism of modern drama, with its fine attention to scenic detail and representative interiors, without the development of the proscenium theatre. In a similar way, advances in technology, as expressed through theatre architecture, have shaped both the way we watch theatre and the kind of theatre available in our own time. From the introduction of gas lighting, which allowed the stage to be lit while the auditorium was kept dark, through the computerized mechanics and video effects of shows such as *Spiderman: Turn Off the Dark* or *War Horse*, our buildings have shaped the plays performed within them, even as emerging technologies such as holographic projections offer a promise of innovation in their "seeing place."

Types of Theatres

Today, the design of most theatre buildings falls into four fundamental types: the proscenium, the thrust, the arena, and the black box. The **proscenium** theatre is probably the most common and well-known arrangement today. It takes its name from its most prominent architectural feature, the **proscenium arch**, which frames the stage and separates the audience's space from the performers' space. The performance in a proscenium theatre is intended to be viewed from one perspective, the front of the stage, and the arch serves as a kind of picture frame around the dramatic world. This is the source of the **"fourth wall"** concept: the audience views the action of the play through the invisible wall in front of the stage. There is often a curtain behind the proscenium that conceals the stage until the performance begins that can be lowered to hide changes of scenery in the course of the performance. The proscenium stage also incorporates additional spaces beyond the performance area (**backstage**). On either side of the stage is called the **wings**, and the area above the playing space is referred to as the **fly space** or **flies**, where scenery might be raised or lowered through a system of lines and pulleys. One of the key conventions of the proscenium theatre is to prevent the audience from seeing these additional spaces through the use of **masking**, black draperies surrounding the performance area that limit what the audience can see. Masking can also be used to hide lighting and sound equipment and elements of scenery not currently in use, and to provide pathways for performers to enter or exit.

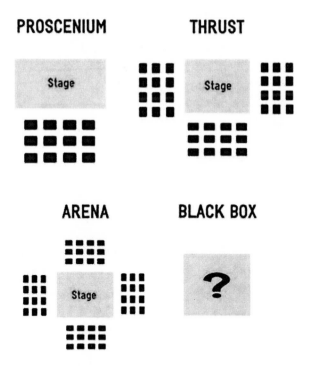

PROSCENIUM

THRUST

ARENA

BLACK BOX

The **thrust** theatre has an opening on one wall, behind which might be found scenic and lighting equipment, but unlike a proscenium, the stage projects forward so that it is surrounded by the audience on three sides. Like the proscenium, there is access between the performance area and the backstage, but like the arena, the designation of the "front" of the stage is somewhat problematic; at any given moment, the actors will necessarily present a profile, if not their backs, to part of the audience. On the one hand, this may seem more "natural"—we do not typically see those around us in a front-on aspect in everyday life. But on the other hand, there is an expectation of the performers being "on display" when seen on stage, and this expectation may not be fully realized when the actors seem to be directing their performances to other different parts of the audience.

The arena stage also presents a complication for any play that requires set changes (different locales or times), because the scenic elements not in use need to be handy to the stage, for speedily and efficiently executing the required changes. While most arena theatres include scenic storage spaces near the stage, the absence of a curtain means that the changes are carried out in full view of the audience. And because much of it is installed above the stage or the audience area, some vital theatre technology is at least partially visible and part of the stage picture. So there may well be provisions for hiding or concealing scenic elements and sound and lighting equipment, but the diversity of audience perspective means that the equipment will be difficult to effectively remove from the overall image of the dramatic world created.

In an **arena** theatre, also called theatre-in-the-round, no part of the stage can truly be considered the front, and there is no direct access between the stage and the backstage. It is very difficult to conceal lighting and sound equipment, so their presence is accepted as part of the performance picture. The stage might be at floor level, and the audience sits in riserlike tiers of seats or the seating may be on the floor while the performers use a raised platform as their stage.

The **black box** type of theatre has few fixed features. For each production, audience and performance spaces can be arranged into proscenium, thrust, arena, or other configurations. Dressing rooms, storage spaces, and the like are necessarily disconnected from the performance areas, and frequently from the room itself. For example, a true black box is essentially an empty room, with no designated stage area, let alone any "backstage" or "offstage" areas. An actor, therefore, might literally have to leave the room through a door near one side of the performance area, in order to get to a door on the other side of the room in order to make an entrance on the opposite side of the performance area. Likewise, lighting and sound equipment are in plain view and made a part of the overall scene. Audience seating is temporary, set up for the specific performance, and might consist of chairs on tiered risers or chairs set directly on the floor. Similarly, the performance space is determined by the needs of each production, and might be flat on the floor or raised above the audience level on a platform or platforms. Mostly, these theatres are small and utilized for more experimental shows. Often, they occupy a building that originally served a different purpose, such as a warehouse, school, or office building.

Each of these architectural types offers a different set of advantages and disadvantages for theatre artists during the course of creating a theatrical production. The proscenium theatre, with its fixed frontal relationship between audience and performer, allows for a kind of realism by offering the prospect of viewing the dramatic world through an architectural picture frame without seeing audience members in the background. Its direct access to the backstage areas permits easy exits and entrances and there is little doubt, since performers disappear behind the masking, whether an actor is in the scene being viewed. **Sightlines**, the unobstructed view from the audience, can easily be controlled so lighting and sound equipment does not intrude visually into the stage picture, and with offstage and overhead facilities, scenic changes are easily effected in a proscenium theatre. Yet these qualities also lend a "two-dimensional" quality to the dramatic world: the depth of the stage is sometimes difficult to estimate, and performers must always direct their efforts toward the front of the stage. The arena and thrust theatres allow performers to be seen more "three-dimensionally," but because audience members must be able to see from three or four different seating areas, the use of scenery is rather limited. The wall with a door that seems so realistic in a proscenium theatre might well block the view of a significant portion of the audience in an arena or thrust theatre. In thrust and arena stages, performers must always be cognizant of the fact that they are being watched from several directions at once, and the director's blocking must move the actors in such a way that no one side of the audience gets a bad view. These are but a few of the ways that theatre architecture affects the presentation of a production.

Setting the Stage

Inextricably influenced by architecture, set design is concerned with the creation of the dramatic world in which a play takes place. It is the world in which the actors breathe life into their characters and the canvas on which directors paint their stage pictures. While actors and directors are intimately associated with the dramatic world, they are essentially users of it.

A set design is expected to be not only pleasing to the eye, but also functional, evocative, and part of an overall production concept. The set expresses the dramatic world as a kinetic space through which the actors move under the watchful eyes of the audience, who can frame the scene for themselves by taking in small details as well as the big picture. If the set moves, or changes, over the course of the play, its movements help to convey the rhythm and pace of the production. The set also becomes part of the performance through the actors' interaction with its elements—doorways, stairs, furniture, and boundaries.

This has not always been the case, nor is it necessarily the norm in theatre around the world. The role of the set in a performance, and of the set designer in particular, is a fairly recent development in the long history of theatre. In many global theatre traditions, scenery reflects a sense of and respect for continuity. Chinese opera, for instance, frequently features a simple arrangement of two chairs, a table, and a rug. Although these simple elements might be set up in different configurations, they are not intended to represent or evoke any particular setting or location. The way that they are used by the actors allows them to define any environment that might be called for by a particular play, from a room in a temple to a mountaintop. The stage used by Japanese *noh* theatre conjures up associations with a Shinto shrine with its highly polished cypress floor, distinctive curved roof supported by four pillars, and a modest backdrop with a painted pine tree. These pillars help actors in full masks to orient themselves while the audience knows that certain pillars are associated with certain characters and prominent actions. Portable scenic elements are used sparingly to create specific locales as needed.

Though Western theatrical traditions followed a different path than those of Asia, a similar continuity and conformity can be seen in stage and scenic design in European and American theatre until the middle of the nineteenth century. Unlike the conventions of China and Japan, Western theatre has privileged innovation, but this is more the result of meeting audience expectations and following patterns that proved successful than of preserving historical practices. Yet even as Western drama evolved and progressed over the centuries, scenic elements—the dramatic world in which the play took place—was not seen as a critical aspect of performance until well into the eighteenth century; a short list of somewhat standardized settings served the needs of most dramas. Scenic elements were often the result of pragmatic financial considerations rather than artistic analysis.

The theatre traditions of Asia and Europe both originated in a context of festival and ritual, strongly influencing the "look" of the environments in which their plays were performed. The theatres of ancient Greece were at first only temporary structures set up for the City Dionysia, an annual religious festival. Though the theatres were eventually built as permanent structures, their use remained tied to the festivals. Questions of décor or representation of specific locales does not seem to have been an important element in the Greek theatre; the architectural elements of the buildings behind their stages seem to have served as scenery for whatever plays were performed. Doorways in these façades indicated the houses or palaces occupied by the characters of the plays. The direction an actor used to enter or exit the stage gave a sense of location—an actor entering from stage left was understood to be coming from the harbor while an exit stage right led to the city. This idea of place was also supported by the costumes worn by the actors and the language of the plays.

The Romans adapted the Greek approach to theatre design and practices. However, they built structures that were significantly more elaborate and ornate. While the theatrical performances of Rome were somewhat disconnected from the religious setting of the Greek theatre, the Romans also felt little need for the sort of detailed scenic environments we are accustomed to today. With the fall of the Roman Empire, records of theatrical activity in Europe effectively dried up and we are left with a temporary impression of theatre coming to an end. The more likely story, as contemporary scholarship is helping to establish, is that theatre continued to be created and performed, but in a much lighter and more easily transportable form that could adapt easily to different social environments.

Theatre began to reemerge in the middle of the eleventh century, now called the late medieval period. Seeking new ways to explain the lessons and meanings of Christianity and the Bible to a largely illiterate population, churches in Europe began staging dramatizations of particular biblical stories on specific festival days of the liturgical calendar. These dramatizations were included in regular church services in conjunction with the reading of scripture passages, at first as a kind of pantomime performed by priests or monks. These performances took place within the churches using symbolic spaces along with clerical objects and attire to recall events such as the Nativity or the Resurrection. These performances soon developed into original dramas—plays based on Christian teachings, but not necessarily based on scripture—and by the thirteenth century had begun to be performed outside the church proper. With this move, theatre once again found a need and an opportunity to create a special environment—a dramatic world.

These performances often involved an entire community. Because there were only a few occasions throughout the year that a large portion of a community's populace would gather—market or trade fairs, as well as certain feast days in the liturgical calendar—the performances were scheduled to fill as much of these special days as possible. This was fulfilled by the presentation of several short plays, each treating a different saint's life or biblical story in sequence. The actors were drawn from the community at large, and seldom did any actor perform in more than one play.

To make the performances as accessible as possible to the whole community, two different approaches were adopted. In the first, "fixed" stages were composed of an open, unadorned playing space surrounded by small scenic units designating biblical locales. The open playing space was known as the *platea*, and the small scenic units were called *mansions*. In the medieval pattern, the actors from each story would enter the *platea* from their appropriate *mansion*, thereby informing the audience of the play's locale. This sense of place was also reinforced by references in the play's dialogue.

In the second approach, plays might be mounted on a special wheeled platform known as a *pageant wagon*, or simply *pageant*. Similar to the floats used in parades today, the *pageants* were drawn from place to place around the community throughout the day, meeting small clusters of the populace and performing their designated play before moving on. Unlike the *mansions*, the *pageants* could be quite elaborate, sometimes including a second story or a space beneath the "stage," and particularized to the needs of a specific play/story. Both of these approaches to staging drama strongly influenced the performance conventions of theatre in England in the sixteenth and early seventeenth centuries. Shakespeare's Globe Theatre, for instance, was built around a largely open stage; his plays require little in the way of scenic elaboration or embellishment, and his texts generously provide significant details to help the audience imagine the locale and time.

With the great interest in all aspects of ancient Greek and Roman culture that characterized the Renaissance, questions of theatre architecture, play texts, performance, and scenic design were prominent in the emerging culture. Classical texts were closely read, and societies sprang up in many cities with a passionate interest in recreating the arts of the ancients. One of the earliest theatres of the Renaissance was the Teatro Olimpico in Vicenza, Italy. Designed by Andrea Palladio, this

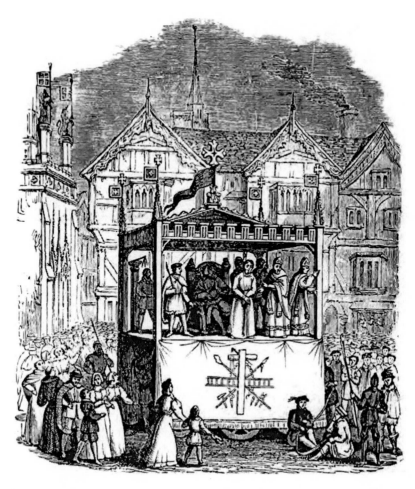

A medieval *pageant* wagon. From Charles Knight, *The Popular History of England* (London: Warne, 1874).

late-sixteenth-century theatre featured an audience area arranged as a semicircle open to a broad raised stage backed by a three-story *scaenae frons*, an elaborate architectural façade found in classic Roman theatres.

Yet the theatre designers of the Renaissance also displayed a degree of creative flexibility in their quest for the classical and made several adaptations to the ancient plans to accommodate the newly understood applications of linear perspective. Within a generation, the Teatro Farnese opened in Parma. Like the Teatro Olimpico, this theatre was patterned

The Teatro Olimpico. Photo by Graeme Churchard.

on a classical Roman plan, but the audience semicircle was elongated into a horseshoe shape and a wall with a large opening was erected between the audience area and the stage. With this first appearance of a proscenium arch, scenery became an inescapable part of the theatrical performance, and scenic design began to take on importance.

Another important influence was Sebastiano Serlio's publication of his multivolume *Architettura* (1545), which included information on his system of three stock settings. Inspired by his readings about the ancients' use of *periaktoi,* a triangular prism with three different painted scenes, Serlio advocated one unique stock setting each for tragedies, comedies, and pastorals. In this use, **stock** suggests a set design guided by the genre of the play (comedy or tragedy, for instance), and that the appropriate stock set would serve the scenic needs of any play of the genre. All three scenes represented exterior locales and emphasized right angles and straight lines, and all were painted so that the edges of the shapes appeared to converge toward a central **vanishing point**. Many theatres, in fact, even sloped the floor of the stage so that the elevated upstage contributed to the perspective illusion; such stages are "raked," in today's parlance. In addition, all three scenes depicted masses that

The Teatro Farnese.

were quite sizable, representing buildings and trees. Yet because of the tricks of perspective, the buildings supposedly farther away were actually painted smaller, an illusion easily shattered by an actor standing in the wrong place. As a result, all of the scenery was placed upstage, behind the proscenium, while actors remained in front of it. Serlio's system proved immensely popular and was quickly put into use throughout the major cities and courts of Europe.

Though the English tended to follow the performance practices of the late medieval period through the sixteenth and early seventeenth centuries, they too began to build the proscenium-equipped theatres popular on the Continent. And while the theatre continued to adopt and adapt to technological advances, little emphasis was put on developing new approaches. Scenic demands were handled by skilled painters, but very few unique set designs were created for specific productions. Set design as a profession would not arrive until the mid-nineteenth century.

Set Design

Serlio's stock setting for tragedy. Courtesy of Hekman Digital Archive.

Two major developments in the nineteenth century challenged the primacy of painted perspective scenery and opened the door for theatrical artists specifically qualified to capitalize on them. The first was the adoption of the **box set**, which represented an interior space by enclosing the stage with three walls of scenery. This environment more realistically accommodated the actors and allowed them greater freedom to interact in a "natural" manner with their dramatic environment. The second was the rise of an intense attention to historical accuracy in all aspects of production, especially scene design. The increasing interest of historians, news reports of archaeological finds in exotic lands, and the steady publication of new books on historical costume, armor, and interior decoration all helped this trend. Set designers began studiously researching their interiors, exteriors, set dressings, and properties with great attention to historical accuracy and authenticity. Whenever possible, actual historical artifacts were acquired for use in performance,

A computer rendering of a box set. 2008 production of *The Late Henry Moss*, St. Louis Actors' Studio, set design by Patrick Huber.

but if historical objects were not available, facsimiles were constructed to look like the originals.

Over time, the set designer became a more important member of the theatrical creative team. The emergence of the variety of visual styles, starting in the early twentieth century, demanded artists who understood not only their principles but also the peculiar demands of mounting a theatrical production. At the same time, new and inventive theatre genres appeared, each requiring its own scenic needs. And while realism continued to be the dominant style through the middle of the century, the experimentation and turmoil of the first half of the century had sufficiently matured by the end of World War II to effectively challenge that style. As the boundaries of theatre expanded to contain all of these changes, the opportunities and the need for the set designer were clear to all.

Process

As for even the most casual reader, a set designer's first experience of a new play is usually in the reading of the script. From this encounter, readers invariably find that their imaginations begin to create the world

Site-specific refers to theatrical works presented outside traditional theatre spaces. A straightforward use of this technique is to transplant a play to a setting suggested by the text (*A Midsummer Night's Dream* in a forest, *The Pirates of Penzance* on a ship, etc.). Performances devised specifically for a found space are capable of more complexity. They can allow the environment and the play to be reconsidered at the same time and can challenge the boundaries between actor and audience.

A 2007 production of *Waiting for Godot* (featuring T. Ryder Smith, J. Kyle Manzay, Wendell Pierce, and Mark McLaughlin; directed by Christopher McElroen) presented in the Ninth Ward of New Orleans, an area devastated by Hurricane Katrina. Seating was set up for five hundred, but hundreds had to be turned away. Photo courtesy of Christopher McElroen.

This set design for the 2012 production of the opera *André Chénier* was built on Lake Constance, Austria, for the Bregenz Festspiel. The design is based on the famous painting *The Death of Marat*, which depicts the radical French revolutionary Jean-Paul Marat murdered in his bathtub. Photo by Kecko/Flickr.com.

The 2010 We Players production of *Hamlet* on Alcatraz Island. The site of the former prison high-lights issues of justice and punishment. Photo by Katie Hatey.

The 2006 production of *Roam* at Edinburgh Airport, a co-production between Grid Iron Theatre Company and the National Theatre of Scotland. It was billed as an "imaginative journey through, in and around the possibilities of air travel"; audiences were moved to a different location for each scene, from check-in to the departure gate and eventually baggage claim. The production was nominated for a Scottish Critics Award for Best Design. Photo by Richard Campbell, www.richardcampbell.co.uk.

inhabited by the characters and events of the play, to a varying degree of detail and specificity. The role and artistry of the set designer, though, lies in transforming the images that arise in the imagination into concrete tangible forms that will fulfill the requirements of the text within the reality of performance. The skills employed are diverse and various, but first and foremost, a set designer must be good at script analysis, able to dig into the text for the details of the characters' environments, and the individual details about each that are expressed by their environments—their economic status, their occupations, and their relationships with one another. The set design may be required to convey information about location, time of day, time of year, and era. Together with the director and other designers (costume designer, lighting, properties, and sound), the set designer creates the dramatic world of the play. And the world thus created must also be one inhabitable by the actors, be affordable and practical within the constraints of budgets and schedules, and comport comfortably with the architectural limits of the theatre itself.

Though each set designer has his or her own approach to these tasks, some common elements are shared by all. Among these are the establishment of time and place; the materialization of a setting that elaborates details of the characters' lives, circumstances, and relationships; the creation of mood and atmosphere appropriate to the production; and the relationship between the audience and the performance itself. Using

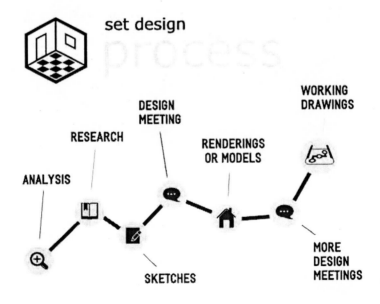

THEATRICAL PRODUCTION

the tools of the craft, which will be discussed next, the set designer—more than anything—helps to tell the story, through visual metaphors, and so facilitates the dramatic action. Starting with the premise that the audience will "read" every aspect of the visual manifestation presented on the stage for significance and symbolic meaning (even if only subconsciously), the set designer is responsible for myriad details and decisions, each of which contributes to the overall theatrical experience and telling of the story. Along the way, there are many decisions driven by pragmatic concerns, such as how the design ideas are communicated to the technicians charged with realizing the design and the selection of materials, arrangements, and finishes applied to the scenic elements. A set designer is, in short, a scholar, researcher, sketch artist, draftsperson, model builder, and communicator.

Many of a set designer's objectives can be considered under the broad heading of "telling the story." While the set designer, like all of the artists involved in mounting a play, forms initial impressions and understandings from the first readings of the script, these immediate reactions do not lead directly to the creation of a set design. Rather, the set designer shares these personal responses to the script with the rest of the creative team, especially the director. This is one of the first steps in the design process, and such discussions are often built into a production's schedule as **design meetings** or **design conferences**. The decisions arising from these meetings both form the agreed-upon vision and understanding of the play and the production and establish a clear set of standards for the individual artists involved to measure their work against.

In addition to "artistic" considerations, design meetings also bring to light specific needs or preferences that the set designer will probably have to address. Such needs might include the number and locations of the entrance and exit pathways the director can expect to have available for blocking the actors' entrances and exits. Similarly, particular items of furniture may be required, and their placement is critical to the "stage pictures" intended for the show. The design meeting is not just about identifying and finding solutions to the problems presented by the script. The participants also talk about their individual understandings of the script and share the visual images each developed during their readings of the text. It is not at all unusual for everyone involved to come away from a design meeting with new insights and interpretations of the story, the characters, and the play itself.

Building on the design discussions, the set designer develops a **design concept**, which in effect expresses the production concept as a complete plan for realizing the decisions and choices made. The set, in other words, becomes a visual metaphor for the abstract ideas discovered through the deep analysis and thoughtful deliberations of the text, in concrete symbolic form. Jo Mielziner's classic design for *Death of a Salesman*, for example, captures the claustrophobic closeness of the Loman household through its multiroomed interiors. Standing against the backdrops of a cityscape or the arches of the Brooklyn Bridge, the tightly connected rooms or the small backyard garden plot also helps to convey the sense that the world has passed Willy by, leaving him out of date and out of touch — with his professional life, his family, even his lost brother. Mielziner's design sets a tone, a mood, a sense of place and time, and provides a wealth of suggestions about the characters' lives and the emotional journey they take over the course of the play's action, and so helps to tell the play's story.

The set establishes the style and tone of the production through the colors, arrangement, and qualities of the scenic elements. In today's theatre, this process begins as the audience enters the theatre and takes their seats. A common practice is to leave the **act curtain** — the main drape that separates the stage and audience — open, so that the set is in full

Rendering of the original 1949 production of *Death of a Salesman* by Jo Mielziner. Courtesy of Bud H. Gibbs.

view of the audience. The audience, therefore, is free to make assumptions about the play before an actor walks on stage or a line of the play is delivered. Heavy, dark, and somber elements might suggest tragedy, for example, while a lighter, brighter, and airy environment might bring comedy to mind. Consider how a set design for Shakespeare's tragedy *Julius Caesar* might present a different view of Rome than that used for the musical comedy *A Funny Thing Happened on the Way to the Forum*.

Style, in its most basic sense, means how something is said or done; style can also refer to a specific, almost codified combination of distinctive features (color, shape, arrangement, and texture). In this latter use, style often carries a specific label that encapsulates particular combinations such as "realistic." However, such labels should always be considered broad descriptors rather than as a tight set of criteria. A set described as "realistic" might be a highly illusionistic setting in which walls of a completely furnished room are recognizable, but it might also describe a more theatrical setting in which some carefully selected practical objects only suggest the full environment.

"The artist should omit the details, the prose of nature, and give us only the spirit and the splendor."

Robert Edmond Jones, theatrical desinger

Other style choices, such as expressionistic, absurdist, epic, or postmodern, also foster a greater degree of abstraction in the design and directing choices. Ramps, levels, geometric or symbolic objects or shapes, or hanging bits of fabric can create an environment in which the actors can carry on in artificial or exaggerated ways, such as directly confronting the audience in their performance. Style also reflects the dramatic genre. The colors, shapes, and arrangements appropriate to a tragedy or serious drama typically are different from those appropriate to comedy. Thus, the set visually introduces the audience to the type of drama they will see and helps them prepare for the dramatic experience.

Whether realistically detailed or suggested abstractly, the set becomes the world of the characters, and so must visually convey the social, political, religious, and economic rules under which it operates. It also

The 2010 production of *Brighton Beach Memoirs* at the Old Globe Theatre. Directed by Scott Schwartz, set design by Ralph Funicello, lighting design by Matthew McCarthy, and costume design by Alejo Vietti. Photo by Ralph Funicello.

conveys important information about the people who inhabit it and provides insights into their tastes, personalities, and occupations, as well as their education and class status. Neil Simon's *Brighton Beach Memoirs*, set in the mid-1930s, requires a set that reminds the audience of the economic hardships the central characters face during the Great Depression, heightening the characters' hopes and aspirations for better days to come. In a realistic style, the set might show worn but cared-for furnishings and distressed carpets or wallpapers, yet also show the attention paid to keeping up the house and making it as pleasant a home as possible; together, these two aspects of the picture tell the audience that the family living in this house is down on its luck financially but held together by bonds of love and trust.

One of the set designer's first tasks, once the production concept has been agreed on and the design concept begins to take shape, is researching the particulars of the play. This research may include a traditional review of written material on the play and playwright, the era and culture in which the action is set, and the lives of the characters (if they are historical figures) or the people of the time and place in general. But set designers also perform a kind of visual research, seeking out images of all sorts—photographs, prints, paintings, and drawings—that represent the architecture, décor, and fashions of a particular time and place or convey the production concept. This visual research often begins even before the design meetings, and the set designer may use it in the discussions with the director. As the old saying puts it, "A picture is worth a thousand words"—this is accepted wisdom in the theatre.

During the research process, the set designer must be open to several different types of information. On a factual level, attention is given to the objective details of the play, especially when the production concept involves a degree of realism. Questions on topics such as color schemes or construction methods and materials must be answered accurately if the set is to represent, say, Paris in the 1930s authentically. In the course of researching, the set designer will often encounter images that express more subjectively the ideas of the production concept or that spur inspiration in a new direction.

In many instances, plays from earlier eras are "updated," that is, set in the familiar present time and place; a production of Molière's classic comedy *Tartuffe* might be set in the American South, for instance, rather than in the play's original seventeenth-century Paris. The set designer is thus obliged to research both periods, looking for the "feel" of the original and ways to express that feeling in contemporary terms. And every time a set designer undertakes this sort of research, the discoveries are filed away in a collection (files, folios, boxes) known as a "morgue"; this collection is often the starting point for the next project.

As the actual design coalesces from the contemplation of the results of the research, the set designer begins next to consider the design in concrete terms: questions of shape, scale, and color are paramount, of course, but so are such considerations as budgets, schedules, and personnel as well as pragmatic questions such as the theatre architecture within which the set will be located. The design process is now focused on identifying problems and devising practical solutions. While each set designer has personal ways of working through these problems, it is common to begin sketching, representing the design ideas graphically along with the limits or restrictions—wall placement, door size, and such—constraining the design. These sketches can also be shared with the director and other designers, and can be modified or adapted in response to feedback from these colleagues. If the play includes numerous scenes or different sets (especially common in musical comedy), the set designer may also **storyboard** the design by presenting a series of sketches that show the set's changes over the course of the performance.

The set designer employs, in many ways, the same tools as any other visual artist: line, mass, color, texture, space, and composition.

- **Line**—vertical, horizontal diagonal, straight, curved or spiral, line helps to define the edges of masses on the stage and to create feelings of movement or distance;
- **Mass**—literally, the size of scenic elements on the stage, or the amount of space they occupy;
- **Color**—in addition to the "hue" (what is often meant by "color": yellow, red, green, pink), color also deals with the saturation or depth of hue (deep or pale);
- **Texture**—qualities of smoothness or roughness, as well as variation of materials, patterns, or colors;
- **Space**—the three-dimensional volume of the stage can be divided into positive and negative spaces, with the scenic elements occupying the positive category, leaving the empty negative space free for the actors; and
- **Composition**—how the scenic elements and the open space between them are arranged within the height, width, and depth of the stage space.

All of these tools work together, as well. Different masses of color can be arranged to complement or contrast, for instance, and the arrangement of the elements can create a composition that is symmetrical or asymmetrical, balanced or unbalanced. These combinations help to convey mood and emotion. Vertical lines, for instance, are often considered "imposing" (especially when the actor's body is part of the visual composition), and certain colors carry distinct emotional connections—red, for example, suggests passion or anger. Yet none of these values is innate; they are learned cultural responses. A set designer is always on the lookout for such cultural connotations and the best way to interpret them.

Though it is actually the responsibility of the **technical director** to determine the appropriate materials and methods of construction for

realizing the set designer's creation, most designers are intimately familiar with both the catalogue of scenic elements and building techniques.
Among the more common scenic elements available in most theatres are
the following:

- **Flats**—two-dimensional panels, often made of either stretched
  canvas or thin plywood attached to a wooden frame. Flats are
  commonly used to create interior or exterior walls or other vertical expanses. They may rise from the stage floor or be suspended
  from overhead and can be joined together to increase the size of
  the mass;
- **Platforms**—large horizontal units, typically composed of heavy plywood on a frame. Platforms can create various levels. Depending
  on the height of its elevation, a platform can suggest a raised floor
  or a second story; spaced far apart, platforms can suggest different
  locations within the same scene;
- **Wagons**—essentially platforms on casters, wagons permit the movement of different levels around the stage space. This movement
  may be integral to the play, like the one used to transport the dead
  bodies in a production of the Greek tragedy *The Oresteia*, or it might
  answer a more practical question such as a quick scene change;
- **Turntable, or Revolve**—a special kind of circular platform, the
  turntable pivots around its center, revealing different aspects to the
  audience at different times. It is a handy scene-change device, and
  some older theatres have turntables built into their stages;
- **Step Units and Stairways**—short flights of steps or full-height stairways, providing access to or from different levels of platforms;
- **Drops**—large fabric panels filling the entire vertical expanse of the
  stage behind the performance area, drops can be of the following
  types:
  o **Backdrops**—usually made of canvas or muslin and painted to
    represent almost any locale, backdrops are typically created to
    meet the particular needs of a play and may be painted many
    times.
  o **Cyclorama**—often fabricated of special seamless canvas, a cy-
    clorama, or "cyc," is typically white or light blue. It is commonly
    used, in cooperation with the lighting designer, to create a "sky"
    behind the set or to present washes of color.

○ **Scrim**—large loosely woven expanses of fabric, scrims have the ability, because of their weave, to appear opaque when lit from the front (audience) side, yet fade into transparency when lit from behind.

In today's theatre, a set designer might also have available some amazing technology, including projections, lasers, and automated mechanics. Indeed, many Broadway hits probably would not have been possible without recent technological innovations.

The set designer's penultimate step in the design process is recording and communicating the myriad details that comprise the design to the technicians and artisans who bring it to life. This can be a rather large set of information and may be communicated through many channels. Among the most important types of information are the spatial arrangement of scenic elements in the stage space, the kinds and dimensions of the scenic elements, their colors and textures, and any changes in the set over the course of the performance. But a set designer must also provide details on the furnishings and decoration of the set.

Some theatres employ a **props designer**, and part of that job involves assisting the set designer, but in many cases the set designer must also include the selection of furniture, carpets, draperies, and lighting fixtures, as well as decorative items like paintings, knickknacks, books on the shelves, and "memorabilia." This last category of prop often affords the set designer great opportunity to help the audience understand the characters' lives. For example, a college pennant on the bedroom wall might recall happier days as a football hero for the character of Brick in Tennessee Williams's play *Cat on a Hot Tin Roof*.

No single channel can communicate all of the details comprising a set design, and so a designer employs several. The sketches mentioned earlier may be refined, with adjustments made to accurately convey proportions and placements, and color can be added to the sketches. In a finalized form, such sketches become **renderings** and these become the guide for building and finishing the set. Some of the detailed information, though, is quite technical—the dimensions of individual scenic elements and their precise placement on the stage, for example—and is best conveyed in mathematical terms. This information is best conveyed by a more formal type of drawing. Whether they are drafted by hand using a straightedge and pencil or digitally through software like AutoCAD

Set rendering for *The Woman in the Dunes*, Hungarian Theatre of Cluj, 2011. Designed by Mihai Ciupe.

or VectorWorks, these mechanical drawings provide accurate measurements that can easily be transferred to the materials in use, as well as particular details about an object (a rounded edge on a piece of wall trim, maybe) or its placement on the stage.

Two special types of mechanical drawing are predominant in the theatre: the **groundplan** view, which represents the stage or object as if looking down on it from above; and the **elevation**, which represents the stage or object as if looking at it directly from one side. These two types of drawings always include the dimensions of each aspect of the object or space, and they complement one another; a single object may require two, three, four, or more drawings to convey all of the information relevant to it.

Imagine a simple cube. To represent it by mechanical drawing, a set designer might offer a plan that shows the top of the cube. This drawing would be accompanied by four elevation views—one for each of the four sides. Finally, a special inversion of the groundplan view (called a *reflected plan*) would present the bottom of the cube. Because the mechanical drawings are fundamentally a channel of communication, though, the set designer can use some obvious shortcuts. In the case of

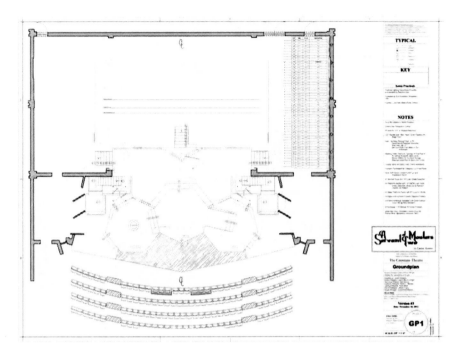

Example of a groundplan. Designed and drafted by Jason Myron Wright.

the cube, for instance, a plan view and one elevation might suffice, if the set designer includes a written note stating that the bottom will be a mirror image of the top, and that all four sides are the same.

Of the two, the type of drawing most used is probably the groundplan. This bird's-eye view shows outlines of the walls of the theatre building, the stage, and the audience area. It also represents the outlines of the scenic elements that make up the set, including the furnishings. When appropriate, the ground plan also illustrates the storage locations of scenic elements not in play during a particular scene, along with the most efficient route these elements should follow during the set change. The set designer's groundplan is also valuable for the lighting designer, who uses it to determine the placement and uses of the lighting equipment, and to the sound designer, who relies on it to plan the installation of microphones or speakers. Certain elevation drawings, especially those portraying the surfaces of scenic elements that will be visible to the audience, can be colored and used as guides for applying the proper finishes to the set. Called *paint elevations*, these drawings usually convey not only the final "look" of the set but also details on the number of different colors that might be used, how these should be applied, and special application information.

The set designer might also build a model of the set, which provides a three-dimensional rendering of the scenic space that is often especially useful to the director. With a model, blocking problems can be worked out, stage pictures can be planned, and a virtual sense of how the performance will appear to the audience can be imagined. A full model is completely and accurately painted, furnished, and decorated just as the actual set will be and can take many hours to complete. It is not unusual, therefore, that either the set designer or the theatre company keeps the models as part of a portfolio or archive. And one final use of the set designer's sketches, renderings, and model might be by the marketing department, as images to be used in advertisements or posters.

While the set designer might be intimately involved in the realization of the design as a finished set, once the design has been recorded in prose, graphically, or as a complete model, it becomes the responsibility of the **technical director** and a group of skilled technicians and artisans to bring it into being. The technical director oversees all aspects of engineering and fabricating the scenic elements and installing them on the stage in accordance with the set designer's intents. The technical director, additionally, oversees the operation of the scene shop, where much of the construction takes place. This work is performed by the scenic carpenters, usually led by a **master carpenter**, and it includes every step from the selection of raw materials, such as lumber, through the dimensioning and shaping of the materials to assembling the parts into completed scenic elements. Scenic carpenters often employ metalworking skills, such as welding and shaping metals, as well as molding, carving, and casting plastics and synthetic foams in today's scene shops as productions adopt new technologies. The constructed scenic elements are finished by the painting crew, often under the guidance of **charge artists**. These artisans are skilled painters, of course, as their crew name suggests, but their purview also includes applied finishes, such as textured plaster, powdered metals, and carved foams.

Together, all of the artists, artisans, and technicians discussed in this chapter collaborate to create the theatrical world in which a play lives.

The set designer is the theatre artist directly responsible, of course, but at every stage there is an ongoing conversation—between the director and designers, between the designer and the researcher, and between the designer and the technicians and artisans—informing and shaping the set design's intentions, style, and shape. Throughout the process, and across all of the conversations, telling the play's story and making the telling as clear and comprehensible as possible is the prime objective. As the most solid visual aspect of a production, the work of the set designer is an embodiment of the production concept.

Sound Design: An Interview with Richard Woodbury

Richard Woodbury is a composer, sound designer, and educator working in theatre, dance, and media arts. Since 1980, Richard has served as music director at the Dance Center of Columbia College Chicago where he is an associate professor and Distinguished Faculty Artist. In 2012, he was named Resident Sound Designer at Chicago's renowned Goodman Theatre.

What are the responsibilities of the sound designer as you see them?

The primary role of a sound designer is to make the storytelling more potent. There are typically two divisions of labor within that task. Job one is making sure that we can hear the actors. Sometimes that's completely passive—you're in a room where that already happens and everybody is happy. And other times, it's about working with set designers to make sure there are surfaces where the sound can bounce off so that the blocking doesn't send all the sonic energy upstage. You try to solve that problem without reinforcement. But at the end of the day, if you can't hear people, you stick microphones on them and reinforce them. Job two is to provide whatever additional sonic content enhances the storytelling and the design concepts of the show. That can be as simple as realistic sounds, realistically sourced, placed within the story. Or as complex as a more cinematic, interpretive, abstract approach where the sound becomes a true design element in framing the story.

When you get a script, what is the first thing you do?

I read it. And I read it the first time with no consideration of anything other than my reading. What's the story? Who are my characters? Then I read it again, thinking in terms of place and practical issues. What are the things the script actually calls for, in terms of sound? Is there a car horn or a doorbell or a phone ring? Continuing into the third reading, I start to figure out how I contribute to this story. What are the environments I might create sonically? Are there transitions that need or might invite some kind of framing music or sound? What might those sounds be? What might that music be?

Are most designers composers?

I think it's a fairly common characteristic in Chicago, less so in New York. Although increasingly across the field, I think the trend is that sound designers pick up some compositional skills and apply them to their craft. I would argue that the line between music composition and sound composition is a fuzzy one at best and that a well-designed and executed sound collage is, in fact, a type of composition. I think where the skill set gets more problematic is when you're doing more tonally based or period or style-based composition, and there is more of a separation.

How did you get involved in sound design?

I was actually a composer and that led me to sound design. I had been doing live music and the reinforcement that goes along with it. I'd been doing work for dance, so I was familiar with crafting music to be an accompaniment for another theatrical presence. A local designer somehow learned of my work as composer and invited me to write music for a production. I had no understanding of where the lines between the roles ended, and so I sort of did the whole production soundwise. Then word got out that I could do this, people started calling me, and the rest is history. I was not trained in it specifically at all.

Do you have relationships with several directors or do you usually work on just one design team?

I have several directors that I work with quite consistently, and [with whom] I've developed relationships over the years, and that's frankly why I do this. I'm fortunate enough that I have a teaching position— I'm the music director at Columbia College's Dance program. I've been here a long time, and I can pick and choose my sound design projects, and I have done so largely based on who I want to work with as a director.

Can you name some favorite designs that you've created?

Well, I think *A True History of the Jonestown Flood* was one of them in terms of the sonic content. I had an opportunity (which I almost never get) to create the key dramatic moment of the play, the flood itself. The play literally turns at that moment. It was two and a half minutes in total darkness where the only storytelling was sound. So I feel like I really delivered. I don't often get the chance to be that foregrounded in a production. Another was *Desire under the Elms.* That production opened with an eight-minute sequence with live action onstage with music behind it. And so, for eight minutes, the only sonic information was mine, and it set the tone for the whole production. It was completely anachronistic to what we were seeing onstage, which was guys hauling rocks and gutting pigs, and you've got this aggressive electronic score going on. Again, that kind of opportunity to be foregrounded is particularly, for my composer self, great moments.

For pieces set in another time, do you find yourself doing a lot of musical research or do you let the mood take you somewhere musically?

Both things happen. I will do research, certainly, on productions that are period set. But there's a line. If I know I'm going to be writing the music, I typically don't. I'm not usually interested in trying to re-create something from a particular period. The people of that period have already done it, and done it better than I can. Why would I ever try to write music that sounds like Bach, when I could just use

Bach? So I'm not a big fan of that. However, I might borrow instrumentation from the period, or I might take some harmonic aspects of a period and borrow that. But if I'm writing music for production, I think of it as my music. It stands outside the period and frames the storytelling in a different way.

What are the tools of the sound designer?

Well, at the risk of sounding precious, I'm going to start with my ears. You listen to the world, you gather information, and you begin to develop an aural imagination and an aural imagery sense that you then seek to bring into the theatre. It turns into technology and techniques after that. Like just about everyone else, I work with Pro Tools, which is a digital audio workstation for manipulating and recording audio. I have a number of portable digital recorders and an assortment of microphones—I'm a big fan of recording my own effects, as opposed to lifting them off CDs. Although I do that too. Musically, I work both in Pro Tools and in another software program called Digital Performer, and I have countless samplers and other virtual instruments in the computer that I can write and compose with. Sometimes those are, in fact, the finished scores, and sometimes those parts are replaced by warm, living human beings. In terms of running a show, I'm a big fan of Cue Lab and also LCS, which is a more fully featured program, for controlling cues and running shows.

What is it you love most about being a sound designer?

There's a lot. You know, there's nothing like sitting with an audience the first night of a preview and seeing it all come together in a way where people who have no connection to all the preparatory work to get to that point. They just receive the experience in a way that, you can tell, moves them and affects them. That's the payoff. But it's also, and I'm constantly amazed at this, any time you are working on a production, you become a member of this family that's intensely devoted to this artistic project together. And over the course of weeks or months, you just have this common experience that has an intensity and focus about it that you don't encounter usually elsewhere in life. That camaraderie and sense of community is, I think, very powerful.

The 2010 Goodman Theatre production of *The True History of the Jonestown Flood*. In this play-within-a-play moment, a theatre troupe reenacts the flood. Courtesy of the Goodman Theatre. Photo by Eric Y. Exit.

5 Costume Design

Stacey Galloway

Costume designers create the entire visual identity of a character. Hair, makeup, accessories, and even body shape, along with clothing, are all a part of this visual presentation, each carefully selected to give clues to the audience about a character and his or her world. By giving these clues, the costume designer is helping to tell the story in a nonverbal way.

Every story has a setting in which it takes place. Sometimes it is specifically defined by the playwright, such as "midafternoon on a cold December day in Maine, present day." Sometimes it is partially defined or not defined at all. No matter how much information is provided by the playwright about the setting of the story, the director and designers must make choices that define the world of the play. Those choices help to convey information to the audience such as geographic location, season and weather, time of day, a particular occasion or activity, and time period. Clothing has many functions, one of which is protection from the elements. For the setting just described, for example, a costume designer might chose to dress characters in snow boots and heavy parkas as opposed to flip-flops and shorts. The choice of clothing could help to indicate a geographic location that has a colder climate, a season that is cold, and weather that includes snow.

Clothing also functions as a statement about the wearer because it offers information about the amount of money the character spent on the clothes, his or her adherence or access to fashion trends, and the degree to which societal rules about appropriateness of clothing are important to this person. We attach meaning to those choices based upon our own understanding, experience, and prejudices. If the characters wear jeans and plaid flannel shirts versus wool trousers and cashmere sweaters underneath the parkas and snow boots, a less urban and more rural location and/or activity can be conveyed. Because fashion is continually changing and there is a recorded history of these changes, the costume designer is able to use choices in clothing, hairstyles, and makeup to help indicate when the story is taking place. All of these choices are visual cues that help orient the audience to the setting of the play.

The costume designer also provides visual cues about the characters themselves, such as gender, age, occupation, and social status. Sometimes the costume can even provide insight into relationships between characters and their psychological or emotional states. We all attach meanings to the visual cues we are given based upon our personal experiences and the culture in which we live. Particular colors evoke emotion or have symbolism—red can mean anger or passion, purple is for royalty—some of which are culturally shared and some of which are unique to each individual. Society creates rules about what clothing is appropriate based upon activity, social standing, and gender (tuxedos are worn by men to formal occasions, pajamas are worn to sleep), which can be followed or broken. Fashion and the amount of money spent in its pursuit have different levels of priority for each of us, and we pass judgment on each other based upon our own level of priority. Exposure or accentuation of particular body parts sends unspoken messages that are based in personal and societal ideas of sexuality. Uniforms are worn by members of particular groups for reasons of identification and cohesion. By understanding and using the meanings attached to these visual cues, a costume designer can impart information about characters through the choices the designer makes in clothing them.

The audience makes some assumptions about the people they see onstage. For example, think about the image of a person wearing jeans, sneakers, and a tank top with long scruffy hair. Imagine that person and think about who they might be—their age, occupation, how much money they make, and so on. What if the jeans are tight and the sneakers are high heels instead? Does that change your ideas about this person? It is possible you are now imagining someone of a different gender and maybe even a different social status. Now imagine the jeans and sneakers are designer brand. Who is this person now? What if those designer clothes are dirty and torn? What if the person has smeared mascara and a runny nose? Or is covered in tattoos? All of these specific choices provide different information to the audience about the character and how he or she fits into the story. The costume designer carefully selects from the many choices available to provide the visual image of the character that will best tell the story.

Sometimes the character is not a specific person, but rather a visual representation of an idea. In this case, the costume designer still makes choices based upon the personal and societal meanings we attach to visual cues. However, they are not made to define a particular person in a particular situation. The designer may choose to evoke a feeling, create an atmosphere, or visualize an idea of something that is relevant to the story, such as the inner turmoil of a character or the environment in which a character exists. These meanings, many times, are operating on a more emotional and instinctive level than meanings based upon rules or fashion that define a person's place within society—but that does not mean they are any less important or well defined. Sometimes these meanings create the visual image that best assists in telling the story.

The choices that a costume designer makes are developed through a multistep process that begins with the script. The costume designer, the director, and other designers first study the script and the information provided within the text; then they combine that information with their individual impressions of the story, the characters, and the world of the play and what they want the audience to understand or feel. The director and designers work together in a collaborative process to determine a particular approach or concept to the visual elements that is unique to that production. This collaborative process involves the sharing of ideas and visual elements, usually through a series of design meetings. Sometimes designers seek inspiration for the visual world or the characters. Photographs, paintings, even music can spark an idea or help express an element of the story that the designers and director want to share. Many times, research is required about specific time periods, events, or locations that will be part of the world that is created onstage. From that research, the designers and director can decide how closely to represent that reality or whether to represent it at all. This collaborative process results in a particular concept or design approach that is unique to the production.

The overall design approach artistically affects all the choices of all the designers. The costume designer must always base his or her designs

Examples of costume research from two historical eras, the turn of the century (19th to 20th) and the 1950s.

on what best supports the design approach and creates the world of the play. These choices are also affected by practical elements that must be determined and accommodated. The most basic practical element is the number of characters and the number of different costumes they require within the production. This information is usually compiled into a **costume plot** or list. Costume designers structure this information in different ways according to their own process, but the objective is to determine the specific costume needs of the production. The compiling of this information can bring clarity to another reality of creating a world on stage: whether the performers must change costumes and how much time they have to do so. Also, the physicality of the performance can impact the particular choices that the costume designer makes. Running, dancing, fighting, even gesturing all impact the particular choices of the design.

Once practical needs are determined and the overall artistic foundation for a production is laid, the costume designer must begin to visualize the specific choices for the costumes. Different designers approach this step of the process in different ways, but the goal is always the same—to

CITY OF ANGELS COSTUME PLOT

ACT 1	PROLOGUE	SC 1 - L.A. HOSPITAL	SC 2 - STONE'S OFFICE/STINE'S OFFICE	SC 3 - BUDDY FIDLER'S OFFICE	SC 4 - STONE'S OFFICE	SC 5 - STINE'S BEDROOM	SC 6 - STONE'S OFFICE/STINE'S BEDROOM	SC 7 - STONE'S BUNGALOW	SC 8 - BUDDY'S OFFICE
STINE			LOOK #1	SAME		LOOK #2			SAME
STONE		LOOK #1 UNDER SHEET?	LOOK #1 W/ COAT & HAT		SAME			SAME PANTS & SHIRT	
GABBY / BOBBI						GABBY LOOK #1 (TRAVEL SUIT)	SAME		
DONNA / OOLIE			OOLIE LOOK # 1		SAME		SAME		DONNA LOOK #1
BUDDY FIDLER/ IRWIN IRVING				BUDDY LOOK #1					BUDDY LOOK #2
CARLA HAYWOOD/ ALAURA KINGSLEY			ALAURA LOOK #1						
WERNER KRIEGLER/ LUTHER KINGSLEY									
GERALD PIERCE/ PETER KINGSLEY									
AVRIL RAINES/ MALLORY KINGSLEY PANCHO VARGAS/ LIEUTENANT MUNOZ									
GENE / OFFICER PASCO		ORDERLY							
STAND-IN / MARGARET									
GILBERT / DR. MANDRIL									GILBERT (BARBER)
JIMMY POWERS								LOOK #1 (CROONER)	
STUDIO COP / BIG SIX								BIG SIX	
STUDIO COP / SONNY								SONNY	
DEL DACOSTA/ MAHONEY		ORDERLY							
CINEMATOGRAPHER (JACK)/									
SHOESHINE / COMMISSIONER				SHOESHINE					

Act 1 costume plot of the musical *City of Angels*.

Costume renderings by Robin L. McGee.

visually represent the physical appearance of the play's characters. Many designers create artwork to visually communicate their intentions, generally called **costume renderings**, a series of sketches, paintings, or collages.

Many designers also compile research to accompany this artwork to act as the visual representation of their designs. Magazines, photographs, illustrations, portraits, and even written information can all help to specify how the characters and their world will appear to the audience. Some designers assemble swatches, examples of the colors and textures of fabrics they wish to use. All of this information and visual representation is used to communicate with the director, designers, and performers how the characters will ultimately appear onstage.

The conceptualization and visual representation of ideas is only half the process of costume design. These ideas must be turned into reality. This realization is a multistep process that involves many elements and, usually, many people. Before beginning the realization of a costume design, the parameters of the process must be determined. For every production, a particular amount of time, money, and labor is available and required. Because this is different for each production, the approach to the realization of the costume design is always different. Sometimes costumes are created, sometimes existing garments are used, and sometimes it is a combination of these two approaches. Whichever approach is used, the costume renderings and/or research serve as the plan for what the characters will look like.

Executing the Design

Depending on the size of the production, other staff may be involved in costume creation and maintenance:

Make-up Designer

Assistant Costume Designer

Craftsperson

Wig Designer

Cutter/Draper or Patternmaker

Wig Supervisor

First Hand

Wardrobe Supervisor

Wig Run Crew

Stitcher

Dressers/ Wardrobe Crew

Costume Personnel

These job descriptions are not all-inclusive and do not apply to all productions. These are intended to be generalizations to help the reader understand the variety of people and activities involved in costume design:

Costume Designer—Conceptualizes the look of all the performers in the production and creates visual representations or renderings of the design. Guides the realization of the design through the production and rehearsal process.

Assistant Costume Designer—May assist the designer in the conceptualization phase through research or illustration. Assists the designer in the realization of the design through sourcing of materials, organization of information, budgeting, scheduling of fittings/meetings, and documentation of design choices.

Costume Shop Manager—Oversees the realization of the designs into physical garments. This may include acquiring materials, scheduling/conducting fittings, hiring/scheduling personnel, budgeting, and organizing information.

Cutter/Draper or Patternmaker—Uses the renderings, research, and other information provided by the designer or design team to create or alter the physical costumes. When costumes are created, this person creates the pattern that is used to cut out and assemble the garment. This person generally oversees the construction, fitting, and finishing of the garment.

First Hand—Assists the cutter/draper. Activities may include altering patterns, cutting fabric, assembling the garments, overseeing stitchers, altering garments, and assisting in fitting garments onto performers.

Stitcher—Sews the garments.

Craftsperson—Creates or modifies elements of the costumes that require skills in millinery, armor, dyeing, painting, distressing, and jewelry.

Wardrobe Supervisor—Oversees the appearance of the performers during rehearsals and performances. Oversees the care and maintenance of the costumes during the run of the show.

Dressers/Wardrobe Crew—Assist the performers in the wearing and changing of costumes during rehearsals and performances. Clean and maintain costumes during the run of the show. These activities may be divided between people who dress the show and people who maintain the show.

Wig Designer—Conceptualizes the look of the hairstyles in collaboration with the costume designer.

Wig Supervisor—Oversees the appearance of the performers' hair (including facial hair) during rehearsals and performances. Oversees the care and maintenance of the wigs and facial hair pieces during the run of the show.

Wig Run Crew—Applies wigs and facial hair to performers during rehearsals and performances. May style performers' own hair. Maintains wigs and facial hair during the run of the show.

Makeup Designer—Conceptualizes and creates visual representations of the makeup in collaboration with the costume designer. The application of the makeup is generally handled by the performers or, occasionally, a makeup artist.

If the costumes are being created, then the rendering becomes a blueprint. The people responsible for the realization of the costume analyze the rendering to determine its elements and how to make them. For the person or persons creating the clothing, they must combine what they see in the rendering with their own training and knowledge of fabrics, construction methods, and historical clothing (when appropriate) to turn a two-dimensional illustration into three-dimensional clothing. Many times this process involves creating a **mockup**—a version of the garment made out of inexpensive fabric. This allows the designer to see the idea in three dimensions and also see how it fits the actor's body, allowing adjustments to be made before the garment is constructed. The costume designer is generally involved in or in charge of selecting the fabrics from which the garments will be made. Many choices are available for different colors, textures, and types of fabric. The costume designer must select fabrics that are appropriate for the construction of the garment and fulfill the plan for the visual representation of the character.

If the costumes are not being created, and existing garments are being used, there are several means of acquiring them: pulling, borrowing, renting, and buying. Many theatres maintain a stock of costumes used in previous productions from which they "pull" items they need. If a particular theatre does not have an item that they need within their own stock, they may be able to borrow or rent it from another theatre that does. There are also businesses that rent items or whole sets of costumes for use on stage. Another option is to purchase needed items from stores, online businesses, or other merchants. It is very common to use a combination of all of these methods to assemble the needed items for a show. The costume designer must be able to coordinate all costume items, whether created, bought, rented, borrowed, or pulled, into a cohesive combination that fulfills the plan for the costume designs.

Whatever the origin of the costumes, the ultimate goal is for them to be worn by the actors onstage. This means that they must go through a process of **fitting**—each costume is tried on the actor and adjustments are made so that the garment fits that particular actor correctly and creates the appropriate image of the character. During this fitting, many of the specific choices for the costume are made—how the garment fits, the extent to which the actor can move in the clothing, which undergarments create the correct look and body shape for the actor, what accessories complete the outfit, and what makeup and hairstyle complete the look of the character. This is the stage of the design process where the character's whole look begins to come together and the costume renderings come to life.

As we have discussed, the visual representations of the characters are made up of a complex set of choices made by the costume designer and many others. These choices must be able to be replicated exactly each night onstage: each actor wearing particular clothes, hair, and makeup in specific ways and at specific times. All of this must be documented, so that it can be implemented each time the actors perform. This documentation varies based upon the organization and the people involved. Some of the common paperwork includes a costume plot and a **pieces list** of every item used in the show. This list can also be used as part of the information given to the wardrobe crew or department. The wardrobe crew is responsible for dressing the actors, making sure they match the design, helping the actors change costumes when necessary, and maintaining the costumes and look of the show for each performance. Their paper-

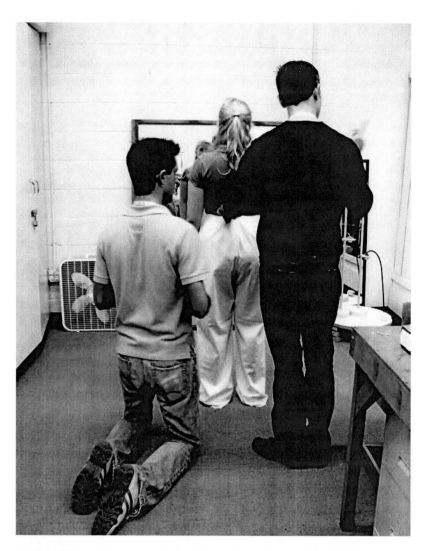

A costume fitting.

work includes information on costume changes, laundry/maintenance procedures, and check-in lists for costume items that have been created from the pieces lists. All of this documentation is crucial for the consistent creation of the visual world represented on stage each night.

The last step for the costume designer is to see everything together onstage during **dress rehearsals**. All the exploration, research, collaboration, planning, construction, fittings, and finishing are done so that the visual elements created and decided upon by the director and designers come together to create the world of the play. Dress rehearsals allow them to see this world for the first time. During these rehearsals, refinements can be made or whole ideas can be reenvisioned. These final necessary modifications ensure that the visual world created for the audience is the best one to tell the story.

Costuming Fantasy and Reality:
A Conversation with Designer Stacey Galloway

When did you know you were first interested in costume design?

I was that kid that started thinking about Halloween partway throughout the year, and was really excited about what I was going to be that year. I didn't realize that it was a possibility to do this as a career until I was in college and I had friends who were in the theatre department. I was looking for an elective in my freshman year and I thought I'd take the costuming class because I knew how to sew. I got hooked.

What was your first design?

I got a work-study job in the costume shop but I wasn't actually in the theatre department or taking courses. Because it seemed like I had interest, the instructor there allowed me to design shows on the side. My first design for them was *Waiting for Godot*. I didn't really know what I was doing. I tried with the guidance of my instructor to figure out how to go about it—how to learn how to draw things out. How to have a dialogue with the director about what we thought it meant. And to bring some sort of concept to it that would help the audience understand the story. And then I took that and tried to make it happen in real life on real bodies on a real stage.

Is there a period or a type of show you like working on more than others?

I don't. I actually get asked that question a lot. I find something interesting in about just about every project that I work on. There's always some part of it that gets me excited about it no matter what type of show, what type of project, what type of period.

Is there any advice you would give someone interested in costume design today?

Wow. So much. I think to be a good costume designer in the long term, you have to have a passion for costume history and history in general, psychology, visual arts. There are so many elements that feed into being a costume designer and the process can be complex. This is not an easy business to be in. We don't make a lot of money. We put in a lot of hours. Your standard, normal costume designer (and there are thousands of them out there) aren't people who are famous or rich. They are just people who are passionate about the storytelling and the creation of these characters that come to life on stage. That is where you get your fulfillment.

If you would, walk me through your design process. You are given the assignment. What's the first thing you do?

Read the script. And read it again. And probably read it again.

Are you looking for specific things each time?

Yes. It's very difficult to process everything you need to about a script in one read. A lot of times I will read the script first just to get the sense and feeling of the story, trying to set aside my costume designer mind and try to experience it as an audience would. That's sometimes very difficult because the costume designer mind wants to take over. The second read is about the design. It's about starting to take down the specifics. Who's in what scene? How many costumes do they need? What do they need to look like? What period is this? What sort of changes need to happen? And that process starts the documentation of the logistics of the design. And for me, I have to start with logistics to begin wrapping my head around the design. I can't process the storytelling without knowing that there are seventeen people and they have five costume changes.

So you have gone through the reading period. What's next for you?

I usually start by creating a costume plot. Every costume designer works slightly different in what they do first and what their paperwork looks like. I start with a costume plot, which is a spreadsheet of every scene in the production, every character in the production. It's essentially a chart of what scenes they are in and what look they need so I can start to process the show as a whole. After conversations with the director, I research the particular period and stylistic choice that the design team is working toward. I begin to accumulate the visuals to feed into the ultimate design.

I'd like to ask you about a design you did a few years ago for a summer stock production of the musical Nine. *First of all, how are musicals different from straight plays from a costume perspective?*

Musicals are generally more complex in the way that the characters function because a lot of times there are characters that are named, that we get to know, and then there is a group of people that are generally referred to as ensemble or chorus members that we don't really get to know. They are background people in scenes. They are singing and dancing in the big production numbers. They transition through a lot of different parts throughout the show, all being played by each individual ensemble member. For example, an ensemble member could be a shoeshine person in one scene, a movie director in another scene, and then they sing and dance in these five musical numbers, and then they are the little street urchin in the final scene . . .

So how do you find an identity for these people where there isn't much to go on textually?

For these ensemble-type designs, it is about creating a feeling of the scene that gives the audience information about location, setting, and mood of the number.

So what were the challenges of designing Nine*?*

Nine is a show somewhat based on the life of Federico Fellini, the Italian film director, and it has realism and fantasy all combined into a show that is grounded in reality but not actual reality. The bulk of the show is about the character Guido (who represents Fellini) and his interactions with all the women in his life. In one particular sequence, titled "The Grand Canal," we go into the fantasy of the movie that Guido is creating about Casanova, the iconic Italian lover.

So the function of the costumes was to show us the difference between reality and fantasy? So we would know by the design of the costumes which world we are in?

Yes. It was challenging to create a distinct difference between the visuals of the interactions of Guido and his women in a more realistic way versus the fantasy world of the movie he is creating. I had to set it within a somewhat historical reference so that the audience understood that this was the movie that Guido was making, not Guido's life. Then I had to impart a distinct surrealism to it that helps the audience understand that the movie Guido's creating is a reflection of the stresses in his life. Therefore, everything within the movie sequence refers back to his relationships with all these women in his life. They are all coming out in this movie is a twisted, surrealistic way.

So you actually have colors and styles that have to refer to other colors and styles?

Correct.

That's kind of a Gordian knot of design.

Right. So when I started talking with the director about the Grand Canal sequences, he distinctly wanted a shift in the feeling of them. There are two versions of it. There is "The Grand Canal" and then there is the "The Grand Canal Reprise." And as it goes through these sequences, the feeling of the number needs to begin to feel threatening to Guido. This is because the messy, tangled relationship he has with all these women comes out during his making of the movie and starts to overwhelm him. I started by talking to the director about the different feelings of the two sequences. We started with the idea that Casanova was in Venice. Venice makes you think of canals. Venice and water and reflection. We also talked about how the movie is a reflection of what is going on in Guido's life and what is going on is kind of ugly.

Venice is also a romantic city, but it also has an ugly side.

Just like Guido's relationships. On the surface, it seems like he has this plethora of women in his life, and yet they are making his life more and more complicated. Venice is also known for Carnival, which is similar in feeling to our Mardi Gras in that everybody wears costumes and masks and it's a big celebration. Then I began thinking about the costumes being see-through. We would see the beautiful silhouette of the eighteenth century, but we would also see the bodies of the performers. It's exterior glamour, but there are real people under there. And real people can sometimes be messy and not as beautiful as we would like them to be. So I started to investigate fashion of the period. It didn't need to be historically accurate: it just needed to represent and reference the eighteenth century. So I started looking at eighteenth-century fashion magazines. And I started seeing there were a lot of sheer garments. Canals and reflective water reminded me of glass, which is also reflective. There are a lot of buildings in Venice with clear and stained glass windows. This inspired me to make the Grand Canal costumes morph into something more threatening by a color change. So I started thinking about the first set of costumes being clear with golds and silvers—beautiful, reflective, and translucent. Then, as it became threatening, it became deeply, richly colored like stained glass.

I also was thinking about the shapes, and how to represent the idea of the eighteenth century without copying it. Since the story is based on Fellini, I looked at his film work, and I saw he had a certain obsession with the circus. So I started to feed in ideas of circus shapes and circus coloration in exaggeration. There is a fun, oversized playful quality about the circus which can also become slightly threatening in that clowns are fun but can also be very scary.

How much change was there between your original renderings and the final costumes?

The idea for this particular project was pretty concrete by the time I got to sketching it out on paper, but it went through a lot of discussion and investigation and exploration between the director and myself. We got to the point where I felt comfortable and that's when I put it on paper.

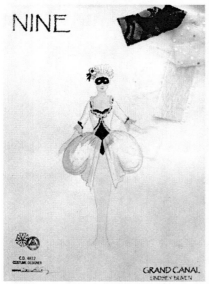

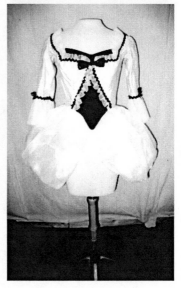

Grand Canal 1, 2, 3, and 4 Costume

Have you ever tossed a design idea into the dustbin and started over?

Absolutely. Yes. Sometimes it just doesn't work out. Sometimes where you think a design is going well but as the project starts to solidify, how the story is going to be told and all the specifics of the

NINE

GRAND CANAL FINALE

NINE

GRAND CANAL FINALE

other design elements, sometimes what you initially thought isn't suitable anymore. The whole point is to serve the storytelling. If a particular costume choice doesn't serve the story, then there's no point in having it.

6   Lighting Design

Kasendra Djuren

Walk outside. Take a look at your surroundings. Think about what you see. Can you describe it in terms of light and shadow? You might see a brilliant blue sky and the dappling of light and shadow as it falls on the sidewalk in front of you. You might notice the pools of light created by streetlights and how the people around you float in and out of light and shadow. Do you see your world differently when you think about the light all around you? How does it change your perception of your surroundings?

Lighting a stage allows the audience to see the world of the play, but it is much more than illumination. The lighting designer must be something of a magician, revealing what must be seen and hiding what needs to be hidden. He or she has the ability to subtly influence the perceptions of the audience and to dramatically transport them from one magical place to the next. Time of day can slowly change over the course of a play or you can go from a scorching desert to a cold, dark castle.

Functions of Lighting

In order to influence the world of the play, the lighting designer works with five basic principles in order to guide his or her work. These are known as **the functions of lighting**, the visual vocabulary the lighting designer uses to communicate with the audience. They are as follows:

- **Selective visibility**. Selective visibility is revealing what the audience needs to see and the manner in which they need to see it. This may vary from scene to scene. Sometimes only a silhouette needs to be seen. At other times, the audience needs to see all the detail of a scene brightly lit.

- **Composition**. This is directing the eye of the audience to a particular place or places on stage. The composition of a scene begins with what the scene designer places on the stage, continues with where the director places the actors, and is completed when the lighting designer guides the audience's eye to what needs to be seen.
- **Revelation of form**. Altering shape is one of the greatest powers of the lighting designer. Figures on stage (and sometimes scenery) must be lit in such a way as to maintain a constant three-dimensional presence.
- **Establishing the mood**. Mood is an inescapable feature of light— color, shape, and visibility must be used to establish the tone of a scene.
- **Reinforcing the theme**. The lighting of the scene must support the action of the scene. By doing so, the designer helps to convey the themes of the play.

Some of the greatest mistakes that a lighting designer can make are ignoring any of these functions. They help to enhance the audience's viewing and interpretation of the play. Ignoring them will confuse the audience and cloud the play's meaning.

The Lighting Designer

A great deal of responsibility is placed on the role of the lighting designer, but who is this person? A lighting designer is someone who strives to "paint with light," to create moments on stage that can capture the meaning and intent of a scene as if it were a painting or a photograph. A lighting designer is someone who spends a great deal of time paying attention to light, shadow, highlight, and shade. He or she will notice how the natural light and color move and strive to recreate these effects for an audience. In sum, the lighting designer tries to bring the natural world to life on stage in order to highlight meaning.

A lighting designer is a team player and a collaborative artist. The actors, director, and set and costume designers bring their work to the stage before the lighting designer. There is a great deal of planning, but the lighting designer cannot begin working on the stage until very close to the end of the design process. Therefore, he or she must be highly involved in the design and production process in order to be able to unify all the elements of the production.

The lighting designer cannot complete his or her tasks without a support team. Typically, an **assistant lighting designer** helps facilitate communication between the lighting designer and the production team as well as helping to complete some of the required paperwork for a production. The assistant lighting designer must be incredibly organized in order to help keep the lighting designer on task and to make sure everything is completed and on time.

Typically, a theatre will have a **master electrician** working for them. This person is responsible for the physical implementation of the lighting designer's work, making sure all the lighting instruments or fixtures get hung and focused correctly. He or she makes sure everything is working and all appropriate supplies are purchased. Often, the master electrician is also in charge of supplying other support staff that may be needed.

A Brief History of Stage Lighting

We all take for granted the electric lights we have in our homes. It is assumed that every space we enter in the modern world will have electricity and other modern conveniences. In our everyday lives, we often forget that even a century ago, amenities such as electric lighting, indoor plumbing, and air-conditioning were new technologies. Many texts on lighting design do not take the past into account. However, when you look at lighting design from a historical perspective, you can gain a greater appreciation of what it has achieved.

Texts dealing with ancient Greek and Roman theatre deal very little with the lighting of plays, stating only that it is assumed that they took place during the day. Since play festivals would have taken place over the course of a whole day, it is thought that torches and shiny pieces of mica were used to redirect the natural light entering the theatre. This would allow actors and moments to be highlighted for the audience, much as modern lighting attempts to do.

Similar practices in lighting continued until the sixteenth century. At the dawn of the Renaissance, theatre experienced a rebirth. Stage settings became more elaborate and stage machinery became more complex. Some theatres began to move indoors. As the physical space of the theatre changed, so did theatrical lighting. Theatres began to use chandeliers suspended from the ceiling and oil lamps hung on walls and scenery to light the stage. This took a great deal of candles, oil, and effort to create enough light.

In the early 1600s, theatre practitioners began to use reflectors to intensify the effects of the candles and lamps used to light the stage and audience. Later, theatres also began using candles or oil lamps at the front edge of the stage as footlights. They also placed them in vertical stacks in the wings to provide additional illumination. While these lights provided significant illumination, they also created a serious fire hazard. Over the years, many theatres burned down because of this method of lighting.

In 1792, William Murdock developed a process for distilling gas from coal, inventing a new form of illumination. Gas lighting quickly gained public popularity and rapidly moved into theatres and other public spaces in Europe and North America. A great improvement over candles and oil lamps, it provided a brighter and cleaner-burning source of light that was also easily controllable. While gas was a great improvement over earlier methods, it still posed a fire hazard as well as producing a great amount of heat and odor.

The angle of light can dramatically alter the mood of a scene. In this scene from a 2012 production of the musical *Urinetown*, the old practice of footlights was used to give the actors' faces a ghastly, menacing appearance. Constans Theatre, University of Florida School of Theatre and Dance, directed by Charlie Mitchell, lighting design by Timothy A. Reed. Photo by Stan Kaye.

The next great improvement in stage lighting came in 1879 when Thomas Edison developed a practical incandescent lamp, or the light-bulb as it is known today. Many lamps used today are variations on Edison's design. By 1900, most theatres had converted to electricity and were using incandescent lamps rather than gaslight. With this innovation, theatres slowly started moving into the twentieth century.

At first, the introduction of electricity itself did not change the way in which lighting operated. Electric lines were run to lights and electric fixtures operated much as gas fixtures had done previously. However, with the advent of the first circuit board electronics, stage lighting technology improved by leaps and bounds in the second half of the twentieth century. One of the biggest breakthroughs came in 1975 when the first computerized **lightboard**—a specialized piece of computer equipment designed and used to control theatrical lights—was used on Broadway by Tharon Musser in her groundbreaking lighting design for the musical A *Chorus Line*. It paved the way for the use of modern technology in lighting design.

Since the introduction of computer technology, lighting has changed almost as fast as the computer market itself. Each new generation of lightboard can process faster, control more lights, and interface more easily with the user. Lighting instruments are brighter and more energy

The first computerized lightboard.

efficient. Automated fixtures have been introduced to the theatre market and continue to grow in popularity and usefulness. Now, LEDs (light-emitting diodes) are being introduced as theatrical lights. They are more energy efficient, produce less heat, and are very controllable. As lighting technology improves, one is sure to see even greater changes in the tools of lighting design.

Lighting Pioneers

Adolphe Appia was born in 1862 in Geneva, Switzerland, the son of a physician who supported music but disliked theatre mostly because of his strict Calvinist views. As a young man, Appia studied music, including the operas of Richard Wagner. Appia disliked the traditional staging of Wagner's operas, with their two-dimensional painted scenery and lack of unity. Instead, he favored the idea of an artistic unity that would blend the acting with the staging, lighting, and music. Appia believed that shadow was as important as highlight. It helped to create depth and heightened the reality of the piece. His use of three-dimensional scenery and lighting to artistically unify a theatrical piece helped to revolutionize the ways in which productions were staged and lighting was used.

Stanley McCandless (1897–1967) is considered the father of modern lighting design. He developed what is known as the McCandless Method, which he published in *A Method of Lighting the Stage* in 1932. His theory was that light cast on the actor from a forty-five-

Lighting visionary Adolphe Appia.

Adolphe Appia's 1896 rendering of the Sacred Forest in Act 1 of Richard Wagner's opera *Parsifal*.

degree angle enhanced visibility and appeared natural. He maintained that there should be two lights at forty-five-degree angles aimed at the front of an actor—one with a warm tint and one with a cool tint. This technique is still used today.

Jean Rosenthal (1912–1969) is considered the first professional lighting designer. She studied lighting design with McCandless at Yale University from 1931 to 1934. During her career, she became the first resident designer for the Metropolitan Opera in New York City. She began working at a time when women were not accepted as professionals in the backstage theatre world. She is perhaps most well known for her work with the Martha Graham dance company; her lighting techniques for dance have become standards in the dance lighting repertoire.

Tharon Musser (1925–2009) began her career in 1956 with her lighting of the premiere of Eugene O'Neill's *Long Day's Journey into Night*. She had a prolific career as a lighting designer and was a pioneer in her field. She was nominated for ten Tony Awards

Jean Rosenthal in 1951. Photo by Carl Van Vechten. Courtesy of Bruce Kellner.

Jennifer Tipton teaching a lighting master class in 2011. Courtesy of the Wexner Center.

throughout her career and won three. She is perhaps most well known for her introduction of the computerized lighting board to Broadway.

Jennifer Tipton (1937–) has truly managed to unify the field of lighting design through her work in theatre, opera, and dance. Tipton has been working in theatre since 1969. She is best known for her use of white light and how it shapes the space. Her work and innovative style are currently influencing designers around the world.

The Design Process

Theatrical design is a collaborative process. Each designer works in his or her own area while also communicating with the production team as a whole. All designers share certain parts of the design process, such as analysis, research, and production meetings. However, the work that each designer produces as a result of these steps in the process is vastly different.

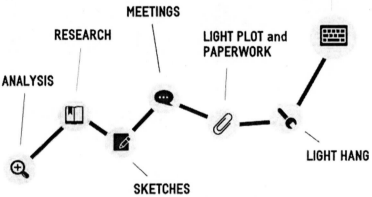

Once a designer is hired for a production, he or she receives a copy of the script from which to work. If the show is a musical, he or she also receives the appropriate accompanying documentation such as a copy of the music, as well as the score if necessary. The first step in the design process is analysis. The designer must read through the script several times, looking for different elements each time. On the first reading, the designer is typically just reading the play through to get a sense of the plot, characters, themes, mood, and atmosphere while noting any mention of lighting in the script. On the second and third readings, the designer reads deeper and looks for the specific shape of the action that leads to the play's climax and ways in which lighting can enhance specific scenes. These readings often happen between meetings with the production team. In these initial meetings, ideas the production team would like to highlight are discussed.

This textual analysis leads the lighting designer into the second step in the design process, the research phase, by doing both the visual and background research for the lighting of the production. For instance, a production of *The Heiress* by Ruth and Augustus Goetz, which takes place in 1880, would require research into gas lighting, which was common for interior and exterior spaces. The lighting designer might look into what gas light fixtures look like, how gas light works, and what color of light it produces.

The lighting designer will also look for visuals that support ideas he or she has about the mood, atmosphere, composition, and theme of a production. These images are used to help convey ideas between the lighting designer and other members of the production team. Visual images will help the lighting designer describe what he or she wants a particular scene or moment to look like. For example, images of light through trees might help the lighting designer describe the front yard for a production of Arthur Miller's *All My Sons*, a play that takes place in the yard of the family home and mentions an apple tree.

Once the production team agrees on certain images and ideas, the lighting designer can move on to creating specific visuals for scenes or moments in the play. Most lighting designers will do light sketches or create CAD (computer-aided design) renderings for specific moments such as the climax of the play or for special moments of visual interest. These sketches or renderings help to further the conversation with the director and the rest of the team. They communicate the "look" of the

The 2010 production of *All My Sons*, featuring Zoe Wanamaker, Daniel Lapaine, David Suchet, Stephen Campbell Moore, and Jemima Rooper; directed by Howard Davies, Apollo Theatre, London. Photo © Robbie Jack/Corbis.

final design in these key moments. These drawings can be reworked until the production team is happy with how the show will look once it is lit.

Throughout this whole process, the design and production team meets regularly, usually a couple of times a week, to communicate ideas and information about the production. Meetings can happen in the same room, if the production team is in one location. They can also happen virtually through the use of technologies such as Skype, e-mail, and file-sharing programs. It does not matter how the meetings happen as long as there is a free flow of communication and information is shared regularly.

After the design ideas for a production are finalized, the lighting designer can move on to the production stage of the design process. This means producing a **light plot** in order for the master electrician to hang lights in the appropriate places to make the lighting designer's vision happen on stage. The light plot will provide three important pieces of information about each instrument—on which part of the stage the light should be focused, what color it should have, and how it is controlled. Color is created by a **gel**, a colored plastic filter placed in front of a lighting instrument in order to change the color of the light it emits. Control is

A light plot. Photo by Keturah Stickann.

achieved by assigning each light a **channel number**. This number is assigned to a light or group of lights to help the designer identify the purpose of the instrument.

At this point, supporting paperwork is produced with lists of all of the lighting instruments and their channel numbers, the order in which they appear on the plot, and their gel colors. This paperwork is supplemental to the light plot and helps to provide more information for the master electrician to complete his or her work. Once the paperwork is in the hands of the master electrician, the physical implementation of the design begins. He or she makes sure the information conveyed in the plot is made into reality in the theatre space. The lights are hung, tested, gelled, and then focused so the lighting designer can complete his or her work.

"I can make you cry. I can make you get excited -- maybe even make you jump to your feet. By doing a light cue in the right way, I can change the emotions of what the audience sees."

Ken Billington, lighting designer

The final step of the design process is the cuing of the show. A **cue** is a change in the lighting on stage. Cuing a show is defining how and when the stage lighting will change. The lighting designer will watch several rehearsals in order to understand the action happening in each scene on stage. Once the designer has a good grasp on what is happening, he or she can begin using the lights that have been hung to shape the look of each scene. These cues take place in a sequence starting at the beginning and building on one another until the end of the show is reached. Each cue has a specific purpose and is used to make the functions of lighting a reality for a particular production. Cues are refined during each technical and dress rehearsal until everything meets the satisfaction of the lighting designer and the production team and is ready for an audience on opening night.

The Tools of a Lighting Designer

All designers have tools with which they work to produce their designs. The costumer works with fabric, needle, and thread. The scene designer works with wood, metal, and paint. The lighting designer works with lighting instruments and the lightboard. To get the different qualities of light needed, he or she can use a wide variety of instruments.

The modern **lightboard**, also called the lighting control console, is a highly specialized computer. Its sole purpose is to control the level, or amount of light, that each fixture puts out. By telling different fixtures what level of light to give and when to turn on and off, the designer can control and dramatically change the look of the light on the stage. Lightboards are manufactured by a variety of different companies. Each one is distinct and operates in a slightly different manner. Some are made to control standard lighting instruments, others to control automated fixtures, but all are produced with the sole purpose of controlling the light output of fixtures on a stage.

The designer can choose from many types of lighting fixtures to achieve different effects. Like lighting consoles, these fixtures are made by a wide variety of manufacturers and have many different looks. However, all of them can be broken down into a few basic categories: PAR fixtures, Fresnels, ERSs, cyc lights, and automated fixtures. Each of these types serves a different purpose. Designers must understand what

A Classic Palette II, manufactured by Strand Lighting. This console is used to control both conventional and automated fixtures. Courtesy of Strand Lighting.

Hog 4 Lighting Console, manufactured by High End Systems. This console is primarily used to control automated fixtures. Courtesy of High End Systems.

each instrument will do when placed above the stage and then carefully choose the correct type. The wrong instrument choice can lead to the wrong look for a scene. However, the right instrument can make all the difference.

PAR fixtures, or parabolic aluminized reflector lamps, are a mainstay of concert lighting. PARs are often referred to as **PAR cans**. The lamp of a PAR is a self-contained unit. This lamp must be placed in a housing to secure it in place. The term *can* refers to the round extruded metal housing that absorbs some of the extra light from the PAR fixture. This extruded metal housing looks something like a coffee can that has been painted black. Hence the term PAR *can*.

One of the unique features of this fixture is its oval beam, which is nearly twice as tall as it is wide. The direction of the PAR's beam may be adjusted only by physically turning the lamp housed inside the PAR's casing. The size of the beam is changed by physically changing out the lamp housed in the can. This fixture comes in four main beam sizes: very narrow, narrow, medium, and wide. The width of the beam is determined by the glass with which the self-contained lamp is manufactured.

The reflector in the PAR makes the quality of light produced by the PAR relatively harsh. The self-contained nature of a PAR makes the light output and the beam difficult to control adequately. The PAR delivers a very bright light. The limited control and the brightness of the light make the PAR a good choice for onstage lighting. The construction of

A variety of lighting instruments: (*top left*) an ellipsoidal reflector; (*top middle*) a Fresnel; (*top right*) a version of a par can; (*middle left*) a striplight (courtesy of Electronic Theatre Controls); (*middle right*) an automated or a motorized fixture (courtesy of Martin Professional); (*bottom left*) a follow spot (courtesy of Altman Lighting); (*bottom right*) examples of gobos (courtesy of Rosco).

the extruded metal casing that houses the PAR lamp ensures that the fixture is virtually indestructible. This makes the PAR an excellent choice for touring and explains its popularity among designers of concerts.

The **Fresnel** (pronounced FRAY-nel) is named for the man who invented its lens—August-Jean Fresnel. He originally invented the lens for use in lighthouses; however, a smaller version of the lens has gained popularity. The Fresnel lens takes a plano-convex lens (a lens with one curved side and one flat side) and cuts curved "steps" into the curved side of the lens to reduce its thickness and weight.

The Fresnel light is known for its soft edge and smooth illumination. The shadows it creates are very soft and do not have harsh edges. Its light also blends easily with other Fresnels as well as with other instruments. Even with the nice, even, smooth field a Fresnel produces, it has few other controllable properties. This makes it difficult to use in any place other than over the stage. If it were placed over the audience, the scattered light beam would provide too much illumination in the auditorium.

The **ellipsoidal reflector spotlight**, or ERS, is the workhorse of the lighting world. The ERS has more features and flexibility than any other conventional fixture on the market. There are several brands of ERSs on the market. However, the Source 4, designed and marketed by ETC (Electronic Theatre Controls), has become the industry standard. The ERS provides for a variety of variations in intensity and focus because it contains shutters that can be used to shape the beam of light. It also has a barrel through which light passes, which can be adjusted to change the quality of light. In this way, the designer can control the sharpness or softness of the light beam. It also allows patterns to be projected when a **gobo** is used. This is a small template made of steel or glass that is placed in a slot in the center of the light between the source and the lens. The pattern is then projected onto the stage.

Cyc lights are special lighting units made to light up a painted backdrop or cyclorama. A **cyclorama** is a large, smooth piece of seamless fabric specially made to catch and spread light, often used as a backdrop. Cyc lights are specially designed to spread a large wash of light evenly over the area on which it is focused. These units, often called *cells*, can come individually or in a group of two to four. Each unit can be controlled individually from the lightboard based on how the designer chooses to control them. While these lights have only a single purpose, they provide a great deal of flexibility and diversity to a designer. A smart designer can create a wide array of color washes and looks with these units, allowing for quick changes of mood and scene on stage.

Automated lights have been used for many years in concert lighting and are beginning to make regular appearances in the theatre world, both on Broadway and off. An automated fixture can provide a designer with a wide variety of option in colors, gobos, and focus areas all in one instrument. The designer only needs to know how to program one of these lights in order to do the job that it might take ten conventional fixtures to do.

Like conventional lighting fixtures, automated lights will have specific purposes. Some are designed to be **wash fixtures**, lights that will cast a large, even field of light. Others are designed to highlight specific people or objects at specific times, create special effects on stage, and draw the audience's attention. These fixtures can carry a variety of gobos, change color, and move with the push of a button.

As technology advances, both conventional and automated lighting instruments are becoming more and more advanced and efficient. For example, companies have developed more efficient lamps for their instruments. They use less wattage and put out more light than their predecessors. A wide variety of companies are also embracing LED technology. Companies are working to create LED fixtures that are just as bright and controllable as current standard lights but will use less energy. As technology continues to improve, the lighting industry will continue to develop alongside it.

The Toys

In combination with lighting fixtures, designers can use other accessories to create a variety of looks onstage. Among these accessories are gobos, fog machines, hazers, strobe lights, black lights, and projectors. All of these accessories interact with or create light that can enhance the mood and meaning of a theatrical experience when used appropriately and in moderation.

Projections made by gobos can be very abstract and used to create texture, or they can be more realistic and used to suggest a realistic object, such as a tree. Basic gobos are patterns cut into small circles of steel, but many companies are now making more complex and complicated gobos out of glass because they can hold more detail and depth than steel. Atmospheric devices such as **fog machines** or **hazers** can also be used to enhance the look of a scene. They pump certain safe chemicals into the atmosphere in order to replicate different atmospheric conditions onstage. For instance, a fog machine can create a dense white fog that will make it hard for both the audience and actors to see, helping to increase the intensity of certain scenes or to direct the eye with the beam of light being cast through the fog. Dry-ice foggers can be used to create low-lying fog that will mimic steam rising from the ground. Hazers will fill the whole theatre with a mist that mimics a very humid day. This

The 2010 production of *The Inspector General*, National Theatre of Cluj, Romania. Set design by Mihai Ciupe.

mist not only affects the atmosphere and the audience's perceptions, but also allows the light beams to be visible to the audience. These beams can be followed from the light source to the area of the stage that it is illuminating.

A wide variety of other special effects equipment can be used in productions; some were specifically developed for theatrical production, and others have been adapted from other fields. These include disco balls, strobe lights, and projectors. Many were developed for specific applications not related to theatre but have been appropriated to create specific special effects. For instance, a strobe light is often used to create a lightning effect onstage, but it was originally developed by Harold Edgerton to freeze objects in motion in order to capture their image on film. This common camera flash technology has been appropriated by lighting designers for many years. When strobes are used, however, care must be taken to inform the audience, as they can cause an adverse reaction with people with medical conditions such as epilepsy.

Disco balls, also known as mirror balls or glitter balls, are round surfaces covered with tiny mirror or reflective pieces. When light is projected at the ball, it is reflected back at different angles, spreading tiny points of light around a given area. The balls are often mounted on a motor to slowly rotate and cast light around a room. While the history of the disco ball is muddy at best, it appears that they were first commonly used in dance halls in the early part of the nineteenth century and quickly became a common element of the dance hall and music scene. For theatrical purposes, disco balls are used to re-create these environments or to create a special effect based on the ideas of the lighting designer and the director. A dream world full of stars or a night sky are some of the possible uses.

All lighting is a form of projection. Specialized projectors are becoming more and more common as lighting tools. These projectors can be anything from a slide projector to a common computer digital projector to highly advanced and interactive large-format screens that can show still images as well as moving video. Projectors allow for lighting to provide scenery. Large blank screen surfaces can be set up and projected upon to create a variety of different looks within any given production. How much projection is incorporated into any production is a decision that must be made carefully by any design team. Overusing projections can detract. However, when used skillfully, they can broaden the scope

The 2012 production of *Roberto Zucco*, University of Florida (featuring Greg Jones, directed by Ralf Remshardt, projection design by Brittany Merenda). Photo by Shari Thompson.

THEATRICAL PRODUCTION

and enhance the beauty of an otherwise ordinary piece. Because of recent advances in computer technology, the options for projectors seem limitless. In fact, many organizations that use projections heavily are investing in **projection designers** whose sole job is to create and program all projections used in a show.

Computers and Design: AutoCAD and Other Programs

Computer technology has not only influenced lighting equipment and control systems, it has also influenced the way in which a lighting designer designs. What used to be created with pencil and paper by a team of assistants can now be completed in a fraction of the time and manpower using specialized computer programs. Today, designers can use programs initially developed for other industries, such as Adobe Photoshop and AutoCAD, to create light renderings and computer-aided draftings.

Highly specialized software programs have also been developed specifically for the theatre lighting designer, such as Nemetschek's Vectorworks for Lighting Design, Lightwright created by John McKernon Software, and WYSIWYG from CAST Software. These products provide highly specialized tools developed especially for the theatrical lighting designer, such as two-dimensional and three-dimensional drawing capabilities. A designer who chooses to work in three dimensions may also have the option of rendering his or her design within the computer in order to visualize what it might look like on stage. He or she also can provide paperwork, which is quickly and easily generated.

The creation of these specific software programs has revolutionized the way in which a lighting designer can work. No longer does he have to waste time and manpower to see how something will look by hanging a light, focusing it, and then playing with the look during rehearsals. All of that work can now be done within a computer-generated model that can be used to create looks the designer intends to use. These images can then be shared with other members of the production team to help visually communicate lighting ideas that were previously left to the imagination until technical and dress rehearsals. Technology of this sort allows designers to work on more shows from their home base and to spend fewer hours in the theatre reworking any given production.

Part Three

Special Topics

7   Genre

Jim Davis

Western culture is obsessed with definitions. People wear T-shirts with slogans and put stickers on their cars to help others define their personalities. Ads explain that new television shows are "wacky comedies" or "exciting dramas." Political candidates distill their ideas and policies down to short, easily digested catchphrases. We list our favorite musicians and athletes on our Facebook pages to help people understand who we are. The cultural need to define seems limitless. Of course, this desire appears in the arts as well. But since creative work is generally subjective and often difficult to describe, defining it can be problematic. Anybody who has ever read a music review that describes a song as "a cross between zydeco and electronica with polka and hip-hop influences" understands this dilemma.

So how do you define something like theatre—especially since a theatrical script is meant to be reinterpreted? We can easily call *Macbeth* a tragedy—but what if we do a production using puppetry? And add music? And change the characters from tenth-century Scottish royalty to professional wrestlers (all of which has been done)? Is it still Shakespeare's infamous "Scottish play," or have we invented a new type of theatre: sports entertainment/puppet theatre/musical/tragedy? Frustratingly, both are correct. The point here is that defining theatre is a tricky business. Theatre artists love to break rules and make audiences think about scripts from new, unexpected perspectives.

In an effort to simplify, this chapter employs two approaches to define a production through generic criticism. The first is by the content of the production's script. The genre is defined by specific actions taking place in the script—if funny things happen, it is a comedy. If tragic things happen, it is a tragedy. However, a production can also be defined by being identified with a specific aesthetic or cultural movement, such as realism or feminism. When it is more appropriate to discuss a genre from its cultural context and not the script itself, we will discuss it from this perspective.

Also, just to complicate this approach even further, a production is rarely just one genre. For example, a production of a broad, Shakespearean comedy or a big, spectacular Broadway musical may both feature elements of realism despite the fact that neither is entirely realistic. Conversely, a realistic script can also contain elements of low comedy and feminist theatre.

Finally, in no way is the list of genres presented here exhaustive. There are many more types of theatre, defined both by the script's action and by the cultural movement with which it is affiliated. The purpose of the following is to provide you with the tools to define theatrical productions in specific ways. Does this seem subjective? It is. But when you are dealing with a topic as fluid as theatrical performance, subjectivity always comes into play.

Classical and Historical Definitions

Genre is a French word that comes from the Latin *generis*, meaning "kind." It is similar to *genus*, a term used in biology to classify living organisms and fossils. The Greek philosopher Aristotle was the first to classify living things based on their similarities in his work *The History of Animals* (c. 350 BCE). Interestingly, he used this same strategy in *The Poetics* (c. 335–323 BCE), a later work about poetry, drama, and literature. In it, he had much to say about the mechanics and functions of drama. He also provided definitions of ancient Greece's two most prevalent forms of drama—tragedy and comedy.

Historians generally believe that **tragedy** was the most common type of theatre in classical Greece. Of all the full scripts from this era that we have, the overwhelming majority of them are tragedies, and this type of drama played a specific role in Greek democracy. Aristotle defined it as "the imitation of an action that is serious and also as having magnitude, complete in itself." In other words, it is a play featuring specific actions that are sad (or serious) involving characters who were important or well-known ("having magnitude").

The final part is important, as Aristotle believed that in order for a play to be truly tragic, it had to feature a character who, while important and heroic, also possessed a "tragic flaw." This mistake in

"Man is the only animal that laughs and weeps; for he is the only animal that is struck with the difference between what things are, and what they ought to be."

William Hazlitt, essayist

judgment because of a lack of knowledge ultimately leads to their downfall and upsets the balance of the universe. Aristotle's belief was that the purpose of tragedy was to instill "pity and fear" in audiences, and it would eventually create a feeling of catharsis or emotional purgation that audiences would find pleasurable. Aristotle greatly admired the play *Oedipus Rex* by Sophocles, considering it the "perfect tragedy," which is not surprising as it fits his definition.

According to Aristotle, **comedy** is "an imitation of characters of a lower type [and features] some defect or ugliness which is not painful or destructive." While tragedy focuses on earth-shattering actions performed by important people, comedy is about common people with common problems. There are numerous subsections of comedies—generally based on the style of humor or type of plot. **Farce** is a type of comedy that has absurdly complicated plots, broad characters who behave irrationally, and lots of physical comedy. Examples include the appropriately titled *Bedroom Farce* by Alan Ayckbourn, Michael Frayn's *Noises Off*, and the Stephen Sondheim musical *A Funny Thing Happened on the Way to the Forum*. **Romantic comedy** is defined by its plot. This genre generally features two sympathetic characters who, because of a series of extenuating circumstances, cannot be together. Fortunately, the two overcome their obstacles and get to enjoy a happy ending. A. R. Gurney's *Sylvia* and Neil Simon's *Same Time Next Year* are examples of romantic comedy.

Of course, tragedy and comedy are not mutually exclusive; some scripts feature elements of both. Those scripts are called **black comedy**. Sometimes, like *The Zoo Story* by Edward Albee, they are comic scripts with a serious ending—other times, like *Rhinoceros* by Eugène Ionesco or Noah Haidle's *Mr. Marmalade*, they are serious plays with happy endings. The hallmark of a black comedy is that it generally deals with dark

The 2009 production of Michael Frayn's farce *Noises Off*, Novello Theatre, London (directed by Lindsay Posner). Photo © Robbie Jack/Corbis.

characters and subjects that one would not generally consider funny. For example, Martin McDonagh's *A Behanding in Spokane* is about Carmichael, a man who has spent years traveling the United States in search of his severed hand. During the play, he encounters a pair of drug dealers who offer to sell him a hand they have stolen from a local museum. When Carmichael learns it is not his hand, he chains them to a radiator and threatens to light them on fire. This is not typical comic fare, but playwright McDonagh finds humor in the terror and absurdity of the situation.

Two other comic genres that are closely related are **high** and **low comedy**. Comic wordplay, humor based on mistaken identities and false assumptions, and characters who flout the conventions of an exceedingly mannered society are all elements of high comedy. Generally, the conflict and humor in high comedy comes from watching "upper-crust" characters try to satisfy their base desires (lust, greed and any other deadly sin you can think of . . .) while struggling to maintain their aristocratic standing. For example, in Oscar Wilde's *The Importance of Being Earnest*, Jack and Algernon, two wealthy Englishmen, invent a secret identity (the titular "Ernest") to woo women. The comedy happens when

The 2013 production of *A Behanding in Spokane*, Keegan Theatre (featuring Manu Kumasi, Mark A. Rhea, and Laura Herren; directed by Colin Smith). Photo by C. Stanley Photography.

the women begin to realize the charade and the men are forced to go to great lengths to keep from being found out. Many plays by the French playwright Molière (1622–1673), such as *The Miser* and *Tartuffe*, also exemplify high comedy.

While high comedy focuses on characters who attempt to follow society's rules, characters in low comedy set out to deliberately disrupt social norms. The humor in these plays comes from watching culturally accepted rules and behaviors disrupted by slapstick violence, exaggerated sexuality, and absurd and scatological behavior. The earliest examples of low comedy in Western theatre are the satyr plays from fifth-century-BCE Greece that were bawdy retellings of well-known stories and myths. This tradition of broadly comic stories performed for popular audiences was also present in *commedia dell'arte*, which began in Italy in the sixteenth century. With roots in satyr plays and comic Roman theatre, commedia dell'arte featured broad stock characters, improvised jokes and stories, and a great deal of physical comedy. There are also elements of low comedy in Shakespeare (such as Sir Toby Belch's misadventures in *Twelfth Night*) and the puppet theatre tradition of Punch and Judy. More recently, plays like *The Nerd* by Larry Shue and *One Man, Two Guvnors*

Oliver Goldsmith's play *She Stoops to Conquer* (1773) is an example of high comedy, also called comedy of manners. It exists in a world of aristocratic, mannered society where wit and gamesmanship in matters of love has high value. (2012 production, University of Florida, featuring Cristian Gonzales and Michelle Bellaver; directed by Judith Williams). Photo by Shari Thompson.

by Richard Bean (and adapted from the eighteenth-century play *Servant of Two Masters* by Carlo Goldoni) feature socially awkward protagonists who upset the status quo.

One of the most influential Western genres was **melodrama**. With their roots in the popular English theatre of the nineteenth century, melodramas were formulaic performances that emphasized plot and action over any character development. In fact, one of the hallmarks of melodrama was simply drawn, one-dimensional characters. These characters were defined by their moral alignment—good characters were entirely good and evil characters were entirely evil. But this moral rigidity allowed a clarity of action that appealed to popular audiences. For example, the villain never had to waste time explaining his actions—he was doing them simply because he was evil. This lack of character development allowed simple plots that focused on action with little time for discussion, as well as happy endings where good triumphed over evil. The popularity of melodrama lay in its adherence to a formula that was simple to follow, was pleasurable to watch, and provided a satisfying, morally redemptive climax.

The 2013 production of Carlo Goldoni's *A Servant to Two Masters*. Goldoni utilized familiar stock characters in commedia dell'arte such as wily servants and hapless merchants but did away with the half masks worn by commedia performers. Produced by the University of Florida School of Theatre and Dance (featuring Joseph Urick, Rob Cope, and Anastasia Placido; directed by Judith Williams; costumes by Robin McGee). Photo by Robin McGee.

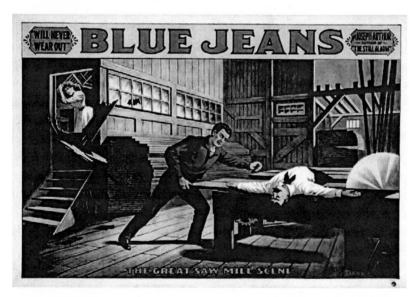

Poster for the popular 1890 melodrama *Blue Jeans*. In a sawmill, the villain ties the hero to a board, where an approaching buzz saw promises certain death. Suddenly his girlfriend, previously locked in the office, breaks free and rescues him. A later silent film ensured that this moment would become a long-standing plot cliché.

While melodrama has fallen out of favor as a theatrical genre, its impact on film and television is undeniable. Many action movies and TV procedurals follow a formulaic plot and feature simplistic, morally absolute characters. While their stories may not be complex, their appeal lies in watching characters—either good or evil—take action and eventually get what they deserve.

The Rise of "Isms"

Theatre always reflects the values and ideas of the culture that produces it. Informed audience members can usually guess when and where a script was written by looking for a few telling cultural clues. With that in mind, the genres discussed next are inextricably linked to a specific cultural or aesthetic movement. Sometimes they are a product of a new cultural ideas or a reaction to an artistic idea, but they are always linked to what is going on in the world around them.

The most prevalent and well known of these "isms" in Western theatre is **realism**. The roots of realism are found in the cultural and technological shifts of the nineteenth century. Scientists and political figures such as Auguste Comte, Sigmund Freud, Karl Marx, and Charles Darwin looked at the world objectively and based theories and ideas on empirical evidence as opposed to ephemeral beliefs based in mythology or spirituality. This shift toward the empirical created a theatre of realism that was used as an objective laboratory to observe human behavior.

The theatre artists of the time responded to this movement by creating work with a high degree of verisimilitude featuring detailed, authentic-looking designs; characters who behaved in a logical fashion; and stories dealing with issues and actions similar to those faced by most people. Shakespeare's playfulness and poetry and the classical values espoused by Sophocles were replaced by plays about poverty, social inequity, and dysfunctional families—a move that outraged some audiences and critics. However, the shift toward a more realistic theatre that portrayed life objectively was unstoppable.

Two of the most influential practitioners of realism are playwright Anton Chekhov and acting teacher/director Konstantine Stanislavsky, who adapted and modified many of the ideas of realism with their company the Moscow Art Theatre. Chekhov wrote scripts like *The Cherry Orchard*

Norwegian playwright Henrik Ibsen is considered one of the most important dramatists of all time. His controversial play *A Doll's House* (1879), the story of a woman who realizes she has been living her life as a plaything, spearheaded an international move toward dramatic realism. Photo by Gustav Borgen. Courtesy of the Digitalt Museum.

The 2006 production of *A Doll's House*, University of Minnesota (directed by Steve Cardamone). Photo by Michal Daniel.

and *Uncle Vanya* for the MAT that depicted the trials and tribulations of the Russian landowning class while Stanislavsky created The System, a method of training that encouraged actors to create characters that behaved in a true-to-life, convincing manner. The style and training practiced by the MAT has informed nearly every major theatre artist of the last century. Realism has infused nearly every aspect of theatrical practice—some scripts that exemplify this movement are *'night, Mother* by Marsha Norman, *Glengarry Glen Ross* by David Mamet, *Last Summer at Bluefish Cove* by Jane Chambers, and the *Shape of Things* by Neil LaBute.

Naturalism

Despite its rapid rise to ubiquity, there was still some resistance to realism. William Butler Yeats (1865–1939), the Irish poet who also wrote elegiac, abstract plays, believed that realism was too limiting and that it removed the "joyful, fantastic, extravagant, whimsical, beautiful, resonant, and altogether reckless" elements that were vital to theatre. While Yeats considered realism too realistic, some theatre artists did not think it was realistic enough. Whereas realists wanted to reflect reality on stage, naturalists wanted to do away with all the theatrical trappings and actually place reality on stage. Naturalists rejected traditional plots and characters to create work that unfolded over real time and consciously avoided dramatic action and climactic moments. For example, there was no traditional intermission in August Strindberg's naturalist script *Miss Julie*. In its place was a folk dance performed by local peasant characters to occupy the time while the main characters were off stage.

One of the most outspoken advocates of naturalism was Andre Antoine (1858–1943), the primary director of Théâtre Libre (or "Free Theatre") in Paris. Antoine produced scripts featuring colloquial dialogue; plots that unfolded in an unhurried, organic manner; and settings that were extremely authentic and detailed—in an 1888 production of *The Butchers*, he hung actual sides of beef onstage. These practices went against the conservative idea of theatre that existed in France at the time. However, as the Théâtre Libre audience was made up of subscribers, it was able to circumvent restrictive government policies. Antoine was with Théâtre Libre for less than a decade, but in that time he produced Henrik Ibsen's *Ghosts* and Leo Tolstoy's *The Power of Darkness*

Photo from David Belasco's 1912 production of *The Governor's Lady*. Source: *Theatre Magazine*, vol. 25, no. 140 (October 1912), p. 104.

in a manner that featured the heightened reality and verisimilitude of naturalism.

Another advocate of naturalism was American producer and playwright David Belasco (1854–1931), who pioneered the use of technology to bring greater realism to the stage. During a production of *Madame Butterfly*, he designed a twelve-minute sequence illustrating a sunset using stage lights colored with gelatin slides. Belasco's most famous attempt at naturalism came about during a 1912 production of *The Governor's Lady* featuring a scene in a Childs Diner, an early American chain restaurant. Not content to simply replicate the restaurant, Belasco bought the actual furniture and fixtures and set up a working diner stocked with food from the Childs chain prior to each night's performance.

Anti-Realism and Absurdism

While the naturalists reacted by trying to be more real than realism, plenty of theatre artists reacted by moving in the opposite direction, too. Following World War I and influenced by existentialism, the French **absurdists** sought to challenge the preconceived notions of conservative European culture. Jean-Paul Sartre (1905–1980), best known as a novelist and philosopher, wrote plays featuring characters forced to reassess their personal values when faced with extreme circumstance. For example, in *Dirty Hands,* an allegory about post–World War II Europe, characters are forced to choose between two unpleasant choices in an effort to resuscitate their failing nation.

Perhaps the best-known absurdist playwright was Samuel Beckett (1906–1989). Born in Ireland, Beckett moved to France just prior to World War II. Beckett's *Waiting for Godot* is arguably the most well-known example of absurdist drama. The script concerns Estragon and Vladimir, who wait for the arrival of the mythical Godot, who never appears. As they wait, the pair discuss their bleak surroundings, whether they should eat a turnip or a radish, and swap hats. While this may seem ridiculous, critics have been seeking the "meaning" of the script since it was first produced in 1953. The popular consensus is that Beckett consciously rejected nearly all forms of Western character development and plot structure in an effort to portray the existential/absurdist belief that the life has no inherent meaning, but with a play as inscrutable as *Godot,* it is impossible to reach a conclusive interpretation. And that may be Beckett's point.

Perhaps the most radical reaction to realism was **theatre of cruelty,** a term devised by Antonin Artaud (1896–1948), a French actor, playwright, and theorist. In his book *The Theatre and Its Double,* Artaud called for a shift away from realistic, text-based theatre to create "spectacles" that were primal and poetic that used a "unique language half-way between gesture and thought" to assault the senses of the audience. Artaud also wanted to do away with the physical separation between performers and audiences, arguing that a "spectator, placed in the middle of the action, is engulfed and physically affected by it."

While Artaud's theories were compelling—and his work influenced major theatre artists such as director Peter Brook and playwrights Samuel Beckett and Jean Genet (as well as rock musicians Patti Smith and Jim Morrison) the scripts he wrote to illustrate his theories were difficult to stage. For example, his script *The Spurt of Blood* contains the following stage direction:

> . . . two Stars are seen colliding and from them fall a series of legs of living flesh with feet, hands, scalps, masks, colonnades, porticos, temples, alembics, falling more and more slowly, as if falling in a vacuum: then

three scorpions one after another and finally a frog and a beetle which come to rest with desperate slowness, nauseating slowness.

While this is certainly a rejection of realism, it is difficult to see how this could be staged in a practical, theatrical style. Nevertheless, Artaud's rejection of the dominant aesthetic style and call for a more visceral, spectacular theatre made him one of the most influential theoreticians of the twentieth century.

Feminist Theatre

Another group of artists rejected realism but wanted to do it in a way that was engaging and accessible while maintaining a critical and (sometimes) satirical edge. With its roots in the civil rights and women's liberation movements of the 1960s, **feminist theatre** addressed the under-representation of women in the American theatre. Feminist critics and artists argued that traditional theatre practice—specifically that which was derived from Aristotle's ideas—focused on stories, characters, and linear plot structures that were customarily considered "masculine" and failed to provide an arena for women's voices. Playwrights like María Irene Fornés, Paula Vogel, and Wendy Wasserstein wrote scripts that addressed the issues confronted by women on a daily basis. Some of the scripts, like Wasserstein's *The Heidi Chronicles*, employed traditional dramaturgy (i.e., a linear plotline, individual protagonist, and realistic characters) to tell the story of a woman's personal and political growth over a twenty-year period. Others, like Fornés's *Fefu and Her Friends*, which was influenced by the women's collective theatre movement of the 1970s, deal with a community of women's treatment within a patriarchal society using a nonlinear narrative structure.

Another important element of feminist theatre is how it deals with mimesis or imitation. While Aristotle said that theatre (tragedy specifically) should be an "imitation of an action," feminist critics believed that mimesis was limiting and oppressive, arguing that theatre and performance should be more abstract to fully illustrate the female experience. An example of this style of theatre is Holly Hughes's *The Well of Horniness*, which uses the style of a 1940s radio drama for a campy, comic, and decidedly nonrealistic exploration of female sexuality.

A vital element of feminist theatre is directly addressing gender inequities in a direct manner. One example is The Guerrilla Girls, artists and activists whose performances address issues of sexism in theatre and the visual arts. And they do it while wearing gorilla masks.

A famous quote states that "writing about music is like dancing about architecture." While that may seem like an absurd statement at first, it succinctly frames the issue that defining and criticizing art is a subjective undertaking. Combine this problem with the inherent fact that theatre is all about reinterpretation, and you have a daunting proposition. Generic criticism is an art, not a science. It is fluid and based on numerous variables, such as style, script, and the intent of the artists that produce it. Even so, understanding genres and how they function helps us understand both scripts and productions from multiple perspectives.

Sidebar: Shakespeare—One Genre Cannot Contain Him

It is rare for the work of an individual artist to be considered a genre unto itself. However, one playwright is so important and influential, his work covers three distinct genres all his own. Of course, we are talking about William Shakespeare. His scripts can generally be broken down into three genres, but as discussed elsewhere, it is never that simple.

The first Shakespearean genre is tragedy. In Shakespeare's case, tragedy means a serious play with an unhappy ending featuring a protagonist who suffers exceptional calamity and loss. Usually there's a single protagonist (*Macbeth, Othello, Titus Andronicus*), but occasionally the calamities happen to two people (*Romeo and Juliet, Antony and Cleopatra*). The trademark of Shakespearean tragedy is a stage littered with dead bodies at the play's end.

Shakespeare's histories generally deal with the War of the Roses, a fifteenth-century English civil war. These scripts provide fictionalized accounts of the exploits of actual historical figures (*Richard III, Henry V*) and deal with the English sense of destiny and identity. Some scholars talk about the crossover between the tragedies and histories—for example, *Julius Caesar* is generally considered a tragedy, but it is about an actual historic figure.

Finally—and most convolutedly—Shakespeare wrote three types of comedies—farcical comedies, romantic comedies, and (most strangely) serious comedies. Shakespeare's farcical comedies are the most recognizable to twenty-first-century audiences as comedy. Scripts like *The Taming of the Shrew* and *The Comedy of Errors* use slapstick humor and are usually based on mistaken identity. Despite the name, Shakespeare's romantic comedies have little to do with Jennifer Aniston's latest movie. These scripts, like *Twelfth Night* and *A Midsummer Night's Dream*, are set in unrealistic worlds and feature characters with supernatural powers.

Despite its seemingly oxymoronic name, the last type of Shakespeare's scripts is the serious comedy. This type is a sort of catch-all for the plays that do not fit any of the other definitions. For instance, they are serious, but unlike the tragedies, end happily. Some examples of serious comedies are *The Merchant of Venice* and *Measure for Measure*.

8   The World of Shakespeare

Jeremy Fiebig

While realism remains the dominant mode of performance today, William Shakespeare remains, by far, the most-produced playwright in the world. He has had the most significant, if not overriding, presence in English-speaking theatre since his work as a playwright, actor, and theatre company co-owner in the late sixteenth and early seventeenth centuries. Many consider Shakespeare to be the greatest writer and dramatist in the English language. In English-speaking countries and the West, experience with Shakespeare signals a kind of "mastery" of theatre, for both companies and practitioners; in many places, performing or seeing a Shakespearean production means one is participating in the most essential or highest form of theatre.

In addition to being a major theatrical presence, Shakespeare is also an object of great cultural fascination, whether part of a high school curriculum, a slate of shows at a local theatre, or the subject of a major Hollywood film. In many respects, he represents a kind of ideal about what it is to use language, make art, create story, and invent character—all expressions we value as part of the way we express ourselves in theatre and culture.

Of course, Shakespeare's influence and permanence can also be problematic: Shakespeare was male, white, and Anglo and has come to represent, for some, a kind of colonial takeover of Western cultures and values. For better or worse, Shakespeare's emergence as a cultural icon—a great writer who has come to represent the good and bad values in English-speaking societies and the West—means that by looking at Shakespeare and his plays, we are looking at ourselves and our roles in Western life. Therefore, we can consider Shakespeare in two main ways: one, as a

Shakespeare(s)

Shakespeare the man represented by art, film, and theatre. (*center*) Title page of Heminge and Condell's 1623 First Folio of Shakespeare's work, engraving by Martin Droeshout, considered the closest representation of William Shakespeare. (*bottom left and right*) The Chandos and Cobbe portraits, c. 1610. Named for the painting's owners, both works are believed to be Shakespeare by some, disputed by others. (*top left*) Joseph Fiennes as the bard in the 1998 film *Shakespeare in Love*, a fictional love story set during the writing of *Romeo and Juliet*. (*center left*) Rafe Spall in the 2011 film *Anonymous* plays an illiterate Shakespeare who is a front for Edward de Vere, the seventeenth Earl of Oxford. This imaginary account is derived from the "authorship question," a position taken by some who believe that only someone with aristocratic ties and education could have penned Shakespeare's plays. (*top right*) Patrick Stewart in the 2012 revival of Edward Bond's play *Bingo*, where an unhappily retired Shakespeare deals with his personal life. (*center right*) Simon Callow's 2010 performance in Jonathan Bate's play *The Man from Stratford* creates a picture of the playwright through snippets of his plays. Sources: Cobbe portrait © Corbis. Chandos portrait © National Portrait Gallery. *Shakespeare in Love* © Bureau L.A. Collection/Sygma/Corbis. *Anonymous* © Sony Pictures. *Bingo* and *The Man from Stratford* © Robbie Jack/Robbie Jack/Corbis.

historical presence, a master of the predominant dramatic form prior to the twentieth century, and two, as a contemporary presence, a figure whose work sits at the heart of today's theatrical and cultural practices.

Who Was Shakespeare?

William Shakespeare, a product of the English educational system and a middle-class family, spent his career as a professional playwright, poet, actor, and company sharer, or co-owner of a theatre company, from the late 1580s until at least 1612. Born on or around April 23, 1564, he was the son of John Shakespeare, a glove maker and sometime city official, and Mary Arden, the daughter of a landowner. He grew up in Stratford-upon-Avon, a town in the vast countryside of Warwickshire, a county well to the northwest of London and Oxford. Few records exist of William's early life, but scholars believe that he benefited from the economic and cultural engagement resulting from Stratford-upon-Avon's status as a market town and from a robust curriculum at the grammar school in town. Shakespeare received no other formal education of which we are aware. At age eighteen, he married Anne Hathaway, about eight years his senior.

A few years later in the early 1590s, he appeared in London having recently written at least a small handful of plays. The historical record is unclear about the reasons for Shakespeare's departure from Stratford-upon-Avon, his decision to seek a trade outside the family business, and his apparent choice to leave his wife and children to pursue a career in London. There is evidence that Shakespeare was surrounded by personal and family dramas such as his father's descent into debt and loss of his city office, his own marriage to a then-pregnant Anne Hathaway, and his

The house in Stratford-upon-Avon where Shakespeare was born and spent his childhood years. Photo by Richard Towell.

coming of age in a time of great political and religious upheaval in and around England.

Though it is not known when exactly he started writing, scholars widely acknowledge his arrival on the London theatre scene in 1592 when another playwright, Robert Greene, referred to Shakespeare as an "upstart crow, beautified with our feathers," possibly referring to Shakespeare's lack of a university education. Shakespeare's writing career began modestly with plays such as *The Two Gentlemen of Verona*, *Titus Andronicus*, and *The Taming of the Shrew* but seemed to hit commercial success—and gain the attention of Greene—with a string of plays about the English civil wars of the prior century. These plays, the three parts of *Henry VI*, catapulted Shakespeare to the top of the London theatre world. By 1594, his reputation as a playwright made him such a commodity that he formed a company with Richard Burbage, one of London's leading actors, and several other stars of the London stage. This company was co-owned by Shakespeare and his fellow sharers and sponsored by the Lord Chamberlain, a highly placed government official responsible for Queen Elizabeth's household. Such patronage indicates the high level of attainment the company and its chief playwright, Shakespeare, had reached by the mid-1590s.

Kelly Kilgore (Lavinia) and Justin Baldwin (Bassanius) in the background; Greg Jackson (Satturinus) and Jean Tafler (Tamora) in Orlando Shakespeare Theater's 2013 production of *Titus Andronicus*. Photo by Tony Firriolo.

The 2012 production of *The Taming of the Shrew* at the Globe Theatre (featuring Samantha Spiro and Simon Paisley Day; directed by Toby Frow). © Robbie Jack/Robbie Jack/Corbis.

By 1599, the Lord Chamberlain's Men had relocated its operation to the Globe Theatre in the south suburbs of London and was performing new plays like *Hamlet* and *As You Like It*. In 1603, after Elizabeth's death, the company received a royal patent, a kind of official license and recognition reserved for achievement with special value to the crown, from Elizabeth's successor, King James. The company was now the King's Men, and this heightened status, along with plays like *Othello*, *King Lear*, and *Macbeth*, cemented Shakespeare's and the company's legacy at the top of the London theatre.

In 1608, the company established a second theatre, this one indoors in London's Blackfriars district, which allowed them to perform at a higher ticket price and for a typically wealthier clientele. The company performed at both Blackfriars and the Globe after 1608. Between this time and 1612, Shakespeare undertook several collaborations with other writers, most notably John Fletcher, who succeeded him as the chief playwright upon Shakespeare's retirement. Shakespeare died on or around April 23, 1616, and was buried in Holy Trinity Church in Stratford-upon-Avon. After his death, the King's Men remained the leading company in London until the closure of the theatres in 1642. In 1623, two of Shakespeare's fellow actors and sharers, John Heminges and Henry Condell,

Detail from *The Long View of London from Bankside, 1647*. This etching by Czech artist Wenceslaus Hollar provides an invaluable representation of London before the Great Fire of 1666. However, the labels of the Globe Theatre and the "Beere bayting" ring (also known as the Hope Theatre) are reversed. Bearbaiting was a popular sport in which a bear was chained to a post and attacked by bulldogs. Gamblers placed wagers on the winner.

collected his plays, some never before published, into a Folio meant to represent and honor Shakespeare's work.

We often overlook many of the conditions that created Shakespeare—or rather that allowed Shakespeare, the son of a glove maker, to become Shakespeare, the successful playwright and cultural icon. He began his writing career at a time when theatre enjoyed an especially prized position in English society. In the century before Shakespeare's birth, Johannes Gutenberg's printing press, a German invention that allowed for movable type and mass printing of all kinds of writing, made its way to England. A society that had been largely illiterate—outside the nobility, the church, and some in the merchant class, most citizens could not read—suddenly had access to printed texts of all sorts. This access to the printed word created an atmosphere of excitement and interest in the English language among the many social classes that could now afford the printed word and the education necessary to read it. As part of this atmosphere, writers were inventing new words, style, and grammar. New verse forms were emerging. Readers were soaking up the novelties of the language and a sense was growing about what it meant to speak, and be, English.

This cultural identity was emerging in other areas of English life as well. The political landscape in England in the half-century or so prior to Shakespeare's theatrical career had changed radically as the English church split off from the governance and authority of the Catholic church, headed by the pope in Rome. Henry VIII, the English king who instituted the split and made himself the head of the church in England, set off a decades-long reimagining of English spirituality and religious life that began to further shape England's cultural identity and put it at odds with the rest of a largely Catholic Europe. In 1588, the English defeated the Spanish Armada in what was widely regarded as a major military upset. Catholic Spain was the chief foreign threat to England; as a result, England's reaction to the victory was profound. After England had spent more than half a century discovering its Englishness, the defeat of Spain cemented the English national identity.

The theatre was a place where the English theatre language, still in flux, could be experimented and played with, and it was accessible to all—both those who could and could not read. English playwrights thrived during this time and together created one of the most vibrant and productive periods in theatre history. Christopher Marlowe, John Lyly, Robert Greene, Thomas Middleton, Ben Jonson, Thomas Kyd, John Fletcher, Francis Beaumont, and a host of other playwrights, along with Shakespeare, produced dozens of new plays each year, written predominantly in verse, that were performed at playhouses in and around the city of London. These new plays were ostensibly "read" for the audience— notice the *audio* part of *audience*—each with new words, turns of phrase, or rhetorical flourishes that made each playhouse a kind of spoken printing press. These spoken presses were cheap—it cost one penny to see a play on the ground floor of the Globe—and one did not need to be able to read to appreciate the play or its language.

The plays also focused on what it meant to be English. As mentioned, Shakespeare's first commercial successes were plays about the English civil war. Many of Shakespeare's contemporaries wrote similarly about events in English history. Many others focused their work even more locally, in what we now refer to as "city comedies"—plays set in and around London proper. Virtually all playwrights referred to or used current events within their English and London society as material for their plays, from the latest ballads sung on London street corners to the exploits of noteworthy Londoners to both significant and insignificant bits of news. In this regard, playhouses in England at this time were not merely spoken presses; they drew upon London, the entire country, and

Shakespeare's Plays

A number of plays are considered collaborations

Comedies

All's Well That Ends Well
As You Like It
The Comedy of Errors
Love's Labour's Lost
The Merchant of Venice
The Merry Wives of Windsor
A Midsummer Night's Dream
Much Ado About Nothing
Pericles
The Taming of the Shrew
The Tempest
Twelfth Night
The Two Gentlemen of Verona
The Two Noble Kinsmen
The Winter's Tale

Tragedies

Anthony and Cleopatra
Coriolanus
Cymbeline
Hamlet
Julius Caesar
King Lear
Macbeth
Othello
Romeo and Juliet
Timon of Athens
Titus Andronicus
Troilus and Cressida

Histories

Henry IV, Part I & II
Henry V
Henry VI, Part I, II, & III
Henry VIII
King John
Richard II
Richard III

Disputed Authorship

Cardenio	Mucedorus
Double Falsehood	Sir Thomas More
Edward III	The Spanish Tragedy
Locrine	Thomas Lord Cromwell
The London Prodigal	A Yorkshire Tragedy

the emerging national identity as they presented plays to the audiences of London.

In this marketplace primed for theatre, playing companies of the period built sophisticated enterprises aimed at negotiating the challenges of making theatre in London while making a profit. All companies in this period used a repertory model when producing plays, which meant that a different play was performed each day, with repeated performances of the same play coming days, weeks, or even months apart. The rapid shift from show to show meant that companies did not have time to build elaborate sets or costumes, which helped keep costs down, and could not rehearse more than a few hours on a single play. With no sets, plays were performed largely on a bare stage, possibly with a couple of doorways, an upper-level balcony, and perhaps only a few props, such as a throne or a bed—used when needed. Sensitive to the cost of paying actors, companies kept their cast size relatively small—usually only twelve to twenty actors for a single performance, with several actors playing more than one role in the course of the performance. Companies, composed exclusively of men because of a combination of aesthetic and cultural preferences and common theatre practice that eliminated women on the

stage, used young boys to play women's roles. In the absence of mean-
ingful copyright laws, playing companies kept only one complete copy
of the script for a play, fearing that an actor might take a full copy of the
script and have it published for profit. Instead, actors learned their lines
using "parts" or "sides" with only their lines written. Without electricity
and effective lighting, companies performed either outdoors during the
daylight hours or indoors under candlelight.

The playing conditions of the time—repertory, actor doubling, limited rehearsal time, bare stages, minimal props, men and boys playing
all roles, working from sides—presented unique challenges to the playwrights and audiences of the period and allowed Shakespeare to emerge
both uniquely English and theatrical. As he responded to the atmosphere
of writing and culture around him, Shakespeare likewise responded to
the conditions around him in the playhouse. With a bare stage, he is
able to shift from Egypt to Rome, or from Sicilia to Bohemia, or England to France with simple word craft. With a balcony, he writes the
balcony scene in Romeo and Juliet. With boys playing women's roles,
he invents lasting characters like Rosalind in *As You Like It* or Viola in
Twelfth Night—women who disguise themselves as young men in the
course of their respective plays. This adaptability and creativity enabled
him to cement a career, along with his playing company, at the top of
the theatre world.

After Shakespeare

Shakespeare's plays resonated in the generations after his death in 1616
and the demise of the King's Men in 1642 and came to define how theatre has been made in English-speaking countries and much of the West
since that time. In 1642, after several decades of a highly productive
English theatre in which Shakespeare, Jonson, Middleton, and others
were able to thrive, the English Parliament voted to close all theatres in
England, believing them to perpetuate lies and attract sinful behavior.
This move was part of a major religious upheaval between a religiously
conservative parliament and King Charles I, which resulted in a bloody
civil war and, ultimately, Parliament's victory and long period of rule
in England. After eighteen years and the restoration of Charles's son,
Charles II, as king, new theatres and theatre companies opened to a society hungry, once again, for "English" theatre. The work of Shakespeare

was performed and adapted by dramatists like William Davenant and Nahum Tate who, along with their audiences, saw Shakespeare and other early modern playwrights like Beaumont and Fletcher as cultural touchstones harking back to the prewar days. Davenant, who had been a playwright for the King's Men prior to 1642, and his rival playwright and company manager, Thomas Killigrew, each received patents, or licenses, to form new theatre companies after Charles II's restoration to the throne. Killigrew's company even reconstituted the title of the King's Men for his new company. Davenant, Killigrew, and Tate performed Shakespeare but usually only after major adaptation. The postwar, post-Puritan London audiences did not, for understandable reasons, have quite the same taste for violence and tragedy as their prewar predecessors, so even Shakespeare's starkest tragedies were reimagined for the Restoration audience. Whereas Shakespeare's *King Lear* is unrelenting in its tragic conclusion—Lear and his beloved daughter, Cordelia, both die in the play's final moments—Nahum Tate's *King Lear* reads as much more of a dramatic comedy. In Tate's version, Cordelia and Lear both live, Cordelia marries, and Lear contemplates a quiet retirement. These two starkly different versions of *Lear* signal us how early practitioners and audiences regarded both Shakespeare and his plays as something to be preserved and a canvas onto which more contemporary values, tastes, and styles could be painted.

In some respects, this early reaction to and use of Shakespeare's plays has continued to characterize how we have approached Shakespeare since. The initial impulse to see the plays as something of value—deeply resonant poetic dramas, reflections of England's politics and culture, current events, frontiers of a freshly emerging language, pieces of art or literature—continued. Shakespeare was at the heart of theatre in England throughout the remainder of the seventeenth century and into the eighteenth century, championed from the London stage by actor-managers like David Garrick and in writing by diarists and critics like Samuel Johnson, each of whom held special positions as cultural tastemakers in Britain. Shakespeare was also exported to Europe, with plays like *Hamlet* being adapted and performed in France and Germany, and even as puppet shows in Italy and America, where his plays were among the first performed in English.

In this period, responses to Shakespeare's work developed into new traditions of academic study, theatrical performance, and cultural expression.

Three characters from *Hamlet*. These antique marionettes were found in the attic of a church in what used to be a predominately Czech neighborhood in New York City. Today, they are used by the Czechoslovak-American Marionette Theatre.

Each of these traditions had its roots in his plays and stagecraft, but also adapted to the new conditions and needs of practitioners, audiences, and cultures. Some practitioners and audiences continued to see the plays in much the same vein as their predecessors: Shakespeare was about being English and celebrating Englishness. By performing Shakespeare, an actor or company was performing the work of the great master of the English language in a way that bought it some legitimacy with its audience. In the eighteenth and nineteenth centuries, as a unified Britain was emerging as a major world power, building its empire, and colonizing America, Australia, Africa, and parts of Asia, the assertion of this Englishness became even more important. At home, Shakespeare's plays and language allowed audiences to celebrate themselves and their great cultural heritage with Shakespeare right at the center of this expression, the literary persona responsible for the culture's crowning achievements. Abroad, in colonies like those that would become the United States, Canada, and India, Shakespeare was simply part of a way to connect to and assert what it meant to be English, to be civilized, and to be Western; volumes of Shakespeare's plays became what English speakers placed on their shelves right next to their Bibles.

In all, Shakespeare's poetic drama had become the predominant theatrical form of the late eighteenth and nineteenth centuries, and this preoccupation with him extended beyond the stage into societies that were increasingly literate and increasingly literary. In some respects, Shakespeare had become both a dramatic and a literary ideal, representing the highest, most essential mode of theatrical performance on stages throughout the West and serving as the singular literary and artistic figure in the culture. At its most benign, thinking about Shakespeare as a genius meant that Britain could assert its position at the apex of Western civilization; as the producer of the world's greatest poet and greatest artistic mind, Great Britain could be articulated as more refined, smarter, or having achieved more than others. As Britain's influence expanded in North America, southern Asia, Australia, and Africa in the eighteenth and nineteenth centuries, Shakespeare's role at the forefront of cultural expression meant that both he and his work were valued not only on their own merits, but as representations of the nation, of cultural superiority, and of genius itself.

This new position meant that Shakespeare's plays were no longer being encountered as the fresh, relevant reflections of England and its language, but as the basic material used for making the best theatre and defining a cultural ideal. Shakespeare's plays were, for actors, audiences, readers, and scholars, part of a canon—must-read, must-watch material that defined what it meant to see theatre and be English. This idea of "canon," a notion that the greatest artistic and cultural works of Europe could be thought of as a collective achievement of a civilization, put Shakespeare's plays into a more integrated role in society. In the schoolhouse, the plays became part of organized curricula. At universities and among the scholarly community, the plays became the subject of scholarly study and writing. Scholars like Edmund Malone began to dig into Shakespeare, both in essays and in newly edited versions of the plays, meaning that Shakespeare was taking his place alongside the great classical and Renaissance writers worthy of serious study. On the stage, stars were made based, in large part, on their achievements in the great Shakespearean roles like Hamlet, Othello, and Richard III. Many actors became "great" only after performing Shakespeare well. For actors such as David Garrick, Sarah Siddons and the Kemble and Booth families,

Shakespeare was a staple of performance. Stars also helped to generate new excitement around Shakespeare's plays. With great actors in Shakespeare's leading roles, theatre in England and the emerging United States reached its heyday—Shakespeare was being reinvented and made relevant again in the performances of the eighteenth and nineteenth centuries. This newness was expressed not only in the performances of the stars, each with their own "brand" of doing Shakespeare, but also in how audiences identified with the Shakespeare they saw.

In Europe, Shakespeare's plays were translated into German, French, and Italian as Romanticism emerged—a movement that, for the first time, put Shakespeare and other Renaissance writers and artists at or above the level of classical authors like Euripedes, Seneca, and Virgil—and composers like Giuseppe Verdi, Hector Berlioz, and Richard Wagner adapted Shakespeare for the opera. In the United States, Shakespeare's plays were becoming part of the cultural landscape for African Americans, with popular black actor Ira Aldridge playing roles like Hamlet and Othello. More broadly, Shakespeare's work represented an ideal mode of performance and of literature; to perform Shakespeare, see it performed, or read or study it was to play a part in the mainstream of cultural life. For Aldridge and others who existed, at least in part, outside

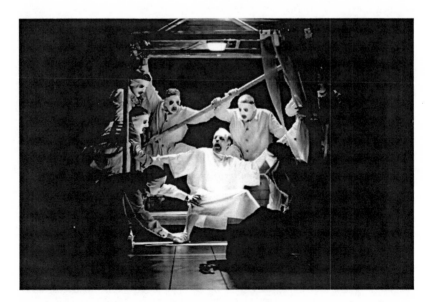

The 2011 production of *Richard III* by the Propeller Theatre Company. Photo by Manuel Harlan.

Ira Aldridge as Othello, c. 1830. Oil on canvas. National Portrait Gallery, Smithsonian Institution.

the cultural mainstream, Shakespeare may have been seen as a catalyst or gateway for blacks, Jews, immigrants, women, colonized populations, and other cultural minorities to converse with and contribute to the otherwise English-speaking, white, male cultural norm.

At the same time, Shakespeare's plays could become the mechanism for distinguishing oneself or one's group from that norm. One such example of this was in the 1849 Astor Place Opera House Riot in New York City. Here, rival actors Edwin Forrest, an American, and William Charles Macready, an Englishman, had presented competing interpretations of Shakespeare's *Macbeth*. The rivalry between the two men was primarily a stylistic one, with each representing a different way of acting the title role in the play. Audiences, however, saw in the two interpretations a break along other, more deeply seeded, lines of social class and status. Many in the American audience, primed with anti-English sentiment that saw Macready and other English as socially elite, turned on Macready and his supporters, and violence erupted, leaving several dead and scores wounded.

Though this example is by far the most extreme, it demonstrates what Shakespeare's plays were becoming by the dawn of the twentieth century, both in the theatre and in society: material that, on one hand,

Engraving of the Astor Place Opera House Riot in New York, 1849. Library of Congress.

represented a kind of cultural continuity—touchstones that signified connectedness and commonality and, on the other hand, could reflect the endless values and conditions with which they came into contact. In this way, Shakespeare's plays were paradoxically both a connection to the larger English-speaking world, a nod to a particular country's—or culture's—English heritage, and a means of asserting a separation or adaptation of that heritage.

What Was Shakespeare?

For theatre practitioners, the ideal Shakespeare encountered in the dynamic, heightened performance in some of today's theatres can be at odds with the educational or academic Shakespeares whose treatment can be comparatively static. Our first engagement with Shakespeare is likely to be reading the play as a literary object rather than a text for performance. For some potential audiences, this notion of Shakespeare as a bookish enterprise—a static, printed thing rather than an enacted, embodied thing—can be intimidating and off-putting. At the same time, some readers who like Shakespeare as something to be read and closely studied might find the theatrical Shakespeare too loud, too garish, or, as with many film adaptations we see today, not as good as the book.

Our responses to Shakespeare can often fall along cultural lines. Shakespeare's identity, his style, the cultural changes that have passed since his career in London theatre, and the role he plays and has played in the culture each allow for different responses based on who we are and what role we occupy in the culture. In some sense, this means that Shakespeare, no matter how ideal, must always answer for the agendas and traditions that have appropriated the playwright and his work over time. If Shakespeare can be identified as a heady poet, a bawdy writer, a male, a symbol of colonial power, an English speaker, a white person, a Catholic or Protestant, a member of the middle class, or any other thing that Shakespeare was in his own day or has become since, our responses will be vastly different depending on who we are. These responses enable our exchange with Shakespeare and ultimately put us into conversation with and about Shakespeare's work. Common critical responses—lenses for looking at Shakespeare in close study—include feminist criticism, performance criticism, and consideration of the historical contexts that influenced Shakespeare's work.

The presence of the many traditions, responses, and understandings of seeing, reading, studying, and performing Shakespeare—and it can be argued easily that there are more to consider—signal how we would think of him in the twentieth century and how we continue to consider the playwright-poet and his work today. Each Shakespearean tradition—theatrical, literary, educational, cultural—is a way of appropriating Shakespeare and aligning the ideals of that tradition with perceived ideals of Shakespeare. For the scholar of English, Shakespeare can be the master poet or the timeless, even universal, artist. For the schoolteacher, Shakespeare can be the "safe," "proper," or "authorized" subject of study. For those in society, literacy in Shakespearean plays and poems can serve as a badge of cultural achievement, a ticket to sophistication. In the theatre, Shakespeare can be an ideal mode of performance—a heightened way of approaching the theatre craft that carries with it a sense of seriousness, authenticity, classicality, or heightened expression.

The Values of Poetic Drama

Though there are hundreds of Shakespeare brands—methods of doing theatre that differ from theatre to theatre and country to country—the Shakespearean theatrical tradition is a rich one, and one that is distinct from the primarily realistic modes of performance we see in many plays and films today. Shakespeare's poetic drama has different values than its counterparts in realism and therefore is a different kind of theatrical expression, one that requires different tools in rehearsal and performance. The following are among the values that set poetic drama apart:

Language as the Primary Means of Conveyance

Poetic drama puts a premium on language in performance. Though language is an important part of most kinds of theatre, poetic drama uses language as the primary means of revealing characters and story. In realism and other modes of making theatre, other means of revelation might be used, from spectacular effects, to dance or movement, to physicality, behavioral acting choices, or subtextual discoveries. One example of language as the primary means of revealing the characters and story is in this speech from *Hamlet* as Hamlet happens upon his uncle, Claudius, the play's villain, who is praying and debates whether or not to kill him:

> Now might I do it pat, now he is praying;
> And now I'll do't. And so he goes to heaven;
> And so am I revenged. That would be scann'd:
> A villain kills my father; and for that,
> I, his sole son, do this same villain send
> To heaven.
> O, this is hire and salary, not revenge.
> He took my father grossly, full of bread;
> With all his crimes broad blown, as flush as May;
> And how his audit stands who knows save heaven?
> But in our circumstance and course of thought,
> 'Tis heavy with him. And am I then revenged,
> To take him in the purging of his soul,
> When he is fit and season'd for his passage?
> No!
> Up, sword; and know thou a more horrid hent:
> When he is drunk asleep, or in his rage,
> Or in the incestuous pleasure of his bed;
> At game, a-swearing, or about some act
> That has no relish of salvation in't;

Then trip him, that his heels may kick at heaven,
And that his soul may be as damn'd and black
As hell, whereto it goes. My mother stays:
This physic but prolongs thy sickly days.

Here, Hamlet is revealing to the audience everything happening in this moment through his language: He has an opportunity to kill his uncle, but his uncle is praying, maybe for forgiveness; if Claudius is forgiven, Hamlet's choice to murder him would be an act of grace, not of revenge; Hamlet wants to kill Claudius anyway and tells us he is raising his sword to do it; ultimately he relents, promising to find another, more opportune moment to kill his uncle, preferably while Claudius is engaged in some sort of sin.

Though there are notable exceptions in realistic drama, Shakespeare's use of language to convey the dramatic moment, the plot, and even the character's thoughts and actions is an essential element of poetic drama. In realistic drama, we might expect to get all of this information but by an array of different means: Hamlet might raise his sword but not necessarily tell us he is doing so. We might see the character struggle psychologically or physically with the idea of killing his uncle but not necessarily reveal that thought process to the audience. Lighting cues, sound effects, or musical underscoring might help tell the story of this suspenseful moment of reluctance. In contrast, in Shakespeare's poetic drama—not only in speeches like this but also in dialogue—the spoken language becomes the primary means of making the theatrical moment.

Heightened Language Leads to Heightened Experience

Especially as compared to realistic drama, poetic drama simply sounds different than realistic dialogue. One of the ways we might describe this difference is that realistic dialogue sounds more or less the way we speak to each other as part of our everyday lives, while in poetic drama, there is a heightened sense to the language—it operates in a special, more intense way. This heightened language is directly tied to the poetry: Shakespeare's language, for instance, does not merely convey ideas, as it might in realism, but conveys rhythm, structure, rhetorical patterns, linguistic flourishes, and image in a complex way. Take the first part of Richard's speech from the opening of *Richard III*:

Now is the winter of our discontent
Made glorious summer by this sun of York;
And all the clouds that lour'd upon our house
In the deep bosom of the ocean buried.
Now are our brows bound with victorious wreaths;
Our bruised arms hung up for monuments;
Our stern alarums chang'd to merry meetings,
Our dreadful marches to delightful measures.
Grim-visag'd war hath smooth'd his wrinkled front;
And now,—instead of mounting barbed steeds
To fright the souls of fearful adversaries,—
He capers nimbly in a lady's chamber
To the lascivious pleasing of a lute.

In this speech, the language works differently than it would if Richard III were a realistic drama. First, the language is poetic: each line has a certain number of syllables and a certain rhythm, the sentence structure is occasionally manipulated to fit a better rhythm or to make for a more beautiful line reading, the images are especially rich (e.g., "grim-visag'd war," the idea that war could be a stern-looking person), and there are patterns built into the language that give the speech its heightened sense. In another mode of drama, this speech could just as easily be:

We're really glad the York family just won the civil war. The sad days for us are over and we're going to trade in our days of war for music and parties.

Instead, Shakespeare's speech has a lot more going on in it—contrasting images (summer and winter), recurrent sounds (the assonance in "clouds," "lour'd," and "house" and the consonance in "bosom," "buried," "brows," and "bound"), the setting up and breaking of rhetorical patterns (the three lines beginning with "Our . . . "), and the expansive word choice (*lascivious*, *lour'd*, and *barbed*).

This heightened approach to the language in the Shakespearean theatrical tradition calls for a heightened experience, both for actors and audience. For actors, speaking poetic drama might mean matching the heightened, more intense, more lyrical nature of the language with a heightened approach to physicality, vocal delivery, or emotional payout.

Finding Patterns in Shakespeare's Language

Now is the winter of our discontent
Made glorious summer by this sun of York;
And all the clouds that lour'd upon our house
In the deep bosom of the ocean buried
Now are our brows bound with victorious wreaths;
Our bruised arms hung up for monuments;
Our stern alarums changed to merry meetings,
Our dreadful marches to delightful measures.

Assonance – similar, recurring vowel sounds

Consonance – similar, recurring consonant sounds

Parallelism – similar, recurring sentence structure

Antithesis – opposing images set against each other

Certainly not all of the patterns have been identified in this selection. Shakespeare's language is full of these and many other rhetorical elements. What other patterns can you identify in this speech?

For the audience, the heightened language can mean a more demanding, more complex theatrical experience.

Language Prompts the Imagination in a Special Way

In part because of the heightened language and experience associated with it, and in part because of its literary nature, poetic drama calls upon both the practitioner and the audience to engage their imaginations in ways that may be less common in realistic drama. In Shakespeare's plays, we can be called upon to imagine the setting; to stretch our imagination to account for a magical character or a fantastical, unrealistic element; or to believe that the woman in the play who is dressed like a man passes muster.

The requirement of imagination is a key element of Shakespeare's plays in particular. One example is **spoken décor**, settings that are described rather than demonstrated, as in this example from *Macbeth*:

DUNCAN: This castle hath a pleasant seat; the air
　　　　　Nimbly and sweetly recommends itself
　　　　　Unto our gentle senses.
BANQUO: This guest of summer,
　　　　　The temple-haunting martlet, does approve,
　　　　　By his loved mansionry, that the heaven's breath
　　　　　Smells wooingly here: no jutty, frieze,
　　　　　Buttress, nor coign of vantage, but this bird
　　　　　Hath made his pendent bed and procreant cradle:
　　　　　Where they most breed and haunt, I have observed,
　　　　　The air is delicate.

Here we do not see Macbeth's castle, which Duncan and Banquo describe, but rather we hear about it through descriptive language—spoken décor. For Shakespeare and other dramatists in early modern England, spoken décor proved an economical means of creating setting for a particular scene. Rather than building a new set for each scene, or even a new set for each play, both of which were very expensive and impractical options for the playing companies of the day, spoken décor called upon the actors to paint a world—Scotland, Rome, Egypt, Italy—that audience could imagine together.

In addition to spoken décor, Shakespeare's plays stoke the imagination in other ways: a few actors might have to represent an entire army, weeks might pass in just a few moments on the stage, or a character might hide in plain sight or adopt what is, to the audience, a very transparent disguise. The Chorus in *Henry V* points to some of the ways audiences might be prompted to imagine:

. . . can this cockpit hold
The vasty fields of France? or may we cram
Within this wooden O the very casques
That did affright the air at Agincourt?
O, pardon! since a crooked figure may
Attest in little place a million;
And let us, ciphers to this great accompt,
On your imaginary forces work.
Suppose within the girdle of these walls
Are now confined two mighty monarchies,

Whose high upreared and abutting fronts
The perilous narrow ocean parts asunder:
Piece out our imperfections with your thoughts;
Into a thousand parts divide on man,
And make imaginary puissance;
Think when we talk of horses, that you see them
Printing their proud hoofs i' the receiving earth;
For 'tis your thoughts that now must deck our kings,
Carry them here and there; jumping o'er times,
Turning the accomplishment of many years
Into an hour-glass: for the which supply,
Admit me Chorus to this history;
Who prologue-like your humble patience pray,
Gently to hear, kindly to judge, our play.

For audiences, imagining and filling in the world of the play is a cue to take a more active part in how the play is made and, ultimately, in its successful performance. Because Shakespeare's poetic drama asks us to imagine that Rosalind, a beautiful young woman, is instead a young man named Ganymede, the ultimate success of Rosalind's disguise depends on whether we allow it to work over the course of the play, *As You Like It*. This stretching or testing of our imaginative will is key in Shakespeare's plays and represents a clear distinction from what can often be a more literal and more plausible way of making theatre in the realistic mode. Though there are myriad exceptions among plays in contemporary theatre—*Angels in America, Parts I & II*, for instance—poetic drama, particularly that of Shakespeare, seems to make these special demands on the audience as a rule.

Interpreting Shakespeare

In the theatrical tradition, the imagination required to engage Shakespeare's plays prompts practitioners—particularly directors and designers—to realize, in production, their own imagined responses to the play. Because Shakespeare is such a presence in the theatre and the culture, the plays can become a bit like a blank canvas onto which modern practitioners can invent new worlds around the play. Directors and designers of modern Shakespeare productions might do this with a stylized

Emily Plumtree as Nerissa and Susannah Fielding as Portia in the Royal Shakespeare Company's 2011 production of *The Merchant of Venice*, which takes place in present-day Las Vegas amid a television dating game in which a blond wig-wearing Portia hosts. Photo © Robbie Jack/Corbis.

Sir Ian McKellen as the titular role in the 1995 film *Richard III*, reset in midtwentieth-century fascist England. Director Richard Loncraine brings the reality of World War II into the Shakespearean world. Photo © United Artists.

production design or "concept." In some of these concept productions, a given play can be reimagined in a different era or setting that resonates with the play's central themes, helps the audience connect the play to other ideas, or makes the play look or feel fresh and contemporary.

These concepts are mostly sensorial adaptations that fill in the imagined setting with an actual one and create a fuller theatrical experience for audiences that have come to expect plays with compelling lighting, sets, and effects while keeping Shakespeare's original texts largely intact. Other concepts might include rewriting or reorganizing the texts, using a limited number of actors (say, in a four-person production of *Romeo and Juliet*), or using a play as the basis for a much more highly stylized performance.

Concept productions are one approach to these imaginative texts, but there are others. Shakespeare's Globe Theatre in London and the American Shakespeare Center's Blackfriars Playhouse in Staunton, Virginia, both reconstructions of two of Shakespeare's original theatres, often attempt to present Shakespeare's plays in an "original" setting with bare stages, live music, "universal" lighting (lighting of actor and audience together with no blackouts as one might see in a conventional theatre), and early modern costuming. Though not all productions at the Globe or the

This 2010 production of *Much Ado About Nothing* featured a cast of eight actors playing multiple roles, including gender-, race-, and age-nonspecific casting. Burning Coal Theatre Company (directed by Emily Ranii). Photo by Jerome Davis.

The Globe Theatre. Built in 1599 and demolished in 1644, it was recreated based on historical evidence and opened in 1997. Photo by Heidi Blanton.

Interior of the Globe Theatre. Photo by David Welch.

Blackfriars are performed with all of these elements, these companies attempt to respond to the poetic drama with simple concepts and relatively few trappings in an effort to return some of the business of imagination to their audiences.

Our imaginative response to Shakespeare—taking our cue as practitioners and audiences to engage these plays in ways that make sense and speak to us—and our awareness of the agendas and traditions that have informed and will continue to inform how we make and remake Shakespeare is ultimately a way of keeping the plays and their ideas and language fresh, contemporary, and alive. Because Shakespeare's words still resonate today, practitioners and audiences are in a unique position to say something back to him and to each other.

Language

Shakespeare wrote primarily in **blank verse**. Verse means that the lines have meter—a regular pattern of stressed syllables that occurs in the poetic line. Blank means that the verse is unrhymed. Therefore, blank verse is unrhymed, metered verse. The meter Shakespeare uses—for the most part—is called **iambic pentameter**. An iamb is a kind of metrical "foot" with one unstressed syllable followed by a stressed syllable, like:

/re WARD/

Penta (of *pentameter*) means "five." So in iambic pentameter, there are five iambs (five feet) in a regular line of verse:

/now, FAIR/ hiPPOL/yTA,/ our NUP/tial HOUR/

Say that out loud and you will hear yourself naturally speak five iambs (/unstressed-STRESSED/). Even if you do not know the identity of Hippolyta, or the definition of a nuptial, this line sounds relatively normal. However, there will be some lines in Shakespeare that sound very strange by comparison. They may be strange for one of two reasons: (a) you may be pronouncing or stressing the words incorrectly (Shakespeare's language does have some oddly pronounced words, like "commendable"—pronounced a bit like "common double") or (b) the line isn't regular. Here is an example of a slightly irregular line:

/to BE/ or NOT/ to BE/that IS/ the QUEST/ion/

This line has five perfectly normal iambs followed by an extra, unstressed, syllable ("ion"). This is called a weak ending and it occurs quite a lot throughout Shakespeare's poetic verse. This is still technically a "regular" line. In Hamlet's speech that follows, however, he has a lot of these weak endings right in a row—and this string of weak endings becomes a pattern unto itself. Patterns like this one are important to notice. In a play about a prince who cannot decide whether to go through with killing his uncle, this series of weak endings makes Hamlet sound like he is waffling (which is true). This is a pattern the actor can use to think about, and perhaps unlock, a choice about how to play this particular moment.

Verse may cause the actor to pronounce words irregularly so that they better fit the verse line. Take this speech from *Macbeth*:

> If it were done when 'tis done, then 'twere well
> It were done quickly: if the assassination
> Could trammel up the consequence, and catch
> With his surcease success; that but this blow
> Might be the be-all and the end-all here,
> But here, upon this bank and shoal of time,
> We'ld jump the life to come. But in these cases
> We still have judgment here; that we but teach
> Bloody instructions, which, being taught, return
> To plague the inventor: this even-handed justice
> Commends the ingredients of our poison'd chalice
> To our own lips.

The lines are mostly regular, but to make them so, Shakespeare had to elide some words. Examples of **elisions** from the preceding speech include *'tis, 'twere, We'ld*, and *poison'd*. This short speech contains a relatively high percentage of elisions and therefore might be a pattern to notice and then address as a potential acting choice, simply: why is Macbeth rushing through his words? Is he anxious? Hurried? When the actor begins to address those questions brought on by the language, he or she has a potential character choice.

Sometimes actors may have to elide words themselves to make the words fit the verse line—she might have a two-syllable "TROYlus "in one line and a three-syllable "TRO-ih-lus" in another, for example. On the printed page, both pronunciations simply appear as "Troilus." The actor must expand or overenunciate the pronunciation of some words, too, to fit the verse line:

> And change misdoubt to resolution

To scan correctly, you have to expand the word "REsoLushun" to "REs-oLUsheUN." Or here:

Had left the flushing in her galled eyes

"Galled" becomes two syllables: "gall-ed." For modern actors and audiences, these pronunciations can seem antiquated and can actually obscure, rather than reveal, a moment in the play. The idea with verse is to notice how it is working, particularly the places where it works differently, and then use the observations as a basis for performance choices.

As the actors begin to do all this analysis, they may find that in the verse line, this "pulse" throughout the poetry often highlights a point—a kind of "thesis" for the character in a given moment. Here is another example from *Macbeth*:

/toMOR/ow AND/to MOR/ow AND/to MOR/ow

This is just a regular line with a weak ending. Now just try to say the STRESSED syllables:

/MORE/AND/MORE/AND/MORE

For a character giving this particular speech in a play about ambition, and who has just learned his wife is dead and enemies are on the way to kill him, a line like "MORE AND MORE AND MORE" speaks volumes—he wanted more and more and more, and now more and more and more bad news keeps coming. Very often, irregularities do not mean nearly as much as this example. The point is to notice them and account for them as an actor by making a choice.

In addition to verse patterns, variations, and rules, Shakespeare's poetic drama is also rich with other kinds of patterns that have more to do with how ideas are constructed. We examined rhetorical patterns earlier in the speech from *Richard III*. **Rhetorical patterns** are what you notice happening in the language that sound like something organized is happening. Alliteration, consonance, assonance, repetition, antithesis—all these are rhetorical devices that, like verse patterns, can help the actor and the audience navigate how a particular character thinks or sounds.

In part because of the unique role of theatre in the early modern period, audiences came to the theatre to hear new words and new uses of the language—Shakespeare was meeting that demand in many ways by offering new words or new uses of existing words. Encountering words that are unfamiliar to us was also experienced by the earliest listeners of Shakespeare. For the actor both in Shakespeare's day and today, the task is to reveal the meaning of those words through gesture, clear acting choices that help to convey meaning, and careful listening to the context of the moment.

Printing Conventions and Modern Editions

For most actors—and for those of us who read Shakespeare—we encounter more than just spoken words, but also punctuation, spelling, typography, and stage directions. Though most of us encounter Shakespeare in an edition that has modern, consistent spelling and punctuation, offset stage directions, clear breaks between scenes, and so on, printed texts from the early modern period are very different.

For most actors and readers today, this text from *The Tempest* in Shakespeare's First Folio is difficult to navigate; there are variations in spelling, some older and out-of-use; inconsistent line arrangements; abbreviations

> *Seb.* Very well.   *Ant.* And moſt Chirurgeonly.
> *Gon.* It is foule weather in vs all, good Sir,
> When you are cloudy.
> *Seb.* Fowle weather?   *Ant.* Very foule.
> *Gon.* Had I plantation of this Iſle my Lord.
> *Ant.* Hee'd ſow't vvith Nettle-ſeed.
> *Seb.* Or dockes, or Mallowes.
> *Gon.* And were the King on't, what vvould I do?
> *Seb.* Scape being drunke, for want of Wine.
> *Gon.* I'th'Commonwealth I vvould (by contraries)
> Execute all things : For no kinde of Trafficke
> Would I admit : No name of Magiſtrate:
> Letters ſhould not be knowne : Riches, pouerty,
> And vſe of ſeruice, none : Contraƈt, Succeſſion,
> Borne, bound of Land, Tilth, Vineyard none :
> No vſe of Mettall, Corne, or Wine, or Oẏle :
> No occupation, all men idle, all :
> And Women too, but innocent and pure :
> No Soueraignty.
>   *Seb.* Yet he vvould be King on't.
>   *Ant.* The latter end of his Common-wealth forgets

for character names; and older uses of punctuation. As practitioners and readers of Shakespeare today, we need to know that the modern, clean, edited versions of the play we might use in production or study in class are different from those used by Shakespeare and his contemporaries. These differences are editorial choices that may illuminate or obscure meaning for the actor, director, or reader. One example from *The Tempest*, earlier, is that a modern edition might say either "ducks" or "docks" instead of "dockes" in an attempt to provide clarity, potentially obscuring the definition here, which is that a "docke" or "dock" is a kind of weed. Other editorial choices in the preceding passage might be to convert some of the many colons to semicolons, periods, commas, or exclamation points so that the passage might read as this one does:

SEBASTIAN: Very well.

ANTONIO: And most chirurgeonly.

GONZALO: It is foul weather in us all, good sir,
    When you are cloudy.

SEBASTIAN: Foul weather?

ANTONIO: Very foul.

GONZALO: Had I plantation of this isle, my lord,—

ANTONIO: He'ld sow't with nettle-seed.

SEBASTIAN: Or docks, or mallows.

GONZALO: And were the king on't, what would I do?

SEBASTIAN: 'Scape being drunk for want of wine.

GONZALO: I' the commonwealth I would by contraries
    Execute all things; for no kind of traffic
    Would I admit; no name of magistrate;
    Letters should not be known; riches, poverty,
    And use of service, none; contract, succession,
    Bourn, bound of land, tilth, vineyard, none;
    No use of metal, corn, or wine, or oil;
    No occupation; all men idle, all!
    And women too, but innocent and pure;
    No sovereignty;—

SEBASTIAN: Yet he would be king on't.

For most, the updates to the punctuation, formatting, and spelling on the page can be helpful in providing clarity and in making the text readable but, depending on the editor, meaning can be changed—sometimes very slightly, as in the preceding example, but sometimes much more substantially—and can affect both performance and reception. Here is an example of how editors might affect our understanding of *Romeo and Juliet*. We see three source texts (Q1 and Q2 are the first two "quarto" editions of the play, and F1 is the "folio" edition of the play) that are later negotiated, shifted, and conflated in the modern (Norton) edition.

Romeo and Juliet

Q1 (1597)

Juliet: Whats *Mountague*? It is nor hand nor foote,
Nor arme, nor face, nor any other part.
Whats in a name? That which we call a Rose,
By any other name would smell as sweet:
So *Romeo* would, were he not *Romeo* cald,

Q2 (1599)

Juliet. Whats *Mountague*? it is nor hand nor foote,
Nor arme nor face, o be some other name
Belonging to a man.
Whats in a name that which we call a rose,
By any other word would smell as sweete,
So *Romeo* would were he not *Romeo* cald,

F1 (1623)

Juliet: What's *Mountague*? it is nor hand nor foote,
Nor arme, nor face, O be some other name
Belonging to a man.
What? in a names that which we call a Rose,
By any other word would smell as sweete,
So *Romeo* would, were he not *Romeo* cal'd,

Norton Shakespeare (1998)

Juliet: What's Montague? It is nor hand, nor foot,
Nor arm, nor face, nor any other part
Belonging to a man. O, be some other name!

What's in a name? That which we call a rose
By any other word would smell as sweet.

Obviously there are major editorial differences between the source texts and the modern edition. These differences range from spelling to punctuation to word choice. The editors of modern editions like the Norton shown here are negotiating the text for the modern reader and making judgments about what should and should not be included based on preference. No editorial choices made to update the text for the modern reader are malignant, but they can affect our understanding of the text, obscuring or clarifying in different ways. For the actor or director, having at least a connection to how the older, original texts look and function can provide helpful insights for performance.

Stagecraft

In addition to understanding Shakespeare's language and how modern editions can affect how we read and perform his plays, it can be helpful to understand how Shakespeare made theatre, and how that stagecraft can provide insight for performance. Though there were many conditions for which Shakespeare wrote, we will focus on a few that can strongly affect production choices.

Universal Lighting

Shakespeare's playhouses—the Theatre, the Globe, the Blackfriars—were lit by a combination of daylight and candlelight. In the absence of electricity and the ability to control lights, as we might in a blackout in the theatre today, both actors and audience were lit together. Perhaps because of this condition, plays from these periods—Shakespeare's and others—almost without exception feature characters that talk to the audience. Though there are exceptions in today's theatre and film (*Ferris Bueller's Day Off* is a classic example), the frequency with which it happened in early modern drama made this direct address a common convention in Shakespearean performance and presents a different kind of challenge for today's actors and directors who may be more used to dealing with audiences in the dark. The challenge of a seen audience is that they move, they occasionally talk back, and they may or may not be paying attention—and so the actor has to account for a number of variables besides his or her own performance.

Song and Dance

Shakespeare's plays have much more song and dance than we might expect in a modern, realistic, play, putting Shakespeare's work somewhere between what we might think of as a play and what we would consider a musical. The presence of song and dance in Shakespeare can enliven the piece, set a certain emotional tone, or convey the nature of a particular moment such as the entrance of a king or queen. While we have some of the original music for many of these songs, other tunes have disappeared. Even with the ones we still have, directors and designers may find that the songs or tunes do not fit an updated concept. These songs, signals, and dances present challenges to actors, directors, designers, and technicians who have to navigate them in performance.

Casting

Shakespeare wrote for a small company composed exclusively of males. Women were forbidden to take the stage in early modern England, so boys who had not yet gone through vocal changes of puberty played the parts of younger women. The economics of playing companies prevented them from hiring more than usually twelve to eighteen actors. These casting conditions have two major impacts on performance today. First, since women were not allowed to perform in Shakespeare's plays, there are fewer women's roles in Shakespeare, meaning practitioners often choose to break conventional casting rules to accommodate their desire for more women in the cast, often either by putting women into "breeches" roles (where women play men) or by making a given character a woman instead of a man.

Second, as a result of the small companies, one actor played potentially several small roles in a given production. In performance today, companies may choose to adopt this Shakespearean practice or cast a fuller company based on the named characters in a script. The latter option is a common one but can often lose what may have been a clever or compelling second layer to the performance. If one actor plays a role, say Banquo in *Macbeth*, who is killed about halfway through the play and returns to the stage later on in the play as Siward, we see an actor who is, in a sense, taking revenge for his own death.

Embedded Stage Directions

In very few cases do Shakespeare's plays state in the stage directions where a scene is taking place, what time it is, what the temperature is, or any of the other given circumstances of the scene. Instead, the plays contain stage directions that are embedded in the dialogue itself or referenced with a prop. If a character is carrying a torch or candle, there's an embedded cue that it's nighttime. If it is nighttime, and dark out, there's a direction for the actor to follow: you probably can't see very well—that's why you brought the light. The impact of this embedded stage direction has a direct impact on performance, telling the actor how to behave and, ultimately, how to tell the story more clearly.

Contemporary Shakespeare

Since productions during Shakespeare's era did not use historically accurate costumes, it can be argued that using contemporary dress for Shakespeare's plays is closer to original Elizabethan practices.

The 2008 production of *Macbeth* by the Shotgun Players, Berkeley, California. Photo by Jessica Palopoli.

Citi Performing Arts Center's 2008 Free Shakespeare production of *As You Like It*. Charles Kelby Akin (left) as Charles the wrestler battles Fred Weller as Orlando (right). Photo by T. Charles Erickson.

The Pilot Theatre 2010 production of *Romeo and Juliet*. Courtesy of Pilot Theatre.

Understanding some of the conditions for which Shakespeare wrote, and the conventions at work in the plays—internal cues, casting considerations, and the like—may help some modern practitioners navigate what can sometimes be a daunting, or obstructed, text. At the same time, there are plenty of other resources—new understandings of the text that scholars or previous productions have unveiled, longstanding performance traditions, critical essays on a given play, careful study of original texts, examination of derivative works, training in classical acting techniques, performance itself, and so on—that can help inform directorial choices and acting approaches. Our own imaginations, dispositions, and ideas can also help unlock Shakespeare, both for ourselves and for potential audiences. While we, as audiences or practitioners, can work to better understand Shakespeare, ultimately the quality of the exchange between Shakespeare and ourselves and with each other does not rely solely upon whether we understand how Shakespeare is supposed to work, but simply whether he does work as we enact the plays, speak the language, and engage in the performance. In this sense, Shakespeare is not Shakespeare, the imposing, weighted (and weighty), antiquated, supposedly perfect, monolith we have come to consider, but rather the fresh, sometimes bad, sometimes very good, "new," alive Shakespeare we can help to create.

9 The American Musical

Margaret R. Butler

What is the American musical? It is many things: a fusion of song, dance, spoken and sung dialogue, and visual elements; an essential form of entertainment in popular culture; a venue for expression of political and social themes that have shaped the American experience; a money-making enterprise, with big-budget productions requiring enormous outlay of funds from wealthy sponsors; and a genre that both shapes and has been shaped by American culture. For many, it is synonymous with Broadway, hence the moniker "the Broadway musical." But the musical is not just on Broadway. It is everywhere, in every major city in America and many smaller ones. Musicals are performed by professional touring companies and amateur community theatre groups and by young people in secondary schools, and they represent an area of study at colleges and universities.

Musicals are increasingly available to larger audiences through films with performances by major stars: Johnny Depp, Renée Zellweger, Matthew Broderick, Catherine Zeta-Jones, Kevin Kline, Richard Gere, Neil Patrick Harris, and many others. Marquee stars such as Harry Potter's Daniel Radcliffe routinely perform in live award-winning Broadway musicals. Popular television shows even occasionally spoof or pay homage to the musical; memorable episodes of *Scrubs*, *How I Met Your Mother*, *The Big Bang Theory*, and *Flight of the Conchords* have featured production numbers in which the lead characters sing and dance.

The musical is a living genre, one whose history is still developing. And as with any history that is still taking shape, scholars who study the musical disagree on important questions and issues, ones as basic as the following: What was the very first musical? What features define different genres? What factors were most significant in the musical's development? Which works and which people were most influential? Which works are most representative of their time? And many others.

Early Musical Theatre: Entertainments and Genres

Musicals throughout history can be said to represent many different generic designations; one way to study the musical is to look at them in terms of these categories. Genre names applied to the musical have come from various sources: some came from the creators themselves, others came from critics, and still others came from specialists who study the musical. Some of these genre names indicate important features of form and structure; others are tied to a work's function in society.

The musical's origins lie in a fusion of different entertainment genres from the eighteenth and nineteenth centuries. These are traditionally called precursors, forerunners, or antecedents of the musical. Such labels imply a bias toward an organic unity that is the result of an anachronistic view. Sometimes the "early genres" are described in terms of what they are not: they are not **book musicals**, the genre that eventually displaced all of them, and one that privileges a traditional, forward-moving narrative, usually serious in tone. Book musicals (also called *musical plays*) are shows generally based on some kind of literary source with a story line that has a clear beginning, middle, and end. This genre came to dominate the history of musical theatre and is still the most popular category today.

Since the entertainments of the eighteenth and nineteenth centuries did not view themselves as forerunners to anything, we will not do that either. These entertainments represent a rich variety of generic types, the defining characteristics of which are not always clear. Many genres overlapped, coexisted with, and borrowed elements from one another.

Perhaps one of the most difficult genres for us to understand today involved white performers "blacking up"—coloring their skin with burnt cork—and imitating black Americans. Over the course of its complicated history, blacks eventually performed it as well. The tradition of both groups is known as **minstrelsy**. What today seems like the pinnacle of prejudice and offensiveness was a form of entertainment that offered black performers an entrée into what was then an all-white world. In fact, during its heyday, it was considered a source of pride.

An example of typical minstrel makeup, 1900. As late as 1978, blackface was used for a long-running BBC show titled *The Black and White Minstrel Show*. Courtesy Library of Congress, LC-USZC4-5698.

Blackface minstrelsy started becoming popular around 1843, eventually coming to rival melodrama in popularity. Early troupes comprised between four and six members who were all white males. Their comic skits involved stereotypes of blacks, dealing with plantation life or other situations, and songs with accompaniments by a minstrel band, in what were essentially variety shows. The so-called golden era was the 1840s to the 1870s. Black Americans started performing in troupes regularly after the abolition of slavery; eventually the troupes grew larger and were transformed—some were all female; some were all black.

In Dahomey (1903) by Will Marion Cook and Paul Dunbar is an early musical comedy drawing on the tradition of blackface minstrelsy. As we will see when we get to musical comedy, its elements are more integrated than in other genres and it has a more continuous narrative structure. An important black performer appearing in this work was Bert Williams. He was hired by Florenz Ziegfeld, an influential figure in the genre of the revue. Williams's participation integrated the revue as a genre.

Several genres in particular exhibit a great deal of overlap in their distinguishing characteristics. They commingled and cross-fertilized each

The 1903 production of *In Dahomey*. The musical tells the story of a group of African Americans who decide to travel to the African country of Dahomey (now Benin) and become governors after a generous donation of rum. The show only had fifty-three performances in New York but moved to London and became a sensation, ran for seven months, and then toured for a year in the British Isles. Bert Williams (fourth in line) later wrote, "The way we've aimed at Broadway and just missed it in the past seven years would make you cry. . . . I used to be tempted to beg for a fifteen-dollar job in a chorus for one week so as to be able to say I'd been on Broadway." Williams played in blackface for most of his career. Photo courtesy of the Jas Obrecht Music Archive.

other during the second half of the nineteenth century. **Pantomime** refers to theatrical presentations that used gestures done in silence. It featured *underscoring*, or instrumental music that occurred during the performance of the gestures and that helped create a particular mood. **Ballet**, in the early history of the musical, simply refers to classical dance with a story line. **Spectacles** featured dance, elaborate scenery and costumes, sets, and sophisticated stage machinery. **Extravaganzas** had all of those components in addition to elements of melodrama and fantasy.

The Black Crook (1866) was an important extravaganza. Frequently cited as the first real precursor to the twentieth-century musical, it was a blockbuster hit. Lasting five and a half hours, it had little innovation but enjoyed great commercial success. With preexisting numbers by other composers (related to the operatic genre of the pasticcio), it offered lots of visual appeal and stage spectacle, complete with a chorus line with more than one hundred dancers. It ran for more than four hundred performances and was revived many times. Agnes de Mille made her debut as a choreographer in the 1929 revival.

KIRALFY BROS. "BLACK CROOK"

Illustration of *The Black Crook* (1866). The title refers to a sorcerer who makes a deal with the devil to deliver souls in exchange for everlasting life. The play was a tired melodrama; its success was a result of interpolated popular songs, dance numbers, and immense spectacle. Library of Congress, LC-DIG-ds-04512.

Burlesque emphasized broad comedy and sexual content. Its texts were full of puns, innuendos, and topical references and spoofed aspects of contemporary society. *Evangeline* (1874) was the first burlesque for which the music was newly written. Based on a narrative poem by Henry Wadsworth Longfellow (*Evangeline, A Tale of Acadie*, 1847), it featured music by Edward Everett Rice and text by John Cheever Goodwin. This show is one of the first among several to be called a "musical comedy," again reinforcing the general disagreement on this point as well as the overlap in characteristics of the early genres. *Extravaganza, burlesque,* and *spectacle* in particular were terms used interchangeably or in combination in the midnineteenth century.

Melodrama, popular by the last third of the nineteenth century, represents the use of short musical passages to heighten affect in drama, either in alternation with or underlying spoken dialogue. Coming from British popular theatre, it eventually developed into full-length melodramatic plays. Underscoring, a significant element in the later musical, grew out of this technique.

A burlesque theatre in Baltimore, one of many in the neighborhood called "the Bawdy Block."

The **revue** emerged in the 1890s and remained popular to late 1930s. A style of entertainment that had become popular in Paris, the revue featured elements loosely related by an overarching theme. It had elements of vaudeville, with which it coexisted, but those elements were more integrated. They combined the components of the extravaganza—fantasy, ballet, spectacular scenery and costumes, and sophisticated stage machinery—with an emphasis on beautiful girls performing skits, solo numbers, and choruses. *Tableaux vivants*—still bodies (usually scantily clad and sometimes partially nude) arranged in attractive formations—lent the revue a sensuousness not seen in other genres from around the same time. Important composers such as Irving Berlin, Cole Porter, Richard Rodgers, George Gershwin, and Harold Arlen (who wrote "Somewhere over the Rainbow") got their start in the revue. Flexible in types of presentation style, revues could be either single-shot (performed just once) or multiple, annual editions on Broadway. *The Passing Show* (1894) was the first successful American revue. Recurring revues had consistent visions that were determined by an impresario—a producer, director, or theatre manager—and were named for that person; the *Ziegfeld Follies*, for example, was a series of revues sponsored by the great impresario Florenz

Sheet music for a song included in the *Ziegfeld Follies of 1917*. The theme of Flo Ziegfeld's revues was "glorifying the American girl," and this was often accomplished through seminudity. Unlike the women in burlesque shows frequently raided by police, Ziegfeld girls did not sing or dance. Instead, they paraded in expensive costumes with dispassionate expressions. Although Ziegfeld spent extravagantly on his productions, all made a profit.

Ziegfeld. Members of his chorus lines were known as Ziegfeld showgirls and represented a romantic model of the ultimate in femininity.

Variety, emerging around the 1850s, had little of the luxury and romance of the revue. Featuring skits, gags, and specialized acts, it was entertainment that was considered highly disreputable. Concert saloons were important venues for variety in the first decade of the genre's popularity. They were patronized exclusively by men who bought drinks and watched the entertainments. Variety theatres began to develop during the 1880s and 1890s; these became the central venues for vaudeville.

Vaudeville might be thought of as variety without alcohol, in a theatre rather than a saloon. Theatre managers invented the term, changing the name of the entertainment in an attempt to attract family audiences (in other words, women) and, in general, to clean up the form and render it more professional in tone and content. (*Vaudeville* was a term long used in French popular theatre, which bore close resemblances to variety.) Vaudeville shows featured skits, gags, and specialized acts like those found in variety but placed a greater emphasis on individual performers and independent acts, with no plot tying things together. Its heyday was the decades of the 1890s and 1910s.

George M. Cohan's *Little Johnny Jones* (1904) is considered the first American musical. Cohan's vaudeville roots led to his rise to stardom. Coming from a family of vaudeville performers, Cohan was the composer, lyricist, producer, director, and choreographer of his shows. His songs, such as "Yankee Doodle Boy" and "Give My Regards to Broadway," became emblematic of vaudeville. Jimmy Cagney immortalized Cohan in the film *Yankee Doodle Boy* in the 1940s, and the vaudeville world forms the backdrop for the musical *Gypsy*, one of the most popular shows in the late 1950s.

Tin Pan Alley is neither a genre nor a real place, but it is important for understanding the musical side of the early musical theatrical genres. It is a nickname both for the area around 28th Street in Manhattan, where many early sheet music publishers were located from the 1880s to the 1950s, and for the type of music they published. Tin Pan Alley songs were the popular songs of America, and many were big hits. Tin Pan Alley helped to publicize the music of American musical theatre in two

George M. Cohan in one of his patriotic musicals.

Cast and dedicated in 1959, this Times Square statue of George M. Cohan came into being through a memorial committee that included composers Irving Berlin and Oscar Hammerstein II. Photo by Stephanie Lynge.

important ways: people either wanted the music that they heard at the shows they saw, or they heard the songs and then wanted to see the shows from which those songs were drawn. In music stores, *song pluggers*, musicians who worked for a publishing firm, played songs on a piano to interest customers in buying the sheet music. Many composers of early musicals became known to the general public thanks to their talents. George Gershwin and Irving Berlin both started out as song pluggers. In terms of general form and structure, most songs took the form of AABA, with a repeating section, followed by a contrasting section, and a return to the familiar material, over the course of thirty-two measures, yielding what came to be known as *song form*.

European opera was of great significance in the development of the musical. American audiences at the end of the nineteenth century loved opera, and elements of opera's music and dramatic language gradually carried over into **operetta**, or light opera. The first of the American musical's great creative teams were the British creators of some of the world's best-known operettas: William Schwenk Gilbert (lyricist) and Arthur Sullivan (composer). Gilbert and Sullivan's operettas feature comic stories that spoof nineteenth-century British society's morals and behavior. Their *H.M.S. Pinafore* (1878), *The Pirates of Penzance* (1879), and *The Mikado* (1885), to name a few, are considered staples of the musical theatre repertory and are still widely performed today. *Pinafore* in particular took America by storm, becoming immensely popular. In 1879, Gilbert and Sullivan traveled to the United States with the D'Oyly Carte company, and their performances influenced later ones by American

The 2009 production of *The Pirates of Penzance*, Hirsch Theatre, Jerusalem. Presented by Encore! Educational Theatre Company (directed by Robert Binder). Photo by Brian Negin.

companies. The colorful film *Topsy-Turvy* tells the story of Gilbert and Sullivan's long and sometimes difficult collaboration.

Operetta in America was also strongly influenced by Americans' passion for the Viennese waltz. Franz Lehar's *The Merry Widow* (1907) and Victor Herbert's *Naughty Marietta* (1910) with its romantic song, "Ah, Sweet Mystery of Life" (famously parodied in the film *Young Frankenstein*), recreate a glamorous world with lyrical waltzes as an important

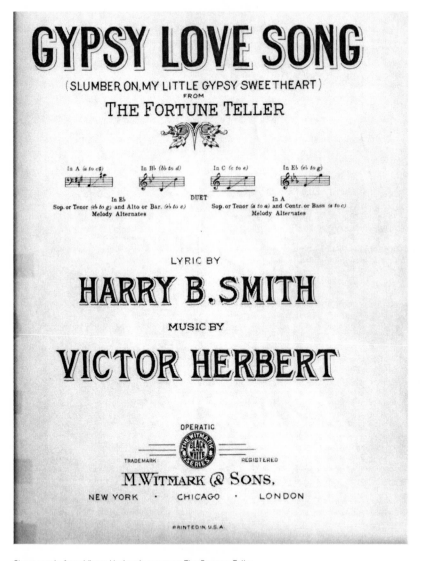

Sheet music from Victor Herbert's operetta *The Fortune Teller*.

element. These and other works evoke the sights and sounds of Viennese operetta, such as *Die Fledermaus* by Johann Strauss II, known as "the waltz king." Other important contributions to operetta are Sigmund Romberg's *The Student Prince* (1924), *The Desert Song* (1926), and *The New Moon* (1928), as well as Rudolf Friml's *Rose-Marie* (1924). The continuous narrative that would become an integral part of the book musical is central to the operetta and is possibly among that genre's most important contributions to the development of the American musical.

Musical Comedies of the 1920s and 1930s

Musical theatre in the 1920s and 1930s was all about entertainment. Dance—particularly tap dance—was a crucial element in the early musical comedies popular during these decades. The plots of musical comedies are usually considered frivolous, a result of viewing them through the lens of today's book musicals. Musical comedies of the 1920s and 1930s, like any other genre, need to be understood in their own time, place, and context. They do have narratives, but they stand apart from book musicals because their emphasis is more on comedy and dance than on drama and character development. The musical language of jazz and other types of American popular music greatly influenced musical theatre of this era.

The brothers George and Ira Gershwin (composer and lyricist, respectively) created many of this era's most popular works. Songs from some of their musicals took on lives of their own, becoming popular in their own right, independent of the shows in which they had their premieres. At the same time, many of the era's big stars had their debuts in Gershwin shows. The title song of *Strike Up the Band* (1927) was the Gershwins' first hit of the 1930s. The catchy tune "Fascinatin' Rhythm" with its driving syncopations was first heard in *Lady Be Good* (1924), the show in which siblings Fred and Adele Astaire made their debut as dancers. The lovely ballad "Someone to Watch over Me" was first heard in *Oh, Kay!* (1926). *Girl Crazy* (1930) introduced Ethel Merman to the theatregoing public. Her performance of "I Got Rhythm," and Ginger Rogers's of "Embraceable You," helped to popularize these songs. The show spawned the partnership of Fred Astaire and Ginger Rogers, one of the greatest dance teams in the history of musicals. Although the show itself, like many of the musical comedies of these decades, did not enjoy lasting

Composer George Gershwin. Photo © Lebrecht Music and Arts/Corbis.

popularity, it took on new life much later, being revamped as *Crazy for You* in 1992. The Gershwins' *Of Thee I Sing* (1931) was the first musical to win a Pulitzer Prize for drama and the first show to have its **book**—the spoken dialogue apart from the song lyrics—published separately.

The best known musical of this era is decidedly not a comedy. *Show Boat* (1927), by composer Jerome Kern and librettist Oscar Hammerstein II, is an actual book musical, widely considered the very first in the genre's history. With its serious tone and treatment of controversial issues of race, this work stands apart from the popular emphasis on comic entertainment that characterized shows from around its time. Based on a 1926 novel by Edna Ferber with the same title, the show deals with issues of race and class, demonstrating the controversy surrounding miscegenation (interracial marriage). Another innovation concerns the integration of the songs into the plot. *Show Boat*'s songs are more central to the narrative than those of earlier (and later) musical comedies. This element would become a defining characteristic of the later book musical. Some of *Show Boat*'s songs are related to each other through similarity of their musical material. For instance, the famous song "Ol' Man River" (in the familiar song form, AABA) is linked to "Cotton Blossom" through inversion of melodic material: the first few notes of the opening of the melody of "Ol' Man River" are the same as that of "Cotton Blossom" when the

The 2013 production of *Show Boat*, produced jointly by the San Francisco Opera, Lyric Opera of Chicago, Washington National Opera, and Houston Grand Opera. Photo by Dan Rest.

This 2011 Portland Center Stage production of *Oklahoma!* was performed by an all-black cast. Traditionally, this story of love in a farming community in 1906 is done with white actors. However, director Chris Coleman discovered through his research that at one point, one third of cowboys in the West were black, and during the time of the play, there were fifty all-black towns in Oklahoma. Photo by Patrick Weishampel.

tune is run backward. Unfortunately, *Show Boat* did not inspire a trend. The work and its innovations would not be influential in the development of the musical until the 1940s, when *Oklahoma!*, the next great book musical and the one to usher in the tradition of greater emphasis on dramatic content, had its premiere. Instead, musical comedies continued to dominate.

Richard Rodgers and Lorenz Hart, the first composer-lyricist team to attain recognition as such, had a hit with *On Your Toes* (1936). The great choreographer George Balanchine created the dances, which were central to the plot, and Rodgers and Hart wrote the book together, in a partnership that would span twenty-four years.

Irving Berlin is known better today for a show that came much later in his career: *Annie Get Your Gun* (1946). His reputation in the 1930s was built on the strength of his songs, many of which were wildly popular, such as "There's No Business Like Show Business," "God Bless America," "White Christmas," "Alexander's Ragtime Band," and "Blue Skies," to name a few. Berlin wrote both the music and lyrics for his songs, as did Cole Porter, one of the most important figures from around this time. Porter, like Berlin, was classically trained in music, and like Berlin, Porter also had a hit later in his career with *Kiss Me Kate* (1948). Porter's songs have a technical complexity unmatched by those of any of his contemporaries. Porter's lyrics are witty and suggestive and often exhibit a sophisticated use of rhyme. His *Anything Goes* (1934) was a vehicle for Ethel Merman (it highlighted her as the star); the title song is typical of Porter's style. Again, dance is a central element in the narrative. The show's recent successful Broadway revival demonstrates its popularity with modern audiences. Porter's turbulent career and personal life is the subject of *De-Lovely*, a biopic with Kevin Kline and Ashley Judd, which presents an intriguing montage of many of Porter's songs (and is named for one of his best-known ones).

The Rise and Dominance of the Book Musical in the 1940s and 1950s

The 1940s and 1950s were dominated by the book musical. Creators and audiences increasingly favored shows that were based on some sort of literary source (such a book, play, novel, or story), many of which were serious in tone and content. They typically featured down-to-earth, realistic characters with whom people could identify and had a recognizable story line. The songs in works during this period were part of the dramatic fabric and essential to the narrative, a result of the close collaboration between the members of the creative teams who conceived the works. In contrast to earlier shows, the musicals of the 1940s and 1950s combined lighthearted and comic elements with those of a greater depth and weight, with characters that are more complex as individuals and in relation to each other. A sense of unity pervades the shows of these decades, with an emphasis on a smooth integration of all the elements.

The musicals of the two great teams of the 1940s and 1950s are the "meat and potatoes" of the genre, classics that are still popular today; many are given regular productions in community theatres around the country as well as revivals on Broadway. The formula they created was expanded upon by their successors, and elements of it are evident in shows throughout the remaining decades of the twentieth century. Shows from this era are sometimes called "symphonic musicals" because they are symphonic in conception and execution, calling for the resources of a full classical orchestra. The composers of these partnerships carefully utilized particular instrumental colors in composing their musical scores, and professional orchestral musicians played in pit orchestras on Broadway.

Richard Rodgers (composer) and Oscar Hammerstein II (lyricist) began to collaborate after Rodgers's partnership with Lorenz Hart came to an end. *Oklahoma!* (1943), based on the play *Green Grow the Lilacs* by Lynn Riggs, was their first collaboration. It was immensely popular, one of most successful musicals ever on Broadway. It broke the record for the show with the longest run, with more than two thousand performances (a record it would hold for fifteen years), and won the Pulitzer Prize for Drama. Its choreographer was Agnes de Mille, whose balletic style transformed theatrical dance and who originated the dream ballet (an extended sequence in which a character's dream is acted out by dancers). The original cast recording helped make the show famous nationally. *Carousel* (1945) dealt with the somber theme of spousal abuse and featured an onstage death. Again, Agnes de Mille's choreography was, like the songs, an essential component of the storytelling. One of the songs, "What's the Use of Wond'rin?" is an example of Rodgers and Hammerstein's expansion of the classic song form, in which a reprise (a vocal coda, which repeats some of the music from earlier) enlarges the scope of the song and broadens it to include participation by the chorus. *South Pacific* (1949) and *The King and I* (1951) share some common features. Both are based on novels, are set in exotic locales, and deal with issues of racism and ethnic prejudice—how it is both created and overcome. *South Pacific*'s "You Have to Be Carefully Taught" addressed this issue explicitly. Both shows also centered on unusual love interests represented by lead characters from different cultural traditions and have many memorable songs that became associated with the music of the era ("Some Enchanted Evening" from *South Pacific*; "Shall We Dance?" and "Getting to Know You" from *The King and I*). *The Sound of Music* (1959) is perhaps their most famous show, known to family audiences through the well-loved film version from 1965 starring Julie Andrews.

Frederick Loewe (composer) and Alan Jay Lerner (lyricist) built successfully on the Rodgers and Hammerstein model. Lerner, unlike most lyricists, had musical training. The two began collaborating in the early 1940s. Their *Brigadoon* (1947), set in a mystical land in the highlands of Scotland, appealed to audiences for its elements of fantasy and exoticism. Their greatest hit, *My Fair Lady* (1956), was based on George Bernard Shaw's play *Pygmalion*. Against a backdrop of class conflict in nineteenth-century Britain, it introduced lively and lovable characters and situations. *Camelot* (1960) recreated the medieval world of King Arthur, Lancelot, and Guinevere, retelling the story of their love triangle. The film versions of these shows brought them to a broad audience. These were often heavily revised versions of the originals, with nonsinging film actors whose voices were dubbed (Audrey Hepburn's portrayal of Eliza Doolittle in *My Fair Lady* is a classic example). These musicals thus developed a national following that shows from the early years of the century never had. The existence of these shows as films contributed greatly to their status as classics that they enjoy today.

Varieties of Nostalgia in the 1950s

The shows of these two towering creative teams were not the only ones to receive acclaim or to introduce innovations. Musicals carried different meanings for different audiences. The themes of the stories and situations dealt with many different issues and topics that were both appealing and thought-provoking in diverse ways and in varying degrees. Several important shows by other composers evoked a nostalgic view of America. They are known as works by their composers alone, rather than as ones that represent a partnership. *Guys and Dolls* (1950), by Frank Loesser, was based on characters from stories by Damon Runyon set in the New York underworld of the 1920s and 1930s (which became known as "Runyonland"). *The Music Man* (1957), by Meredith Willson, another classically trained musician, is the love story of a librarian and a traveling salesman set in small-town Iowa. Audiences loved the sweet, romantic view of urban and rural surroundings depicted by these two shows. *Gypsy* (1959), by Jule (pronounced JOO-lie) Styne, can be viewed as representing nostalgia of a very different type. Set during the vaudeville era, it was based on the autobiography of the stripper Gypsy Rose Lee. Dealing with hard-edged subject matter, it was among the first shows to reveal the unpleasant side of human relationships, with several emotionally wrenching scenes and songs for Gypsy's strong-willed mother, Mama Rose. The collaboration among members of the personnel was complex and is a good example of the strong influence performers could exert in the creation of a musical. Ethel Merman was engaged to play Mama Rose and was brought into the planning stages early on. She insisted that Styne was a better choice as composer than Stephen Sondheim, who had made his mark as lyricist for *West Side Story* two years earlier. In the end, Sondheim, who was slated to compose the music and lyrics for *Gypsy*, partnered with Styne, creating many of the songs and retaining his role as lyricist. *Gypsy* featured other *West Side Story* collaborators as well: Arthur

A 2011 national tour of *West Side Story*. The choreography, a blend of modern dance and ballet styles, uses dance as a means of expressing territoriality and violence in much the same way as modern "dance battles" depicted in movies. Photo by Carol Rosegg.

Laurents, who wrote the book, and Jerome Robbins, a significant figure in theatrical dance in later decades, who created the choreography.

Leonard Bernstein

Leonard Bernstein is a towering figure in the history of American music. His contributions to the musical world as composer, conductor, and educator are unsurpassed by those of any other artist in America in the second half of the twentieth century. Bernstein composed concert works in various genres and film scores as well as musicals. *On the Town* (1944), his first musical, took its inspiration from a ballet he and Robbins had created called *Fancy Free*. It exhibits the thorough integration of book, music, and dance so important to Bernstein's creative vision and that would become essential to the musical's later development.

West Side Story (1957) epitomizes Bernstein's genius as a craftsman of musical theatre and has earned its place as a classic in the genre. Opening the same year as *The Music Man* (demonstrating contemporary audiences' widely ranging tastes), it involved the collaboration of the era's leading artists: Sondheim as lyricist, Laurents as author of the book, and Robbins as choreographer. Themes of discrimination, racism, and love play out in a retelling of Shakespeare's *Romeo and Juliet* set in 1950s New York highlighting the relationships between members of rival gangs and their families. The film version of 1961 won the Academy Award for Best Picture. The show's music is rich in melodic and harmonic invention. The ensembles are particularly challenging to coordinate, with dense textures and complex rhythms. The "Tonight" ensemble is operatic in conception, with energetic interplay between individual lines as well as choral groups. Like the best opera composers, Bernstein portrays characters and their contrasting emotions through the changing qualities of the music they sing. "America," with its driving rhythms and shifting accents, is another high point of the show; both ensembles require performers who are skilled dancers as well as exceptional singers.

Expansions of and Alternatives to the Book Musical in the 1960s–1980s

Starting in the 1960s, creators of the musical began to experiment with new ways of telling stories, exploring new narrative structures that did not rely as greatly on the book musical's plot-oriented approach. The book musical never disappeared or went out of style, however, and is still the most prevalent genre in popular shows of today. But certain aspects of its conventions have been influenced by stylistic developments that started to occur in the second half of the twentieth century. Some of the categories we will explore here are not actually different genres, but are ones that place different amounts and kinds of emphasis on the traditional musical's various components.

Breaking the Mold

Perhaps the most significant change to occur in the book musical's development around this time is the continued broadening of the types of subject matter that came to be considered acceptable for presentation on the musical stage. *Gypsy*, with its gritty realism, might be considered the first show to have initiated this trend and achieved success. Three shows of the 1960s and 1970s—musicals with strong dramatic subjects by new creative teams—stand out as examples: Jerry Bock and Sheldon Harnick's *Fiddler on the Roof* (1964), John Kander and Fred Ebb's *Cabaret* (1966), and *Chicago* (1985). *Fiddler* and *Cabaret* were directed by Hal Prince, whose later collaborations with Sondheim would continue transforming the genre. Both shows deal with ethnic prejudice and discrimination, exploring issues of Jewish cultural identity in different times and places. *Fiddler* set a new record, garnering more than three thousand performances and winning many awards. Jerome Robbins choreographed the dances, which were increasingly important to the action, figuring even more greatly into the plot than those of earlier decades. The film version featuring Zero Mostel is now considered a classic.

Cabaret plays with generic convention perhaps more than any of its predecessors, the role of the narrator (the emcee of the Kit Kat Klub, originated by Joel Grey) playing an important part in that process. In addition, many of the songs are commentaries on the events in the plot. Based on Christopher Isherwood's *Berlin Stories*, its serious subject—the encroachment of Nazism in 1930s Germany—was given a darkly ironic treatment. Kander and Ebb had another hit with *Chicago*. Against the backdrop of prohibition and Al Capone's crime world, *Chicago* integrated vaudeville-influenced songs and images with the edgy choreography of Bob Fosse. The recent movie version with performances by film stars Richard Gere, Catherine Zeta-Jones, Renée Zellweger, and John C. Reilly gave the show new life.

The most important alternative to the book musical to emerge in the 1970s was the **concept musical**. Shows in this genre are more nonlinear meditations on various themes—explorations of concepts—than unified stories. *A Chorus Line* (1975) is perhaps the first concept musical to gain critical acclaim, winning nine Tony awards. It is also called a "fully integrated" musical, a reference to the prominence of dance in the action. Bob Fosse created the dances, continuing his rise to prominence as the leading choreographer/director of the decade. The experiences of dancers auditioning for a place in a chorus line, and their individual stories, form the dramatic material. Two songs from the show in particular became well known: "One" and "What I Did for Love."

Stephen Sondheim

Stephen Sondheim, arguably the most significant composer in the history of American musical theatre, is truly in a class by himself. His eclectic works exhibit a dazzlingly broad range of styles and types of dramatic and musical expression. His shows dominated Broadway during the 1970s and much of the 1980s, garnering numerous awards including six Tonys for Best Broadway Musical. Sondheim was classically trained in music, having studied with the modernist composer Milton Babbitt, but his true mentor was Oscar Hammerstein II. After he collaborated in *West Side Story* and *Gypsy*, Sondheim's first show for which he composed all the music was *A Funny Thing Happened on the Way to the Forum* (1962), a hilarious throwback to the tradition of musical comedy. A recurring theme in his subsequent shows is the many different ways people communicate with each other—or do not—in relationships. He creates complex characters who feel deeply. His shows not only explore his characters' inner lives but address basic, larger questions about what motivates people to do the things they do. The complex psychological portraits he creates emerge as a central feature of his dramatic language. Sondheim's shows often defy categorization because of his innovative approaches to form and structure and his tireless search for new ways to manipulate generic conventions.

Company (1970) was the first of Sondheim's collaborations with director Hal Prince, a partnership that would last about a decade and result in *Follies*, *A Little Night Music*, *Pacific Overtures*, and *Sweeney Todd*. *Company* is a concept musical exploring the theme of communication; its action centers on the lead character, a single man named Bobby, and his relationships to his married friends and girlfriends. Sondheim both links him with and sets him apart from the other characters through the use of a particular musical motive—a short two-pitch unit that is repeated and transformed throughout the course of the show. The motive is manipulated in specific ways to reflect Bobby's relationships with the characters, and theirs with each other. *Follies* (1971) recreates the lavish world of the Ziegfeld Follies, within which characters reexamine their life choices and the consequences of those choices. One of several of Sondheim's shows to play with time and its passing in intriguing ways, *Follies* uses flashbacks to the characters' youth as a central feature of the narrative. *A Little Night Music* (1973) is sometimes referred to as an operetta for the central role played by the waltz as its predominant musical style; its heartfelt ballad "Send In the Clowns" was made famous by the 1970s pop singer Judy Collins.

Sweeney Todd (1979) has been described as a musical thriller. Its subject matter—a deranged barber who kills his customers and sends them to his neighbor, who then turns them into meat pies to be eaten by the unsuspecting public—is at once disturbing and irresistible. The story's passion, tragedy, fascinating characters, and suspenseful situations have made it a modern classic that is both hair-raising and heartbreaking. Inspired by melodrama and British lore of the nineteenth century, it is an adaptation of the story *The Demon Barber of Fleet Street*. In contrast to conventional musicals, *Sweeney Todd* is almost entirely sung throughout (like many operas) with very little spoken dialogue and extensive underscoring. The original cast included Angela Lansbury and Len Cariou, and in a creative recent revival featuring Patti LuPone, the cast played all the instruments onstage (an approach also taken with the revival of *Company*). The movie version with Johnny Depp and Helena Bonham Carter highlighted the plot's elements of horror.

Sondheim's prominence lasted into the 1980s and 1990s, during which he continued to experiment with form and nonlinear ways of storytelling. In *Merrily We Roll Along* (1981) everything runs backward, but audiences found this reverse narrative structure hard to follow (and consequently the show was later revised). *Sunday in the Park with George* (1984), winner of the Pulitzer Prize for Drama (one of the few musicals to do so), ushered in the era of partnership with James Lapine, the writer-director who wrote the book. Sondheim and Lapine also created *Into the Woods* and *Passion* and revised *Merrily We Roll Along*. Based on the famous painting

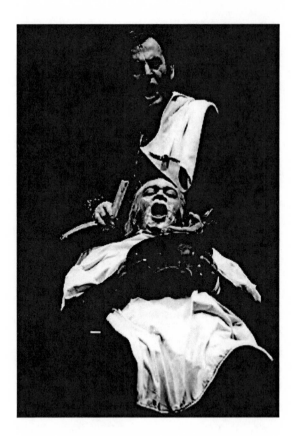

The 2003 production of *Sweeney Todd*, Royal Opera House Covent Garden, London. Photo © Robbie Jack/Corbis.

of *A Sunday Afternoon on the Island of La Grande Jatte* by the pointillist painter Georges Seurat, *Sunday in the Park* explores the nature of the creative process, playing with time and dramatic structure in new ways.

Into the Woods (1987) exhibits still more innovation. Lapine and Sondheim won Tony Awards for best book and best musical score. The show is about community responsibility, as characters in different fairy tales gradually begin to interact with and learn from each other in how to live life. One excerpt in particular stands out for its role in the creation of musical and dramatic structure. Sondheim rarely used reprises—repeats of pieces or sections of them—in his shows, believing that if characters grow and develop emotionally, it doesn't make sense for them to sing the same music over again. The first-act duet, "Agony," sung by Cinderella's and Rapunzel's princes, presents interesting and effective characterization, as they try to outdo each other with descriptions of each maiden's beauty and inaccessibility. But when the duet is presented as a reprise in the second act, another layer to the men's emotional development, or lack thereof, is revealed: they reprise their earlier music to demonstrate that they have indeed not grown or matured—and they go on just as they have before.

Assassins (1991) is a concept musical and a pastiche—an eclectic mix of musical styles drawn from diverse sources and influences. Presidential assassins (both actual and would-be) from different periods of history tell their stories and reveal their motivations and goals, reflecting on their shared experiences as alienated outsiders. *Passion* (1994) represents in some ways a return to more traditional storytelling and musical language. The show is based on the Italian film *Passione d'amore*, and its musical style is overtly romantic, with lush harmonies and soaring melodies. Its use of flashback recalls *Follies*. It is perhaps the most sensuous of Sondheim's musicals.

New Developments from the 1980s and Beyond: Diversity Continues

The development of musical theatre from the 1980s to the present has seen a proliferation of new genres as well as an ever-increasing overlap among the characteristics that define them. Questions as to what constitutes the major new trends and how musical theatre will develop in the future continue to occupy creators, critics, and audiences. Important genres taking shape since the 1980s are based on factors such as dimensions and scope, musical style, reuse of earlier music, and relation to film. And many shows belong to more than one genre.

New Genres and Approaches

Megamusicals are those in which the visual spectacle is the main emphasis and is larger than life. Many have enjoyed widespread popular appeal. *The Phantom of the Opera* and *Les Misérables* are classic examples, shows that are known to audiences worldwide. *Cats* (1982), which is also a concept musical, can also be added to the list. *Phantom* and *Cats*, both by British composer Andrew Lloyd Webber, are among Broadway's longest-running shows, and songs from them have become known to the point of becoming clichés ("Memory" from *Cats* and "Music of the Night" from *Phantom*, among others). *Cats* closed in 2000; *Phantom*, still running on Broadway, opened in London in 1986 and New York

Anne Hathaway and Hugh Jackman in the Universal Pictures film *Les Misérables* (2012). Photo ©
Universal Pictures.

in 1988. *Les Misérables* (1987), by the French team of Claude-Michel
Schönberg and Alain Boublil, won eight Tonys, running from 1987 to
2003. These works are sometimes called *poperas*, with music that is influenced by popular idioms and is continuously sung throughout, with no
spoken dialogue.

Many successful shows are based on musical styles from past decades
for which their genres are named. The **rock musical** is one of the most
difficult genres to define, primarily because rock-influenced music has
been part of the musical since at least the 1950s. It is a category that is still
in flux, with the boundaries of its definition still being formulated by specialists. Those who define the rock musical's parameters are concerned
with the use of rock as a musical language (whether as the show's primary
one or as one style among many) and whether a show is or is not called
a "rock musical" by its creators or commentators, among other considerations. *Hair* (1967), *Jesus Christ Superstar* (1970), *Godspell* (1971), *The
Wiz* (1975), and *Rent* (1996) are generally considered to be rock musicals. Subcategories based on specific popular musical styles have also
emerged: *Dreamgirls* (1981) is a Motown musical, and *City of Angels*
(1989) represents the jazz musical. The pervasiveness of popular musical
idioms in musical theatre is one factor in the development of a related
genre, the **jukebox musical**. Shows in this genre, also sometimes called
"compilation shows," consist of existing pop songs, whether by a single

group or artist or by different ones from a particular era: *Mamma Mia!* (2001), *Movin' Out* (2002), *Jersey Boys* (2005), and *Priscilla, Queen of the Desert* (2011) belong to this category.

Intersections with Film

The musical's relationship with film has been a significant part of its history since the 1930s. Many of the great shows of the 1940s and 1950s were made into well-known films, some of which won Oscars for Best Picture and have become known as classics (such as *West Side Story*, *My Fair Lady*, and *The Sound of Music*). And some musicals that began life as films were produced on the stage, such as Rodgers and Hammerstein's *State Fair*, Lerner and Loewe's *Gigi*, and *Singin' in the Rain*. The Disney variety, such as *The Lion King* and *Beauty and the Beast*, represents particularly interesting crossovers from screen to stage. (These are sometimes called "movicals"; they also qualify as megamusicals.) Different kinds of crossovers are stage shows that are adaptations of nonmusical films, of which *The Producers* represents a recent success. Setting a record in 2001 for winning a total of twelve Tony Awards, Mel Brooks's show, starring Nathan Lane and Matthew Broderick, started out as his 1968 film, which starred Gene Wilder and Zero Mostel. The movie version featuring the original Broadway duo (joined by Will Ferrell and Uma Thurman) came out in 2006. Another show with a similarly circuitous route is the campy *Little Shop of Horrors*: the popular stage show of 1980, based on a bizarre science-fiction movie from 1960, was made into a movie featuring Rick Moranis and Steve Martin in 1986 (newly released on DVD in 2000). The aforementioned *Priscilla, Queen of the Desert* is similarly based on a nonmusical film, as is *Billy Elliott* (2008).

Revivals, Reworkings, and New Shows

Many of the best-loved shows from the past have enjoyed successful recent Broadway revivals: *Oklahoma!*, *Anything Goes* (with Sutton Foster), *How to Succeed in Business Without Really Trying* (with Daniel Radcliffe), and *Annie Get Your Gun* (with Bernadette Peters) are a few examples. Some revivals represent reworkings, such as the recent production of *West Side Story* in which some of the dialogue was sung in Spanish. But many newly created shows are being offered regularly, and many of these represent the enduring tradition of the book musical. Some of the most original and exciting new works draw upon tried-and-true elements

Creators of musicals continue to push the envelope of what is considered acceptable subject matter for musicals. In *Avenue Q* (music and lyrics by Robert Lopez and Jeff Marx), a familiar children's puppet show is used as a vehicle to discuss adult themes. 2013 production, Hippodrome Theatre, Gainesville, FL (featuring Michael Hull, Marissa Toogood, and Jennifer Lauren Brown; directed by Lauren Caldwell and Charlie Mitchell).

of the familiar structure of traditional narrative but offer exciting new opportunities for its expansion and elaboration. These include the wildly successful *Wicked* (2003), the frank and energetic *In the Heights* (2008), and the emotionally wrenching *Next to Normal* (2009), to name a few. *Wicked*, with music and lyrics by Stephen Schwartz (the creator of *Godspell* and *Pippin*, popular shows from the 1970s), is based on Gregory Maguire's novel of the same name, in which L. Frank Baum's fantasy *The Wonderful Wizard of Oz* is retold from the Wicked Witch of the West's point of view. *Wicked*, still running since its opening in 2003, won numerous Tony Awards including Best Musical, and hit upon what seems to be the modern formula for success: a familiar story (but one that offers a new twist); strong dramatic situations with complex characters who wrestle with conflicting emotions (Elphaba and Glinda's relationship); larger-than-life spectacular moments that are integrated into the drama (Elphaba's thrilling ascent in "Defying Gravity"); big stars with name recognition (Joel Grey, Kristin Chenoweth, Idina Menzel); and affecting music in a range of styles that creates a broad array of contrasting moods.

10   World Theatre

Michelle Hayford

When approaching the topic of world theatre, it is necessary to first dispel some popular myths about theatre forms that are outside the traditional Western theatre aesthetic or canon. For the purposes of this chapter, selected examples of world theatre, including theatre of the Western world, are explored. However, there is a focus on the historical trajectory of traditional performance forms of non-Western countries. With the exception of efforts to *preserve* these traditional forms, it is important to note that "world" theatre is not code for static performance that resists evolution. Nor is world theatre "primitive" or simple. In this postmodern globalized age, performance that is "authentic" to its origins or home culture is less common than hybridized forms. Performance and theatre forms around the world continue to evolve to remain relevant. With the prevalence of intercultural exchange, theatre practitioners must approach their craft with cultural sensitivity and integrity, honoring difference and creating dialogue rather than falling into the traps of easy appropriation and exploitation. Armed with knowledge, the theatre and its audiences are only inspired to understand the human experience, wherever that experience may unfold on our planet.

India

Vedic Chanting

For thousands of years, Indian spiritual practices have utilized drama and performance as vehicles for making spirit manifest and expressing devotion—the Indian philosophy of *maya-lila* embraces the inherently playful and creative force of the universe. Chanting of the Hindu Vedas, or sacred hymn books, is an embodied practice of spiritual devotion that is learned only in an intimate master/apprentice relationship and entails intense physical training and exercise as well as mastery of the Vedic chants. It is thought to be the oldest surviving oral tradition, dating back to the Iron Age. By way of oral transmission and physical exercises that include the master's placing of his hands on the apprentice's head to move the head to the rhythm of the chanting, the apprentice learns the exact nuance and intonation of each syllable, thereby preserving the world's most stable oral transmission through generations.

The Mahabharata and Ramayana

The *Mahabharata* and *Ramayana* are the two ancient Indian epic poems that are often dramatized in traditional Indian theatre. The *Mahabharata* is more than two hundred thousand verse lines long, about eight times the length of Homer's *Odyssey* and *Iliad* combined. It is traditionally thought that Vyasa authored the *Mahabharata*, but some believe that many scholars penned the epic. The oldest sections of the text are dated to 400 BCE. The epic includes the Hindu scripture of the *Bhagavad Gita*, philosophical tales, stories of gods and royalty, and Indian mythology. The *Ramayana*, authored by Valmiki, is told in twenty-four thousand verses and is dated between 200 BCE and 200 CE. It is concerned with morals, dharma (Indian philosophy of "natural law"), and relationships, as told through avatar characters, or earthly incarnations of deities, namely Rama.

Sanskrit Drama

Through the oral transmission of Vedic chants and the performance of the Indian epics, the *Mahabharata* and *Ramayana*, India can claim to have had the most highly developed theatre from 1000 BCE through the second century CE. Sanskrit drama of this time period was performed in accordance with the rules of theatre and performance systemized by Bharata Muni, an Indian sage, in the *Natyasastra* treatise (written between 200 BCE and 200 CE). Performances of Sanskrit drama were performed by male and female actors who specialized in particular characters. *The Little Clay Cart* by Bhasa (second or third century CE) and *Shakuntala* by Kalidasa (late fourth or early fifth century CE) are examples of Sanskrit drama, which ceased to be produced in the thirteenth century as other performance forms came into prominence. Traditional Indian theatre forms share a common aesthetic of codified movement and dance, voluptuous costumes, colorful and dramatic makeup, and spare stages that focus attention on the bodies of the actors.

Kutiyattam is an Indian performance style that is a regional derivation of Sanskrit drama developed in Kerala in the tenth century under the patronage of King Kulasekhara Varman. It differed from Sanskrit drama in that it utilized local language and deviated from strict performance rules of the *Natyasastra*. *Kutiyattam* was understood as a visual sacrifice to the deities of the temples in which it was once exclusively performed. Men and women continue to train in *kutiyattam*, with women exclusively playing the female roles.

Kathakali performance of Kerala is closely related to *kutiyattam* and dramatizes devotion to the Hindu god Vishnu. Traditionally, *kathakali* dancers are all male and perform the physically demanding, martial arts–inspired choreography after many years of rigorous training that includes strenuous exercises for strength and flexibility and body massage. Specific characters are immediately recognizable to the audience because of the consistent makeup and costume codes for each role. In

A *kathakali* performance in Fort Cochin, Kerala, India. Photo by Steve Curati.

1975, Tripunithura Kathakali Kendram, an all-female *kathakali* performance troupe, debuted in Kerala and still trains women in this traditionally male theatre form.

The *Natyasastra*

Bharata's *Natyasastra* is a comprehensive treatise on Indian drama, dance, and music, considered the fifth Veda available to all Indian castes. The *Natyasastra* specifies technical, psychological, and physical requirements for producing theatre, including the architecture of performance spaces and the actor's state of mind, as well as gesture and costume. It defines *rasas* and *bhavas* and the relation between the two in a complex and comprehensive system of specific hand gestures, body movements, costumes, and makeup for every distinct type of character. *Bhavas* are states of being embodied by the actor, and *rasas* are the states of consciousness that are "tasted" by the audience. In order for the *bhavas* to be successfully performed and the *rasas* adequately "tasted," actors undergo extensive physical training that enables them to hold specific dance postures and *mudras* (Indian hand and finger positions) in performance that the audience then interprets. For example, if the drama calls on the audience to "taste" the *rasa* of *sringara* (to feel amorous), then the performers must accomplish the *bhava* of *rati* (love) through the embodiment of specific gesture, facial expression, *mudra*, and pose. Bharata believed the theatre should educate and entertain.

Traditional Indian Theatre Makeup and Costumes

Various Indian performance traditions use ornate makeup and costumes to differentiate among common characters played on stage. For example, in *kathakali*, there are seven archetypal characters denoted by the color painted on the face and the appropriate corresponding costume. The "green" archetype is codified for divine characters and requires the actors to paint their faces green and don a white skirt with orange and black stripes. In this way, the audience familiar with *kathakali* conventions is able to determine who the character is as soon as the actor steps onstage, increasing their enjoyment of the performance.

Kathakali performer Kalamandalam Gopi meticulously applies his makeup. Photo by Navaneeth.

Another *kathakali* performer waits to enter the stage. Photo by Steve Cox.

Ramlila, Parsi, "Bollywood," and Beyond

Ramlila has been performed in India from at least 400 CE into the present, drawing millions of pilgrims to participate in the commemorative drama as spiritual pilgrimage. Pilgrim/performer participants reenact the events of the Hindu Lord Rama's life over at least a three-day period, sometimes in performances that continue for more than a month. The collective performance pilgrimage culminates in the festival of Dussehra, where good is celebrated as having conquered evil. All performers in *Ramlila* are male, and many roles passed down through generations in the same family. The performers are amateurs but full of devotion as they act out Lord Rama's life through tableaux and the procession of pilgrims from one sacred site to another.

Parsi theatre became popular in India in the 1870s as India's first modern theatre form by incorporating Urdu-language dramas and poetry into melodramatic performances with ornate set designs. Parsi theatre appealed to South Asian and English audiences and included female actors in troupes that toured India into the 1920s. With the advent of the film industry, Parsi theatre's popularity waned.

Previously called Hindi cinema, "Bollywood" is now one of the largest film industries in the world. The name *Bollywood* is a combination of *Bombay* (now Mumbai) and *Hollywood*; however, it should not be understood as merely a Hollywood wannabe industry. A highly lucrative

On the last day of Ramlila, these giant effigies of the demon king Ravana and his brother and son will be set on fire. Performed in New Delhi, India, 2012. Photo by Megan Knight.

film industry, Bollywood exports Indian culture globally and meets the demands of Indian audiences who evaluate Bollywood actors by praising a successful actor as *paisa vasool*—translated literally as "worth the money" spent on the movie admission. Bollywood draws on many traditional Indian performance forms for inspiration, largely aiming to appeal to a broad-base family audience with melodramatic musical films that feature dance, music, and often romance. Bollywood actors have attained international celebrity, and the conventions continue to evolve with the pressure to assimilate Hollywood film practices. The highest-grossing Bollywood film to date (at more than $60 million worldwide and $6.5 million in North America) is 3 *Idiots*, a comedy about three engineering students released in 2009 by Vinod Chopra Productions.

In 1944, a very popular film actor, Prithviraj Kapoor (1901–1972), founded the touring company Prithvi Theatres, which popularized a more restrained and "realistic" acting style and toured until 1960. Subsequently, Prithvi Theatre was founded in Kapoor's honor in Mumbai and continues to be a popular theatre, with staged performances daily. The 2012 season included a Hindi play titled S*x, M*rality, and Cens*rship,

Bollywood actress Hrishita Bhat rehearses with other dancers on the set of *Kisna* in Bombay, 2004. © Arko Datta/Reuters/Corbis.

The 2012 production of *S*x, M*rality, and Cens*rship* by Sunil Shanbag, a Hindi play about theatrical censorship in the 1970s. Photo by Kartikeyan Shiva.

by the Mumbai-based Arpana theatre company, that is a reflection on the controversy stirred by the 1970s theatre production *Sakharam Binder*, by the Indian playwright Vijay Tendulkar (1928–2008). Originally performed in 1972, then banned in 1974 because of its explosive handling of the oppression of women in postcolonial India, *Sakharam Binder* is still performed today, and Tendulkar's socially conscious plays continue to inspire contemporary Indian theatre productions and adaptations.

Yours Truly Theatre, based in Bangalore, India, is a theatre company founded in 2003. With a dedication to the efficacy of applied theatre, it brings interactive theatre, including "complete the story" and "theatre sports," to nontraditional venues and non-actors through the dedication of more than a hundred company members. They offer workshops for children, adults, and nonprofit agencies that serve underprivileged communities. In 2011, they presented a devised musical play titled *Bhagwaan Dhoondo* (*In Search of God*), that featured a "complete the story" ending determined by the audience and improvised by the actors.

Today, India's theatre landscape is one of preservation and evolution of classical forms, as well as innovation in response to global media's dissemination of popular "Bollywood" performance and aesthetics.

Japan

Kagura

Japanese who engage in Shinto worship participate in a ritual performance art as part of devotional practice to welcome and honor gods, nature, and ancestors in villages all over Japan. Known as *kagura*, it has been in practice since the eighth century, takes many forms, and has become a traditional source of Japanese collective culture, regardless of the diversity of faith. It consists of ritual music and dance practices that have their own creation story, as follows: The sun goddess Amaterasu was angry with her brother and hid in a cave. When she went into the cave, she took all the light with her. To lure her out of the cave, Uzeme, the goddess of music and dance, performed a dance in which she exposed her genitals and stomped loudly. Uzeme's titillating dance made the other gods laugh raucously, until Amaterasu's curiosity at the proceedings made her exit the cave. This dance, the original *kagura*, is therefore responsible for bringing light back to the universe.

Kagura is performed as an expression of Shinto devotion and recognition of the *kami*, or spiritual essence of all things, as well as a funeral rite to appease ancestors. *Mi-kagura* is the winter festival ritual *kagura* performance. In *mi-kagura*, performers wear masks to portray demons and spirits and remain unmasked to comically portray human characters.

A *kagura* at a sacred shrine. Photo by Giya (Velvia)/Flickr.com.

Kagura consists of slow, circular, and elegant choreography that emphasizes the four directions and uses handheld fans and bells.

Noh

When Japan's Prince Shotoku (573–621) converted to Buddhism, he opened Japan to influence from Korea, China, and India. The continental influence was embraced in part by the introduction of Chinese performance forms. Eventually, a popular performance style called *sarugaku* was developed, a bombastic medium of acrobatics, pantomime, and magic that was adapted by Buddhists in the twelfth century to demonstrate the Buddha's teachings.

A form called *noh* emerged under Kan'ami (1333–1384), a *sarugaku* performer, and his son Zeami (1363–1444), who developed the refined court-patronized art form with accompanying treatises. Patronized by the shogun, Zeami and *noh* were elevated to a high status equivalent to the aristocracy who frequented the performances. In fact, in an effort to maintain *noh*'s elite status, commoners were forbidden to learn *noh* dance and music until the end of the Edo period, at the end of the nineteenth century. *Noh* demonstrates the concept of *yugen*, or quiet

A *noh* performance in 2004. © Toshiyuki Aizawa/Reuters/Corbis.

elegance, and was strongly influenced by Japan's embrace of restrained Buddhist philosophy. While never enjoying mass popularity, it remains Japan's oldest theatre form and has survived with most traditional elements intact, including the exclusion of female performers.

The *noh* conventions call for a main actor (*shite*), supporting actors (*waki*), a chorus (*jiutai*), musicians (*hayashi*), and the five *noh* plots, interspersed with short comic performances (*kyogen*): the "god" play, the "warrior" play, the "woman" play, the "present-day" play (often about an insane woman), and the "demon" play. *Noh* main actors use masks for some characters, taking time to stare at the mask and embody the emotion of the mask before donning it. Demon characters are often portrayed with a full-face mask, intensifying the performance. Even if taking place indoors, a traditional *noh* theatre recreates the outdoor *noh* pavilion with painted pine tree background and roof and an elevated stage to allow space for empty drums underneath the actors to amplify their stomps. Because there is no set to speak of, the costumes and masks are ornate and attention stays with the main actor as the storyteller.

Bunraku

Bunraku, Japan's puppet theatre, emerged during the Tokugawa shogunate (1603–1867), but there is evidence that puppet theatre existed before that period. All puppets are operated by at least three puppeteers: one operates the feet and legs (*ashizukai*), another operates the left hand (*hidarizukai* or *sashizukai*), and the main puppeteer (*omozukai*) manipulates the right hand and head. The puppets are built with movable eyes and mouths and jointed fingers, and some are designed to transform into demons. The puppeteers are dressed in black and, according to troupe conventions, may even cover their heads in a black hood. The *tayu* is responsible for chanting the text from a lectern, including creating different voices, pitches, and facial expressions for all characters. Next to the *tayu*, the musician plays the *shamisen*, a Japanese banjolike instrument. *Bunraku* puppeteers must first learn manipulation of the feet and legs, then the left hand, and finally the right hand and head. This process can take thirty years to master. *Bunraku* puppets are usually three to four feet in height, with human and yak hair and ornate costumes. Double-suicide love stories are common in *bunraku*, many of which were penned by "Japan's Shakespeare," Chikamatsu Monzaemon. Traditional *bunraku* is carried on today by two male-dominated institutions in Japan, employing the rare woman as a builder rather than a performer.

Bunraku performance in Kyoto, Japan, 2002. Photo by Susan Hunt.

Kabuki

In the late 18th century, *bunraku* began to decline in popularity as *Kabuki* ascended. Kabuki continues to be the most popular of Japan's traditional theatre forms. Having overcome its associations with prostitution and crime due to its humble origination, Kabuki now enjoys international exposure as a highly esteemed art. Izumo no Okuni, a female shrine dancer known for performing domestic stories full of sexual innuendo, is credited with inventing Kabuki performance and popularizing the all-female Kabuki performance troupes in 1603. These early troupes also participated in prostitution, and an urban underground culture grew up around Kabuki theatres. The upper class shogunate in power did not approve of the hedonistic Kabuki culture and the practice of prostitution by Kabuki actresses. Therefore, Kabuki performed by women was banned in 1629. However, the handsome young boys who were then cast in female parts subsequently also encouraged prostitution. Taking another tack, in 1652 the shogunate then allowed only adult men who shaved their forelocks (this was thought to make them less attractive and therefore less likely to engage in prostitution) to perform Kabuki. This is largely still the convention today, with popular male Kabuki actors known for their female

Japanese Kabuki actor Nakamura Tokizo performs in Tokyo, 2004. © Yuriko Nakao/Reuters/Corbis.

SPECIAL TOPICS

roles (*onnagata*) appearing in film and television in female roles. Some notable Kabuki conventions include codified makeup, *mie* (discussed shortly), and the stage "tricks" that allow for quick reveals. *Hikinuki* is often used, in which a stagehand dressed in black (traditionally thought of as invisible) comes onstage to pull a string that reveals a radically different costume layer underneath to effect a character transformation for the actor. Revolving stages, lifts, and cables allowing for "flying" characters are also popular Kabuki stage tricks.

Similar to Indian *kathakali* makeup, Kabuki makeup or *kesho* is elaborately painted on actors' faces according to the codified character colors: purple for nobility, green for the supernatural, and so on. Kabuki actors often strike dramatic poses and hold them to heighten emotional affect, a practice known as *mie*. In combination with *mie*, the mask-like Kabuki makeup translates into memorable and striking performances.

Western Influence

Called "new school" as opposed to "old school" Kabuki, *shimpa* theatre introduced Western-style drama and conventions to Japan in the 1880s, including the occasional use of female performers. This was followed by *shingeki* or "New Theatre," which performed Western drama with the conventions of realism. During this time Jiyu Gekijo, or Free Theatre, would retrain professional theatre artists to perform in the Stanislavsky "method" so popular in Western actor training.

After World War II, *noh* was recognized as a national treasure and the National Noh Theatre opened in Tokyo in 1983. The Bunraku Association was formed in 1963 to preserve the art form, and the National Bunraku Theatre opened in Osaka in 1984. Kabuki also has been deemed worthy of preservation with the opening of the Japanese National Theatre in 1966.

The 1960s were a time of global civil unrest, and Japan was no exception. The Shogekijo (small theatre) movement that sprung up in unconventional venues at that time was in reaction to the strict formalism of traditional Japanese arts. One of these companies, Jokyo Gekijo (Situation Theatre), founded in 1963 by Kara Juro (b. 1940), was also called Red Tent Theatre in homage to the red tent they often set up on vacant parcels for performances. Jokyo Gekijo continued to create works until 1988 and now operates under a different name, Gekidan Kara Gumi (Shogekijo). *Butoh*, an avant-garde dance form and theatre of protest, also developed in the turbulent 1960s and is known for the white body paint donned by the performers as well as slow and hypnotic movement. Sankai Juku is a *butoh* performance troupe founded in 1975 that continues to perform internationally.

Many significant Japanese artists were affiliated with Shogekijo, Suzuki Tadashi (b. 1939) among them. Suzuki created an actor training method that utilizes strenuous lower-body physical exercises inspired by martial arts, Kabuki and *noh*, called the Suzuki Method. This method of actor training is taught in acting programs all over the world. In 1976, Suzuki founded the Suzuki Company of Toga (a remote mountain village in Japan), which continues to host regular performance seasons and workshops throughout the year.

Chelfitsch

Baby-talk for "selfish," *Chelfitsch* is an innovative Tokyo-based theatre company under the direction of Toshiki Okado (b. 1973). Okado founded *Chelfitsch* in 1997 and the company has found an appreciative audience for its striking choreography, exploration of daily life, and use of everyday language. Okado writes and directs postmodern plays that do not privilege text but treat the words actors deliver equal to the attention given to gesture, movement, lighting, and set design. With *Five Days in March* (2004), Okado deals with his feelings about the Iraq War within the context of his daily life, using the stage to reframe the everyday with characteristically dynamic choreography.

2010 production of *Who Knows We Are Not Injured Like the Others?* Photo by Kazuyuki Matsumoto.

China

Theatre's Evolution through the Dynasties

Performance has played an important role in Chinese cultural life through the millennia, with each dynasty innovating art forms and privileging some performance over others. It is not until the Shang Dynasty (1767 BCE) that there is archival evidence of various court entertainments, including mime, dance, and music. By the time of the Han Dynasty (206 BCE–220 CE), there is a flourishing of the "hundred plays" entertainments at court, fairs, and marketplaces, which include present-day circus acts like tightrope walking and juggling as well as athletic feats, music, and dance. Chinese emperors established the first institutions to nurture performance art forms, including the Imperial Office of Music created by Han emperors (104 BCE) and a training school created by Emperor Yang-Di during the Sui Dynasty, responsible for hosting a festival that included at least eighteen thousand performers.

Emperor Xuan Zong of the Tang Dynasty (618–907) created the Pear Garden school for entertainers in 714, with a mission to innovate art forms and create a distinctively Chinese theatre. The Pear Garden served more than eleven thousand students who studied music, dance, acrobatics, and dramatic text. During the Song Dynasty (960–1279),

Chinese shadow puppets. Photo by Ernie Reyes.

popular novels were narrated by professional storytellers in teahouses and performed in puppet and shadow-play theatres, the most popular theatre forms of the time.

The Yuan Dynasty (1279–1368) is known for ushering in the golden age of Chinese drama written by intellectuals who were banished by the Mongol court and therefore forced to turn their attention to non-government-related concerns. Happily, for theatre's sake, these intellectuals rediscovered earlier Chinese music-dramas and penned classic works that have stood the test of time.

Chinese literary drama conventions were regional. The "northern" or *zaju* style of Chinese theatre that developed in Beijing during the Yuan Dynasty was a highly prescribed form that was made up of four acts including up to twenty songs all sung by the protagonist, while the other characters merely recited their dialogue. There was an orchestra, plots that privileged good over evil, male and female actors, ornate costumes, and simple stage design. Theatre companies were often named after the lead actress in the troupe. It is estimated that more than seven hundred plays were penned in the Yuan period. Of these, Guan Hanqing (c. 1245–c. 1322), the "father of Chinese drama," is said to have written sixty-seven plays, eighteen surviving.

The "southern" or *hangzhou* regional theatre style was favored by the Ming Dynasty (1368–1644), and therefore this style prospered and eclipsed the *zaju* style in popularity. Conventions of the southern style include individually titled acts that totaled around fifty and singing by any character (not the protagonist alone, as in *zaju*) to a slower tempo with a spare orchestra. The southern style was in practice for some five hundred years in China, eventually giving way to the predominance of Beijing opera.

By 1850, Beijing opera reigned as China's most prevalent theatre form. Emperor Qian Long's eightieth birthday party in 1790 prompted the development of Beijing opera when the celebration brought all the best performers of each region to Beijing. Many of the performers stayed and perfected an art form that blended regional performance conventions and created a codified Chinese theatre that privileged performance elements over text. Beijing opera shifted China's performance focus from literary concerns to the formalizing of dance, song, and acting.

Beijing opera usually consists of several different acts, interspersed with acrobatic performances. Actors do not need to adhere to a specific

A Chinese opera performance at Chang'An Theatre, Beijing, 2009. Photo by Gustavo Thomas.

text while performing a story, and as long as the tale retains its happy ending, unique interpretations of major works are expected. All movement is dance in Beijing opera, as it is in sync with the orchestra and systemized: for example, similar to the Indian *mudra*, there are specific finger patterns to indicate numerous plot developments or emotions (such as sword battle or femininity), and the flick of a sleeve may denote disgust, or surprise when paired with a hand thrown above the head. There are four types of characters: male (*sheng*), female (*dan*), painted face (*jing*), and comic (*chou*). The actors are dressed in rich, colorful costumes and, as with Indian *kathakali* and Japanese Kabuki, distinct makeup. The painted-face characters have codified patterns and designs on the face that amplify the archetypal characteristics of the general, dragon, or hero, to name a few.

When the Chinese Republic of 1912 replaced the former empire, a new age in theatre ushered in the *spoken drama*, to differentiate itself from "sung" traditional performance. Most often these spoken dramas were translations of contemporary popular Western works. The most renowned Chinese playwright of the twentieth century, Cao Yu

(1910–1996), is credited with founding spoken theatre in China with popular works like *Thunderstorm* (1933), which dealt with the controversial topic of incest.

Beijing opera, however, remains the most recognizable Chinese theatre form, having survived mandates to conform to communist doctrine in 1949 and the oppression of the Cultural Revolution after 1966. China's Cultural Revolution (1966–1976) limited permissible theatre to eight "model" plays promoting the communist government's agenda. The eight model works favored socialist realism and consisted of two ballets, a symphony, and five "revolutionary operas." The Cultural Revolution was cruel to theatre practitioners, subjecting actors and directors (as well as intellectuals, doctors, teachers) to violence, imprisonment, and forced "re-education" via hard labor in the countryside. In the post–Cultural Revolution era, Chinese theatre flourished with a restoration of traditional plays and a fusion of traditional and modern forms. New plays were self-aware and presentational, combining spoken drama and traditional Chinese performance aesthetics. However, the mid-1980s witnessed a swinging of the pendulum as these modern plays suffered a backlash and

A performance of *Legend of the Red Lantern* at Chang'An Theatre, Beijing, 2009. It tells the story of communist resistance during the Japanese occupation in World War II. Photo by Gustavo Thomas.

were accused of Western-influenced "spiritual pollution." Then government opinion swung in the other direction and theatre saw a period of experimentation coinciding with more widespread cultural liberalization. This ended with the crackdown culminating in the Tiananmen Square protest of June 4, 1989. Since this student-led "democracy movement," the arts continue to be subject to government censorship.

Cross-Dressing in Performance: *Dan, Hijra*, Takarazuka

Female performers were banned in Beijing by the Chinese emperor in 1772; therefore *dan* roles were performed by men in Beijing opera. By 1870, women were unofficially acting in *dan* roles, and in 1912 the ban was lifted. The ban resulted in a complex training in feminine performance by male actors, which in itself became an art form. Before the ban on female actors in Beijing, women participated in Chinese theatre and both men and women practiced cross-dressing in performance. In 1923, it became more common for men to portray men, and women to portray women, onstage, a marked departure from traditional Chinese theatre forms.

The *hijra* of India are a community of transgendered women (many have male physiology, but identify as women) lobbying for official recognition as a "third gender" on passport documents. The

A group of Indian *hijra*. Photo by Daniel Lofredo Rota.

hijra have a long history in India; since 400 BCE to 200 CE, they have been an integral component of Indian marriage traditions and male birth ceremonies via their traditional dances and songs thought to bring blessings from the *Buhuchara Mata*, the Indian mother goddess. They are a marginalized community otherwise; many *hijra* beg for alms and engage in prostitution to survive, underscoring the urgency of their current demand for equal rights.

While it began in 1914, Japan's Takarazuka Revue certainly appeals to postmodern performance sensibilities of today. Consisting only of young women, the cast of the revue train for many years in their particular parts, and in an inversion of most traditional Japanese theatre forms, young women are trained to portray male characters (*otokoyaku*). The Takarazuka Revue still thrives today with an enormous fan following—young Japanese girls are especially fond of the *otokoyaku* actors. In Takarazuka, we see an example of the traditional Japanese convention of cross-gender acting and audiences that continue to respond positively.

Takarazuka Review poster on the Kyoto subway. Photo by David Z./Flickr.com.

The National Theater Concert Hall

The National Theater Concert Hall (NTCH) in Taipei City was built in 1987 to host Chinese and international performance and serve as an experimental theatre venue. Recent productions include an adaptation of *Peach Blossom Fan*, by Qing Dynasty playwright Kong Shangren and performed by ½ Q Theatre, a postmodern Chinese theatre company established in 2006 that blends traditional Chinese opera with experimental modern drama. NTCH played host to another contemporary Taiwanese theatre company, Mobius Strip Theatre (founded in 2005), with a recent production of *Spider in Meditation*, a poetic rumination on modern city life. Mobius Strip Theatre is known for their provocative audience engagement and site-specific environmental performance.

Zhongzheng District, Taipei, Taiwan. Photo by Miguel Vicente Martínez Juan.

Censorship in China

Many theatre productions have been censored by the Chinese government. *The Peony Pavilion* is a twenty-hour-long work penned by Tang Xianxu in 1598 that has long been barred from performance because of a plot that government officials have found objectionable: the passionate story of a girl who finds a lover in her dreams.

In 1998, a production of *The Peony Pavilion* was commissioned by New York's Lincoln Center as the centerpiece of its annual festival. The Shanghai Kunju Opera Company, directed by Chen Shi-Zheng, rehearsed in Shanghai until a mere three weeks before their scheduled departure for New York, when the Shanghai Municipal Bureau of Culture denied the company permission to perform. Concerned about foreigners' perceptions of China, Ma Bomin, the bureau director, seized the set pieces and costumes, insisting that the show change what she called its "feudal," "ignorant," and "pornographic" elements (including a chamberpot prop and effigy burning). The cast was relocated to a country house outside Shanghai and instructed to rehearse changes; however, the Bureau of Culture was not placated and the performance was ultimately canceled.

A year later, in 1999, Chen Shi-Zheng's *The Peony Pavilion* was remounted at Lincoln Center and performed in its entirety, followed by a successful U.S. tour. In January 2012, the China Arts and Entertainment Group, under the administration of the Ministry of Culture for the People's Republic of China, approved the U.S. premiere of a condensed dance adaptation of *The Peony Pavilion* by the China Jinling Dance Company of Nanjing again at New York's Lincoln Center. The history of *The Peony Pavilion* on the international stage illustrates the still fraught relationship Chinese theatre has with government officials. Chinese theatre artists continuously negotiate the approval and censorship of their craft.

The Peony Pavilion performed at Peking University Hall in Beijing, China, 2006. Photo by sweet_vickey/Flickr.com.

SPECIAL TOPICS

The Middle East

Theatre has been a relevant and vibrant art form in Israel since its independence in 1948. A forum for its citizens to reflect on the difficulties of new statehood and the continuous Arab-Israeli conflict, theatre has been a necessary site of negotiation of Israeli identity. Theatre education programs are popular, and the theatre is a reliable source of critical cultural analysis in Israel. The state of Israel is unique in the Middle East in this way, as theatre is a more contentious undertaking in Islamic Middle Eastern countries. With a few notable exceptions, theatre as understood in a Western conventional framework was not performed in Islamic countries until the nineteenth century. While theatre has not developed as a major art form, certain forms of storytelling, mime, and shadow puppet performances have long been popular.

The Sufi Islamic doctrine that equates humanity to a shadow manipulated by its creator infuses shadow puppetry with a spiritual dimension that can perhaps explain the popularity of the shadow puppet play in Islamic countries. The fact that holes were purposely made in shadow puppets in the late Middle Ages illustrates the major point of tension between the art of theatre and Islamic theology; the holes disrupted the audience's perception of the puppet as a "real" representation and proved the puppets were not alive, and therefore the performance could not be accused of idolatry. Without the holes, the puppets could have been interpreted as creating an image of a person or animal, even unrelated to religion, which to some Islamic theologians violates the prohibition of idolatry. Idolatry is a contentious concept that is rife with subjective interpretation, including what does and does not count as idolatry. Some Islamic theologians interpret idolatry, in part, as giving undue regard toward created forms other than God; theatre, as a created representation, is met with disapproval by those who hold this view.

Theatre may not be a state-sponsored institution in the Islamic Middle East; however, the literature, architecture, and visual arts of the region have inspired many Western play adaptations, notably tales from *The Thousand and One Nights*, which was first translated in 1704 and continues to enchant Western audiences. Of course, the tales from *The Thousand and One Nights* were born out of an ancient Middle Eastern storytelling tradition orally transmitted over many generations, in which storytellers, called *hakawati*, performed various folk tales and mythic stories sometimes with the accompaniment of a one-string viol. The *sha'ir*, or poet-musician, is another pre-Islamic Middle Eastern storyteller who figured predominantly in nomadic tribal life. *Sha'irs* performed song poems that praised their own tribe, satirized enemies, and channeled supernatural forces. The most acclaimed storytellers attracted *rawis*, "reciters" who memorized the tales and kept their oral transmission alive. Competitions in poetry and musical performances were held regularly among the best pre-Islamic poet-musicians in the Ukaz marketplace in Mecca. After the death of the prophet Muhammad, a new type of storyteller emerged: the *qussas*. The *qussas* told stories from the Qur'an that were often embellished but nonetheless popular.

Iran

After the murder of Imam Hussein in 680, whom the Shi'ite people honor as the martyr grandson to the prophet Muhammad who was denied his right to be caliph, *Ta'ziyeh* is performed annually in Iran (and sometimes in Lebanon and Iraq). *Ta'ziyeh* is a commemorative passion play that dramatizes Hussein's martyrdom in battle at Karbala. It is a mourning ritual for Hussein and a site for keeping cultural memory alive. The performance usually takes place in the round under a large tent and calls on the audience to participate. Actors sing and read their text, horses are used to recreate the battle at Karbala, and self-flagellation is part of the ritual mourning.

Ta'ziyeh, an Iranian religious play about the martyrdom of Imam Hussein. Courtesy of english. tebyan.net.

Turkey

The Turkish sultans who ruled during the time of the Ottoman Empire (1299–1922) sponsored their personal troupes of actors as well as acting companies and were accustomed to lavish pageants at court that included dance, circus acts, and theatre. The Ottoman aristocracy mimicked the court entertainments in more modest open-air performances throughout the empire.

By the sixteenth century, the Turkish shadow puppet play, called *Karagoz* for the main "Black-eye" puppet character, was a highly popular theatre form. The *Karagoz* puppet master needed to be adept at performing many voices, manipulating several puppets, and playing musical accompaniment. Some puppet masters had an assistant and one or two musicians. There were also at least twenty-eight stories to memorize (one performed for each night of Ramadan) that are either historical or indecent and included improvised humorous arguments between the two lead characters, Karagöz and Hacivat.

When the Turkish Republic was founded in 1923, it took a favorable stance toward the arts. The republic began subsidizing theatre companies, a drama school, and an opera house and allowed Muslim women to work in the theatre.

Egypt

In 1910, Jurj Abyad, a Christian from Syria who had studied theatre in Paris, began an Arabic language theatre troupe in Egypt that performed European and Arabic works. Naguib al-Rihani (1892–1949) was an Egyptian actor known as the "Charlie Chaplain of the East" and thought of as the father of Egyptian comedy. He is known for his "Kesh Kesh Beik" character, whose antics revealed social class issues. Egyptian dramatist Salah Abd al-Sabur (1931–1981) was inspired by T. S. Eliot to write free verse drama and modernize Arabic poetry. His *The Tragedy of Al-Hallaj* (1965) won the State Incentive Award for Theater in 1966.

Contemporary Middle Eastern Theatre—Highlights

Saudi Arabia. Saudi Arabia does not allow men and women to be in the same theatre, and women are not allowed to act. Therefore, men play all roles, donning masks and wigs to play women. Children are allowed to perform with male adult actors.

2012 Tehrik-e-Niswan's production of *We are the Dispossessed*. Moving between past and present, this multimedia production shows how war affects women through violence, loss, rape, and displacement. Courtesy of the Hawler International Theater Festival.

Pakistan. In Pakistan, the Tehrik-e-Niswan (Women's Movement) theatre and performance troupe have been advocating for women's rights since they formed in 1979. Through their plays and dance performances, the women actors continue to communicate their feminist message.

Syria. Saadallah Wannous (1941–1997) was a Syrian playwright whose politically infused productions sometimes met with government censorship and often included an Arab *hakawati* storyteller character. He believed his work was not totally suppressed in Syria so that he could be an example to Western critics of Arab freedom of speech; he stated in an interview, "My very existence is propaganda." He wanted theatre to serve as a forum for Arab peoples to consider political failures and imagine Arab unity.

Israel. Since 1980, the Acco Festival for Alternative Israeli Theatre has occurred annually in Acco to showcase the best of submitted new works. Often, the theatre performances are political in nature, taking on current cultural debates and crises. The festival has also grown to demonstrate coexistence among Arabs and Israelis, with Arab theatre work featured in the festival. The festival takes place over four to five days with street theatre, workshops, and international theatre troupe performances in addition to the presentation of original works selected in competition.

Lebanon. There is a resurgence of interest in the Middle Eastern *hakawati* storytelling tradition as evidenced by the annual storytelling festival held in Beirut since 2000 by the Mannot Theatre, showcasing regional Arabic tales. Ahmad Yousuf, of the United Arab Emirates, is a *hakawati* storyteller who keeps the tradition alive when he rehearses adaptations of classics with a troupe of twenty actors at the Sharjah National Theatre.

Iraq. In 2003, al-Najeen (the Survivors), a theatre ensemble in occupied Iraq, produced *They Passed by Here*, a play that struggled with the concept of freedom, in the al-Rachid National Theatre ruins that had been recently bombed and looted during the war. The stage remained amid the rubble, but there was no electricity, and the actors often spoke their lines over each other and in constant motion as they explored the tensions of occupation. The actors said about the play, "We have to create [hope] ourselves."

Kuwait. Kuwaiti theatre director Sulayman Al-Bassam (b. 1972) founded Sulayman Al-Bassam Theatre (SABAB) Kuwait in 2002. Al-Bassam has an international reputation for his adaptation of classic works, including *Richard III: An Arab Tragedy*. The D-CAF Downtown Contemporary Arts Festival was held for the first time in Cairo, Egypt, in 2012 and featured SABAB's timely work *The Speaker's Progess* by Sulayman Al-Bassam, set in an unspecified Arab country suffering postrevolution stagnation.

West Africa—Highlights

The first *griot*, a West African storyteller and living archive, was Balla Fasséké, personal griot to Sundiata Keita, the founder of the Mali Empire in the thirteenth century. Griots accompanied kings and were transferred as "presents" from one king to his successor. Many villages in northern Africa still have their own griots—the "praise-singers," the keepers of local history, current events, genealogy, and mythic tales. The griot also performs songs passed down through the oral tradition with musical accompaniment, such as the *kora* or *komsa*. There are also women in this tradition, called *griottes*.

The Yoruba people of West Africa have a rich history of ritual performance to practice divination and to mark the installation of a new chief, births, and deaths. Yoruba ritual performance is marked by the

A *griot* sings at an engagement party in Mali, 2006. Photo by Emilia Tjernström.

The role of the *griot* was used for the play *Fly*, produced at Ford's Theatre, Washington, D.C., 2012. It depicts the experiences of the Tuskegee Airmen, African American officers and pilots during World War II. The cast included the "Tap Griot," a dancing storyteller who expresses the inner emotional world that the soldiers cannot show. Featuring Omar Edwards (directed by Ricardo Khan). Photo by Scott Suchman.

improvisational nature of the performance events and the agency of the participants in their ritual journey. Ritual performance in Yoruba may take the form of parades or processionals and involve masks, costumes, dance, and music. Since 1370, the Osun Oshogbo Festival has taken place at the same sacred groves in Oshogbo, Nigeria. Upon settling there and preparing the ground for planting, the people felled a tree, and it landed in the Osun River. The settlers then heard the river lament her destruction, and the people began singing to the river to placate the goddess who resides there. The Osun grove draws tourists from all over the world to witness the two-week ritual proceedings to honor the river goddess Osun and the founding of the Oshogbo kingdom.

Sierra Leone. The Temne Rabai initiation ritual in Sierra Leone does not have a known origination date but is a practice passed down from the ancestors that prescribes a formal set of ritual performances and ceremony to circumcise young boys and metaphorically crown the "little kings" into manhood. The ritual is a community celebration of sexuality and includes the "abduction" of the young boys by their guardians to a clearing where rebirth practices, such as shaving of the head, are undertaken before the boys are circumcised.

The Mende people of Sierra Leone have a story performance tradition called *domei*, which draws on a regular stock of archetypal characters, such as the Defiant Maid and the Stubborn Farmer, in order to engage in critical debate through an improvisational storytelling form. The *Kaso* (spider-trickster) and *Musa Wo* (trickster-hero) fall in the *njepe wovei* narrative category, which utilizes music and a basic plot of transgression followed by punishment. *Kaso* is the most performed character in the Mende story performance tradition.

Nigeria. Wole Soyinka (b. 1934) is a Nigerian playwright who won the Nobel Prize for Literature in 1986, the first African to receive that honor. He was a dramaturg at London's Royal Court Theatre in 1958–1959. In 1967 he called for a cease-fire during Nigeria's civil war and was then imprisoned in solitary confinement for twenty-two months. His plays are influenced by Western drama but retain his Yoruba cultural heritage with African music, dance, and mythology.

Ghana. In the 1920s, a popular form of traveling theatre emerged in Ghana; it was created by Bob Johnson and was known as the *concert party*. While popular, these performances did not fall under the traditional African performance forms, nor were they given the status of dramatic literature. The concert party depended on quality musicians to provide musical accompaniment for the cabaret-style performances, which included dance and minstrelsy in a style inspired by popular minstrelsy and film in the United States, as well as African American spirituals, Latin American music, Ghanaian flag dancing (*asafo*), and "highlife" (West African jazz and guitar) music. The heyday of the concert party in the 1950s and 1960s is considered a golden age for Ghanaian theatre. In 2006, Ghana's first minister of chieftaincy affairs and culture, S. K. Boafo, announced his intention to revive the concert party theatre.

Efua Sutherland (1924–1996) founded Ghana Drama Studio in Accra in 1957 and was instrumental in establishing modern Ghanaian theatre as a director, playwright, and patron. She advocated for the study of African theatre at universities, and her own plays interwove traditional African performance with references to Western classics.

South Africa

Athol Fugard (b. 1932) is a South African playwright whose early plays revealed the pain of institutionalized apartheid. His *"Master Harold"* . . . *and the Boys*, an autobiographical play, is about Harold, a white boy, who chooses to assert his dominance and reinforce systemic racism by sabotaging his friendship with "the Boys," Sam and Willie, black men employed by his parents. The Fugard Theatre, named in his honor,

Athol Fugard directing his play *Blood Knot* for the Signature Theatre in New York City, 2011. Photo © Erik Carter.

opened in 2010 in District 6, Cape Town, South Africa. District 6 is the former site of apartheid's cruel deeds—once a black neighborhood that was savagely demolished with its inhabitants forcibly relocated. In its debut season, the Fugard produced *The Train Driver*, a work that Fugard claims is his most important play. *The Train Driver* is a meditation on the harsh realities of social, economic, and racial dynamics, inspired by a newspaper article about a South African black mother who walked from the squatter camp where she was living to commit suicide with her three children in her arms, on the train tracks. Fugard's work is an example of a South African theatre tradition that bears witness to real stories of struggle for social equity.

Latin America

The performativity of Latin American cultural practices dates back to Mesoamerican Mexica, Aztec, Maya, and Incan civilizations that practiced diverse performances such as the rituals that marked Aztec human sacrifice to the gods, Incan festival parades with the divine deceased, and the Mayan *Rabinal Achi*. Many of these performances, as early as 3000 BCE, seek to commune with an afterlife or to understand human life and death as a continuum rather than in opposition. With the colonization of the New World (sixteenth to nineteenth centuries), indigenous performance practices took on greater significance as the primary means by which the colonized could retain their traditional culture and resist the violence of stolen heritage. Performance was more difficult to censor, did not require literacy, and was a site of rich embodied practice of community that persisted in the face of the conqueror's mandates to assimilate European culture and religion.

Ancestor Worship in Performance:
Rabinal Achi, Day of the Dead, and *Egungun*

In *Rabinal Achi*, a Mayan performance that originated in the fifteenth century, masked actors represent the dead, performing communion with ancestors and allowing the audience to make contact with the deceased. The play puts the character of Cawek on trial for betraying the inhabitants of Rabinal. Spanish conquerors

Dancers of the *Rabinal Achi*. Photo by Rosemary Burnett.

were threatened by the play's interrogation of the dynamics between rulers and their subjects and tried to censor the performance, especially Cawek's "decapitation." In 2005, the dance drama from *Rabinal Achi* was named one of the Masterpieces of the Oral and Intangible Heritage of Humanity by UNESCO.

Present-day Mexico continues to undertake ritual performance to honor ancestors with the **Day of the Dead** festival celebrations, a legacy of an Aztec festival to honor the goddess of the afterlife. Day of the Dead festivities may include the creation of altars, wearing a costume to imitate the deceased, cooking the favorite foods of the dead as an offering, and other ways to publicly perform the connection to ancestors. Latin American performance that honors the dead continues to be an important aspect of cultural heritage.

Since the fourteenth century, the African Yoruba people annually participate in *egungun*, a ritual performance involving dance, masquerade, drumming, and improvisation that honors the ancestors and encourages the living to meet high ethical standards. The robed *egungun* performers become possessed with the spirits of ancestors and, in doing so, spiritually cleanse the community. *Egungun*

Egunguns waiting to begin, Cové, Benin, 2009. Photo by Dietmar Temps.

that honors one's blood relatives is named *Baba* (Father) and *Iya* (Mother), while the rest of *egungun* performances honor Yoruban ancestry, traditions, and heritage more generally.

Mexico

Sor Juana Ines de la Cruz (1648–1695) was born in Mexico as the illegitimate daughter of a Spanish captain and a Criollo woman and registered as a "daughter of the church," since her parents were not married. From these humble beginnings, she overcame the obstacles to receiving an education and was a celebrated and self-taught intellectual. She became a nun in order to continue her studies and intellectual life, including writing fifty-two dramatic works and teaching drama to young women. She is most famous for her poetry and her courageous treatises on the rights of women to an education. However, her significant work as a dramatist is often overlooked. She contributed to various genres of Mexican drama—the *falda y empeño* (petticoat and perseverance, plus the love and mythology subgenre), the *auto* (sacramental, hagiographic and biblical), and *loas* and *villancicos* dramas.

Mexico experienced a revival in folk performance during the 1920s as well as the rise of experimental theatre, as demonstrated by the short-lived but influential Teatro de Ulises, established in 1928 as an experimental theatre that performed works by international playwrights. Rodolfo Usigli (1905–1979) was a Mexican playwright and director called "the playwright of the Mexican revolution." His play *El Gesticulador* (*The Impostor*, 1938) was popular with the public but met with criticism by the Mexican government when it was finally staged in 1947. The first play that dared to script contemporary Mexican politics and the "death" of the Mexican Revolution, it was ultimately censored by the government when several performances at Palacio de Bellas Artes in Mexico City were canceled. Usigli was an advocate for women's rights and mentored men and women in Mexican theatre who continued his legacy of using the theatre to tell the truth.

From the midtwentieth century, the National Autonomous University of Mexico has fostered the development of Mexican avant-garde theatre and nurtured Mexico's experimental dramatists. From 1956 to 1963, the Poesia en Voz Alta (Poetry Out Loud) festival, hosted at the university, accomplished the aim of encouraging Mexican dramatists to step away from Spanish romanticism and canonical works and instead experiment with staging, realism, and colloquial language. The influence of the Poetry Out Loud festivals reverberated into the theatre of the 1970s.

Mexican theatre of the 1980s reflected the political and economic turmoil of that time with plays that relied on realism and the use of personal narrative, called the New Mexican Dramaturgy. By the 1990s, economic depression and lack of government financial support resulted in the fragmenting of the theatre into individual companies with no unified Mexican theatre movement or style. An exception was the 1990s movement in Mexican theatre called *theatre of the body*, which called for the body to be used as theatrical fodder. A group of women directors founded La Rendija (The Slit), and took on the theatre of the body, with avant-garde theatre pieces that foreground corporeality and make use of alternative performance spaces. Still an active theatre company today, La Rendija hosts an annual festival to encourage the development of new works.

The first Festival of Mexico City occurred in 1984 and continues to be organized annually to showcase art forms of all kinds, including theatre. The festival events transpire over two and a half weeks and feature Mexican and international performers. Mexico has many diverse festival offerings such as the International Festival of Street Theatre, which has taken place every year in October in Zacatecas since 2002.

Jesusa Rodriguez (b. 1955) is a Mexican performance artist, playwright, and activist who has been instrumental in shaping and contributing to postmodern Mexican performance. Her wife Liliana Felipe (b. 1954) is an Argentine composer and actress who fled Argentina before the Dirty War, which claimed her sister and brother-in-law as "disappeareds." They are the founders of the political cabaret theatre El Habito (now called El Vicio) in Mexico City, which serves as a space of civil cultural resistance. Rodriguez's performances often called on the audience to participate in sounding off about the politics of the day. Home to the performance arts of the cabaret space, including avant-garde gender transgressive drag acts that celebrate non-normative sexuality, El Vicio has been an important home for many contemporary Mexican performance artists. Rodriguez and Felipe operated El Habito and Teatro de la Capilla, another alternative performance space, until 2005. However, El Vicio still thrives as a cabaret performance space. Typical of much of Rodriguez's explicitly political work, *New War New War* is a *carpa* (Mexican vaudeville) performance that addresses the foreign policy effects of the post-9/11 era and explores the role of humor in dealing with tragedy. Rodriguez insists on the ". . . necessity to protest and resist through pleasure."

Argentina

Argentina experienced a "glorious decade" of theatre (1904–1914) that produced *genero chico* and naturalist plays. *Genero chico* plays are generally one-act satirical comedies with dance that stage the realistic lives of local people. In the 1920s and 1930s the *grotesco criollo* play became popular in Argentina, influenced by the Italian grotesque playwrights, such as Luigi Pirandello. The *grotesco criollo* plays staged the horrible truths of impoverished and oppressed immigrant communities, grotesquing the immigration policies of the day.

From 1950 to 1956, the most compelling productions in the Argentine theatre were produced in independent theatres opened as a reaction to the commercial and politically controlled popular theatres. The theatre happening in the independent venues at this time introduced plays that were unafraid of social commentary during great political unrest. While the independent theatres did not survive long, they managed to plant the seeds of a new realism aesthetic that continued to take shape in the Argentine theatre of the 1960s. The 1960s saw the infusion of the avant-garde movement into the theatre landscape, which continued to affect Argentine realism on the stage. The Argentine plays of this decade centered on disaffected antihero protagonists unable to overcome life's difficulties. The Centro Experimental Audiovisual Instituto Torcuato di Tella in Buenos Aires opened in 1958 with the strident mission to avoid realism altogether in favor of new performance modes that would reinvent the theatre, until the government closed the theatre in 1971. By the end of the 1970s, many theatre practitioners were forced or compelled to leave the country; such was the political climate that stifled freedom of artistic expression. During the Dirty War (1976–1983), some theatres were closed and the Picadero theatre was burned down, while writers were kidnapped, tortured and murdered.

In 1981, the Teatro Abierto was established and managed to produce works that were critical of state terrorism by way of disguised critique that audiences easily deciphered as resistance to the regime. But with the new democracy in 1986, the theatre ceased to exist, its function no longer necessary. By the end of the 1980s, Argentine theatre had dealt with the terrorism of the Dirty War so extensively that the focus of the theatre shifted to lighter fare, as artists and audiences alike did not want to suffer the reliving of recently passed atrocities. It turned to issues of social concern and identity, including grappling with feminism, sexuality, gender, and "machismo."

One of the most accomplished avant-garde dramatists and writers of Latin America to work at the Instituto di Tella was Griselda Gambaro (b. 1928), Argentina's most acclaimed playwright. She courageously penned plays that dealt with the horrors of the political turmoil that eventually culminated in the Dirty War (1976–1983). Her works focus on political crisis (e.g., *The Walls*, 1963) and the "disappeared" (e.g., *Information for Foreigners*, 1973)—Argentines whose bodies were never recovered after the violence of kidnappings and murder perpetrated during political upheaval. She situates her work squarely in the uniquely Argentine *grotesco* genre and uses parody, black comedy, collage, and encoded language (to avoid censorship) to explore the violence, complicity, and what she calls the "schizophrenic" nature of her home country. Gambaro continues to write novels, essays, short stories, and plays, with her *Teatro 7* (seventh collection of plays) published in 2005.

Brazil

Julia Lopes de Almeida (1862–1934) was a Brazilian writer and playwright whose best-known dramatic work was *A Herança* (The Heritage), a psychological romance. This work was performed in 1908 at the Teatro de Exposição Nacional. Notable as one of Brazil's first women to be socially accepted as a writer, she also used her position to advocate for greater equality for women and abolition. It is thought that her husband was elected to the Brazilian Academy of Letters as a stand-in for his wife, given the gender constraints of the time.

São Paulo Teatro de Arena, or Arena Theatre, was established in 1953 and closed in 1972. It succeeded in creating a national theatre that adapted classics to speak to Brazilian life, such as Augusto Boal's 1956 adaptation of Steinbeck's *Of Mice and Men*, and then became a platform for new work by Brazilian playwrights.

Grupo Macunaima, a São Paulo theatre company founded in 1978 by Antunes Filho, still operates as it always has: staging authentically Brazilian performance, whether through adaptation of classics (1992's *Macbeth* adaptation, *Throne of Blood*) or the work of Brazil's native playwrights (1993's *Path of Salvation* by Jorge Andrade). Leading Brazilian theatre through the transition out of the "reign of terror" dictatorship and into democracy, Grupo Macunaima called on a collective Brazilian identity and dramatized Brazil's mythology as well as its reality.

Conclusion

An active traditional Japanese *bunraku* performance company operates in Missouri with the slogan "Traditional Japanese Puppetry in America." Rohina Malik, an American Muslim playwright who resides in Chicago, wrote *Unveiled*, a play about Muslim women reflecting on their identities post-9/11, and it is currently enjoying international production. She was recently commissioned by the Goodman Theatre to write *The Mecca Tales*, which explores the diverse motivations for five Muslim women to embark on pilgrimages to Mecca. In each case, intercultural exchange that interrogates traditional performance conventions is being performed in the heartland of the United States. As Micaela Di Leonardo argues, the "exotic" has come home and culture is "a foreign microbe run wild." The theatre and its audiences are increasingly the benefactors of the connectedness forged through our hybridized culture staged in performance venues around the globe. In a postmodern age, "world" theatre is difficult to pin down—preserving traditional forms becomes elusive when *we* are the world.

Contributors

Kevin Browne is an associate professor of theatre at the University of Central Arkansas. Dr. Browne has nearly thirty years of experience in both the professional and academic worlds as a performing artist, director, and teacher. He has performed in film and television, off-off Broadway, in professional tours, in summer stock, and in academic theatres.

Margaret R. Butler is an assistant professor of musicology at the University of Florida. Her book *Operatic Reform in Turin: Aspects of Production and Stylistic Change in the 1760s* was based on research she conducted as a Fulbright Fellow. Dr. Butler has contributed to the *Cambridge History of Eighteenth-Century Music*, and her articles have appeared in the *Journal of the American Musicological Society*, *Early Music*, *Cambridge Opera Journal*, *Eighteenth-Century Music*, and *Music in Art: International Journal for Musical Iconography*.

Jim Davis is an assistant professor at Kennesaw State University, where he directs plays and has created numerous solo and ensemble works for puppet theatre. Dr. Davis has worked with a variety of arts organizations, including the Center for Puppetry Arts, the Atlanta Lyric Theatre, the Chicago Historical Society, the Mississippi River Museum, Blackhawk Children's Theatre, and Horizon Youth Theatre. His research has been featured in *Northsiders: Essays on the History and Culture of the Chicago Cubs*, in the reference work *Graphic Novels*, and at numerous national academic conferences.

Kasendra Djuren is a freelance lighting and scenic designer. She has designed shows at Concordia University, Brevard College, Minnetonka Performing Arts Center, Missouri State University, and the Helen Hocker Performing Arts Center. She also has taught courses such as stagecraft, script analysis, and introduction to theatre.

Jeremy Fiebig is an assistant professor of theatre at Fayetteville State University and a graduate of the Mary Baldwin College/American Shakespeare Center program in Shakespeare and Renaissance Literature in Performance. A director, designer, and scholar-practitioner, Professor Fiebig serves as editor-in-chief for *The Shakespeare Standard* and is the managing director and co-director of education at Fayetteville's Gilbert Theater.

Stacey Galloway is an assistant professor of theatre at the University of Florida and a freelance costume designer, assistant, and technician. She has worked at theatres such as Manhattan Theatre Club, New York Theatre Workshop, Papermill Playhouse, Playwright's Horizons, Long Wharf Theatre, McCarter Theatre, Goodspeed Opera, Yale Repertory, and La Jolla Playhouse.

Michelle Hayford is an assistant professor of theatre at Florida Gulf Coast University, where she teaches performance theory as well as directing original ensemble productions based on interview narratives. These ethnodramas combine Dr. Hayford's passion for creating live plays with utilizing the craft of theatre as a necessary response to community and civic engagement.

Mark E. Mallett is an associate professor of theatre at Richard Stockton College, where he heads the design and production programs. Dr. Mallett has presented research findings to the Mid-America Theatre Conference, the Southeastern Theatre Conference, and the Association for Theatre in Higher Education and has published articles in *The Journal of American Drama and Theatre* and *Theatre Symposium*.

Charlie Mitchell is an assistant professor of theatre at the University of Florida, where he teaches introductory theatre and improvisation. For three years, he was an artistic associate and company member of the award-winning Chesapeake Shakespeare Company, and he has worked as an actor and director for a variety of theatres in New York City, Chicago, and Baltimore. In addition to his teaching and production work, Dr. Mitchell is the author of *Shakespeare and Public Execution* and co-edited *Zora Neale Hurston: Collected Plays*.

CPSIA information can be obtained at www.ICGtesting.com
Printed in the USA
LVOW08s0853150714

394385LV00002B/2/P

9 781616 101664